EARLY HiSTORY OF IDAHO

By
W. J. McCONNELL
Ex.-U. S. Senator and -Governor

WHO WAS PRESENT AND COGNIZANT
OF THE EVENTS NARRATED

PUBLISHED BY AUTHORITY OF THE
IDAHO STATE LEGISLATURE

CALDWELL, IDAHO
The Caxton Printers
MCMXIII

The Caxton Printers, Caldwell

The author of "The Early History of Idaho" respectfully dedicates this book to the pioneers whose camp-fires and cabins first marked the advent of civilization into the mountains and valleys of Idaho; the men and women who transformed the silence of nothingness into the hum of industry and enterprise. May their children, and their children's children long enjoy the boon of freedom and prosperity bequeathed to them by their valiant and worthy ancestors.

—W. J. McC.

The author of "The Early History of Idaho" respectfully dedicates this book to the pioneers whose camp-fires and cabins first marked the advent of civilization into the mountains and valleys of Idaho; the men and women who transformed the silence of nothingness into the hum of industry and enterprise. May their children, and their children's children long enjoy the boon of freedom and prosperity bequeathed to them by their valiant and worthy ancestors.

—W. J. McC.

CONTENTS

CHAPTER I.

INTRODUCTORY.

HALF a century has elapsed since the author of this narrative first came to the then wilderness which is now embraced within the boundaries of the State of Idaho. Buoyed up with the hopes and aspirations of early manhood, I faced the duties and hardships incident to life on the frontier; secured my share of the harvest of gold then being garnered in the placer mines; and, more precious still, I won the friendship of many of those who came here at the same time and on the same errand—the hope of securing money to enable us to return to our former homes and begin life among our earlier associates.

Many succeeded and carried out their original intentions; a few lost their lives in the effort, and others, I among the number, remained, each doing his part toward transforming the wilderness into a paradise of homes.

As I take up my pen to begin the manuscript of a narrative, or history, of the events which happened in this country during its marvelous transformation within the last fifty years, my mind takes me back in rapid flight over the intervening years and events to the old days of the trail before wagon roads were built; the days of the camp fire, the coffee pot and the frying pan; the day when men loved their friends and, if needs be, fought for them to the death; the days of bacon and beans, of black coffee, and bread baked in the frying pan before the camp fire.

Where are the gallant men who braved the dangers of our mountains and deserts in the early 60's, the men who made the long marches cheerful, who vied with one another as to which should occupy the post of greatest danger?

In retrospect I see them all as in the days gone by; their voices echo in my ears with the cheerful comradeship of old; they are nearly all gone across the Divide to that other Camp, whence no prospector returns. I should prefer to write of them, prefer to extol their individual characteristics; prefer to record their deeds of valor, their every-day lives as, all unconscious of the good they did, they bore the brunt of the battle for civilization which resulted in the creation of a new state—the addition of another star to the galaxy of our national banner. But as the forthcoming pages are to be devoted to the gradual development of a new country, rather than to a pæan of praise for those who accomplished its transformation, I approach the task of writing of events in which they participated with reverence and awe, and with a mind replete with the thoughts that had we known one another better, we would have loved one another even more.

History is relentless, once made it cannot

be unmade. Hence the importance of recording for future reference and information a correct chronicle of events before all who participated in them are gone. Mr. W. A. Goulder, now dead, recently published a valuable and entertaining book, entitled "Reminiscences of a Pioneer," in which he makes the following statement: (Chap. 33, pp. 275-276:)

"The history of Idaho cannot be properly written and successfully placed in the hands of the reading public before the last decade of the present century for the reason that it will require the whole of that time to retire permanently from the scene the host of distinguished personages, all of whom were prominent and active in the making of that history. Until the last one of these is dead and buried, it would be the extreme of rashness and reckless disregard of life, and all that life holds most dear, for any one to venture upon the task of writing a true and impartial account of what has been done in Idaho.

"Take up any one of the many alleged histories of Idaho, and you will find that it has been written and gotten up by the representatives of some eastern publishing house who came very late to the state and who stayed just long enough to gather the material for the work they were hired to do. An inspection of the work will present you with a mass of biographies of unknown celebrities whose many brilliant achievements are

2 E. H. I.

duly chronicled and whose pictures—resembling, for the most part, those of heroes of Falstaff's army—embellish its pages and all printed and published, as a friendly critic has said, 'at so many dollars per pic and per biog.'

"History, at the best, may be defined as the art of selecting, grouping and presenting facts and dates in the way required to produce the effect that the writer has in view, and has been very aptly compared to a child's box of letter blocks which can be made to spell any desired word.

"These reflections should not be understood as excusing any one from the task of exempting him from the duty of writing what he chance may know of history or about history. All of us can write a little, some of us can write a great deal, while there are others who can write entirely too much. The better and safer plan is for each individual to write what he knows to be true; what he has seen; what he has done himself, and what he has seen others do; provided, he can feel reasonably certain that the people of whom he writes are all dead."

With the foregoing in mind, yet without fear of the living, and imbued with the sacredness of correctly recording the acts of those who are dead, I shall pursue to the end the task I have set for myself; glad that some are still alive to commend or to censure a narrative in which I shall endeavor to include as much of the "good" and the "bad" as is pertinent to the subject.

History is not history unless it is true, and there can be no excuse for the alleged historian who indulges in flights of fancy when the truth, if written, would be stranger and more interesting than modern fiction. A great deal of interesting matter has been left out of the historical works relating to Idaho which have been published in the past. The reason for this inadvertence has not been that the writers were fearful that those of whom they would write, and their relatives, were not dead, but that they felt that those things were now past and gone, and that those acts which were discreditable to the individual or community should be allowed to slumber in oblivion. Such considerations are commendable, but they are hardly consistent with the stern duty of the historian.

A very kindly old man, long a resident of Boise, and now bravely coming down the last lap of an eventful and useful life, has written and published a history of Idaho. In his commendable and kindly effort to portray the lovable people who came here among the first arrivals, he states; "I think I may truthfully say that ninety-five per cent of those people were good, industrious, honorable and enterprising, and to all appearances desired to make money in a legitimate way." (*Hailey's History of Idaho*, p. 91).

There were, at the time of which he writes,

at least fifteen thousand people in the Boise Basin and if ninety-five per cent of them were good people, the others, or five per cent, by inference, must have constituted the bad; five per cent of fifteen thousand equals seven hundred and fifty, and if there were that number of bad men distributed throughout the limited area included within that district, it will be readily understood that conditions were sometimes rather tropical. But it is probable the writer who made the foregoing statement, did not take time to calculate in round numbers how many bad men he was charging up to that community.

I do not believe that at any time the proportion of what would have been called *"bad"* men —even in those days—exceeded one-half of one per cent, but, true to the maxim, "birds of a feather flock together," they always succeeded in making their presence felt—whether in saloons, precinct primaries, nominating conventions, or at the polls.

The *Century Dictionary* defines politics as: "The science of government; that part of ethics which consists of the regulation and government of a nation or state for the preservation of its safety, peace and prosperity;" and defines "Political" as "pertaining to policy or to civil government and its administration."

The foregoing applies equally to a territory as to a state or nation; hence, the policy under which the affairs of Idaho were conducted, as well as its safety, peace and prosperity, were in

the hands and under the control of that political
party, or organization, that cast the largest vote
at the general elections. True, the governor and
most of the territorial officers were appointed by
the president; but the legislature which enacted
the laws, the county officers, including the sheriffs, and the justices of the peace, who enforced
them, were elective.

Therefore, the question of politics inevitably
enters into the history of Idaho, as well as that
of all other territories. But in no place is its
importance so keenly felt as in a new territory
such as Idaho, which was largely devoted to the
mining industry and where a majority of the
population were migratory, and few if any of
those who came among the early arrivals intended
to remain.

It was the misfortune of the Democratic
party in Idaho to be in the ascendancy during
those years; that they were, and why, has been
explained by Mr. W. A. Goulder in his "Reminiscences of a Pioneer," pp. 282-283.

In writing of the general election held in
1864, at which E. D. Holbrook was elected delegate to congress from Idaho Territory, Goulder
says:

"During the interval that had elapsed since
the election of Wallace, what was then known as
'the left wing of Price's army' had been scattering its red plumes and feathers all over the
vast intermountain region at that time embraced

within the boundaries of Idaho Territory. The warriors composing this contingent of the Confederate Army, having become tired of the restraints and hardships of military life, and the apparently hopeless task of confronting the hordes of 'Northern Abolitionists' who continued to invade and over-run the fair land watered by the 'Big Muddy' and its tributaries, had concluded to resign in a body and migrate westward, where the more congenial task of taking charge of the political destiny of Idaho awaited them. And so they came, and continued to come, with the ox-whip in one hand and the ballot in the other; and by frequent and persistent voting, soon changed the complexion of things political.

"They were all from Missouri; all Democrats by birth and lineage, and had voted for Andrew Jackson from times immemorial, until in the later days they had transferred their allegiance to 'Jeff Davis.'"

While the foregoing is probably right so far as the political affiliations of these overland arrivals is concerned, yet it is a mistake to credit all of them, or, for that matter, any great number of them, with having belonged formerly to the Confederate Army. A few had, possibly, at one time followed some confederate leader, but nearly of them were refugees trying to escape the horrors of civil war. Husbands and wives, with their children and such of their possessions as they had rescued from the wrecks of their former homes, turned westward, in fact, fled from the internecine strife which was dotting the land with graves. They came in hope of finding peace, rather than to engage in contests, political or otherwise.

Upon their arrival in Idaho they found the political parties here as firmly aligned, and as fully hostile to each other as in the country they had abandoned. The members of the two political factions were called "Republicans" and "Democrats," the same as before the war; but, at the time of which I write, there was only one dividing line, one paramount issue: *Shall the Union remain intact, or shall it be dissevered, dismantled?*

The Republicans in Idaho advocated the Union side of the discussion, while the Democrats were distinctly and declaredly, as an organization, in favor of the secession of the southern states and the establishment of a confederacy with human slavery as its cornerstone. Naturally, the male members of the early overland immigration continued with, and supported by their ballots, the nominees of that political party to which they had, heretofore, given their allegiance. For, are we not, after all, creatures of environment?

Had Henry Ward Beecher or Rev. Starr King been born and educated in Constantinople, they would probably have been strong adherents to the tenets of Mohammedanism; had Robert Ingersoll been born and reared in Canton, he would doubtless have been a follower of Con-

fucius, and had Jefferson Davis and Alexander
H. Stephens, of Confederate fame, been born
and educated in Massachusetts, it is more than
likely that they both would have been radical
abolitionists.

Exceptions are found to nearly all rules,
and accordingly, notwithstanding the influence of
slavery which permeated all the slave-holding
states, many brave officers and men within the
borders of the Confederacy remained loyal to the
Union and the flag. But it is the exception to
find the individual who has the moral stamina
or self-assertiveness to rise above, or shake himself free from the religious or political environ-
ments of his youth and early manhood or womanhood. Then, why should we censure or criticize
those immigrants who crossed the plains to
Idaho in the early 60's, bringing with them, as
they did, the political prejudices that were inherent?

They were, as said by Goulder, "Democrats"
and the greater number of them were probably
Secessionists, but they brought with themselves
those other traits which go to make good citizens in any country—honesty and industry.

I met and became acquainted with nearly all
who became home builders in Idaho during those
years, and it has never been my fortune to meet
a more kindly, neighborly or honest class of men
and women than they.

I was reared in Michigan on the line of the
so-called "Underground Railroad," where colored

men and women passed in their endeavor to gain freedom by reaching Canadian soil. My father was a "Free Soil" Abolitionist, hence, as might be inferred, I was a Republican, and a Unionist, and, as such, I met these people in both a social and a business way, and I stand ready now, as I did then, to vouch for the many estimable qualities and lovable characteristics of those who were called "The left wing of Price's Army."

Their arrival at that time was not conducive, however, to the peace and good government of the territory, for the reason that the lawless element which had come before their arrival, had, for their own protection, taken sides with, and really controlled the stronger party, which happened to be the Democratic. Hence the addition of the immigrants to the voting strength of that party, gave it full control.

In those days few men of either party, other than the toughs and adventurers, attended primaries or nominating conventions; hence, it can be understood that with their voting strength reinforced by the incoming refugees, the nominees named by the objectionable element were easily elected; not because the rank and file of the Democratic party were lawless or bad men, for quite the contrary was the case, but because then, as too frequently happens now, many of our citizens do not attend the primary elections or participate in the nomination of a ticket. On election day they are partisans, and claim to vote their principles, and thus frequently assist in placing into office those who are totally devoid of principle.

Therefore, I reiterate what I have heretofore said: "It was the misfortune of the Democratic party to be in control, under the circumstances." Having made the foregoing prefatory statements, I shall now proceed to embody such historical data as will, I hope, be of interest to this and succeeding generations.

CHAPTER II.

ORIGIN OF THE NAME IDAHO.

"IDAHO" is generally supposed to be a corruption of an Indian word meaning "Gem of the Mountains." This, however, is disputed. Joaquin Miller, the poet, writes as follows on the subject:

"The distinction of naming Idaho certainly belongs to my old friend, Colonel Craig (now dead) of Craig's Mountain, Nez Perce county. As for some fellow naming it in Congress—Bah! The name was familiar in 5,000 men's mouths as they wallowed through the snow in '61, on their way to the Oro Fino mines, long before Congress, or any man in Congress, ever heard of the new discovery.

"The facts are these: I was riding pony express at the time, rumors reached us through the Nez Perce Indians, that gold was to be found on the headwaters and tributaries of Salmon River. I had lived with the Indians, and Colonel Craig, who had spent most of his life with them, often talked with me about possible discoveries in the mountains to the right as we rode to Oro Fino, and of what the Indians said of the then unknown region.

"Gallop your horse, as I have done hundreds of times, against the rising sun; as you climb the Sweet Water Mountains, far away to the right you will see the name of Idaho written on the mountain top—at least, you will see a peculiar and beautiful light at sunrise, a sort of diadem on two grand clusters of mountains that bear away under the clouds, fifty miles distant. I called Colonel Craig's attention to this peculiar and beautifully arched light. 'That,' said he, 'is what the Indians call E-dah-hoe; which means, the light, or diadem, on the line of the mountains.' That was the first time I had ever heard the name. Later, in September, '61, when I rode into the newly discovered camp to establish an express office, I took with me an Indian from Lapwai. We followed an Indian trail, crossed Craig's Mountain, then Camas Prairie, and had all the time 'E-dah-hoe Mount' for our objective point.

"On my return to Lewiston I wrote a letter containing a brief account of our trip and of the mines, and it was published in one of the Oregon papers—which one, I have now forgotten. In that account I often mentioned E-dah-hoe, but spelled it 'I-d-a-h-o,' leaving the pronunciation unmarked by any diacritical signs. So that, perhaps, I may have been the first to give it its present spelling; but I certainly did not originate the word."

A writer in "The New West," who is, apparently, well informed, declared that "Idaho" is not a Nez Perce word, adding:

"The mountains that Joaquin Miller speaks of may be named with a somewhat similar appellation, but most likely the whole story grows out of the fertile imagination of the poet. Idaho Springs in Colorado were known long before Idaho Territory was organized. The various territories, at their organization, should have been given some appropriate local name. Colorado was named after the river of that name—though it is not within its boundaries. It should have been called 'Idaho,' which was the first name placed in the bill organizing it; but which was afterward changed."

Ex-Senator Nesmith of Oregon gives still another account, as follows:

"The bill first passed the House of Representatives designating the present territory of Idaho as 'Montana.' When it came up for consideration in the Senate on the 3rd day of March, 1862, Senator Wilson of Massachusetts moved to strike out the word 'Montana,' and insert 'Idaho.' Mr. Harding of Oregon said: 'I think the word Idaho is preferable to Montana. Idaho in English signifies 'The Gem of the Mountains.' I heard others suggest that it meant, in the Indian tongue, "Shining Mountain," all of which are synonymous. I do not know from which of the tongues the two words Ida-ho came. I think, however, if you will pursue the inquiry among those familiar with the Nez Perce, Shoshone, and Flathead tribes, that you will find the origin of the two words as I have given it above."

Thus it is shown that among those who were in the country at the time it received its name "Idaho," there is a diversity of opinion as to its derivation, as well as to its naming. The fact is, however, now beyond dispute that whether the word "Idaho" means "Gem of the Mountains," or otherwise, as applied today, it is the cognomen of a state which is a "mountain gem" among the sisterhood of states. And the women and men who reside within its borders are satisfied with the title, and proud of their accomplishments; proud of the accomplishments of their predecessors who transformed the wilderness and desert into an Eden of happy, contented homes.

EARLY HISTORY.

The first authentic account we have of any part of Idaho, is that given by Lewis and Clark, who crossed the Bitter Root mountains and came down through Weippe to the Clearwater river, thence down that stream on the way to their destination—the Pacific Ocean.

When the account of the Lewis & Clark expedition became known, great interest was aroused, especially among what was then the western frontier towns, one of the results being the formation of the Missouri Fur Company, which established a fort at what was called Fort Henry, in 1810, but which was soon abandoned.

In 1811, William P. Hunt, and a party of sixty belonging to the Pacific Fur Company arrived at Fort Henry. Moving westward on the 19th of October of that year, they proceeded down the Snake river in fifteen canoes, but encountered so many dangers owing to the rapids, that at last it was decided to abandon the boats and to divide the party into two sections. Hunt, with his guides and eighteen men, to take the right bank, and the remainder under the leadership of a man named Crooks, to take the left. Thus they proceeded down the river in the hope of reaching the Columbia. They had no knowledge of the country nor of the distance to be traveled, except such indifferent information as was gleaned from the published narratives of the Lewis and Clark expedition, which had crossed the divide much farther north.

Through the remainder of November and up to the middle of December, the two parties stayed apart. What they suffered from the cold during that tedious separation may be imagined by those who today are familiar with the climate on the headwaters of the Snake river during late November and December.

One morning, approximately a month from the date of their division, while Hunt's party was breaking camp, the voices of their late companions were heard calling across the river for aid.

"A vague and almost superstitious terror," says Washington Irving, "had infected the minds of Mr. Hunt's followers, enfeebled and rendered imaginative of horrors by the dismal scenes through which they had passed; they regarded the haggard crew, hovering like specters on the opposite bank, with indefinite feelings of awe and apprehension, as if something desperate and dangerous was to be feared from them."

A species of boat or raft was hastily constructed out of poles, covered with the skin of a horse they had killed the day previous for food. On this frail craft a little meat was ferried over to the half-famished men. One of the men was drowned at this point, while several others were ill. Thus, being unable to proceed encumbered with the disabled members, it was necessary for the others to go on and leave them. On the 24th day of December, they arrived at what was afterward the site of old Fort Boise. Being still in two parties, one on each side of the river.

"With great difficulty," says W. H. Bancroft, "the river being full of floating ice, and the men half starved and half frozen. Weak and dispirited, Hunt crossed with his party to the other side and joining their comrades, proceeded on their westward way."

This was the first authentic report of white men ever having visited and traveled through what is now known as Southern Idaho.

No mention need be made of the suffering they endured, to those who are familiar with the volcanic and sage brush wastes over which those weary men made their way.

No record exists of the final end of those poor fellows who were left to perish alone, their only probable companions the lizards and horned toads; their last requiem the howl of the coyote.

Who can conceive the horrors of such a tragic end? Yet, had the blank unwritten pages of the early history of our former territories been filled in, it might have revealed many similar incidents.

The next expedition to enter the future Idaho was that of Captain Bonneville, who with one hundred men in 1834, camped on Port Neuf river near where is now the city of Pocatello.

In the same year Fort Hall was established by Nathaniel Worth, accompanied by a well equipped party of sixty men. The location was selected on the 14th day of June, 1834, on the east bank of Snake river, north of Port Neuf.

"The post became famous," says Bancroft, "and performed good service during the several great overland emigrations. The emigrant trail was made to pass by it, and it was central and valuable in scores of ways."

"From this point in time radiated roads in every direction—to Missouri, to California, to Utah, to Oregon, and to British Columbia. It was near the old war ground of the Bannocks, Blackfeet, and Crows, and prevented many a massacre. It was several times attacked, and nearly burned, but stood to its duty nobly."

3 E. H. I.

In 1836 Weyth was forced to sell Fort Hall to the Hudson Bay Company. This company having the year previous, (1835) erected what is known as "Old Fort Boise" near the mouth of Boise river. The original building fell down in either 1847 or 1848, but was rebuilt a short distance north of where the old building stood. The new buildings continued to be occupied by the Hudson Bay Company until the United States acquired undisputed title to the land.

Forts Hall and Boise were established, at the dates given, for the sole purpose of trading for furs with the Indians. The hardy and adventurous men who constituted their first garrisons had no idea that in their immediate neighborhood would arise, within less than a century, prosperous and enterprising cities. Yet the progress of American ardor and enterprise has been such that today, standing on the ground where the Bannocks, Shoshones, Blackfeet and Arapahoe Indians formerly assembled to trade their peltry for such articles as the white men had to offer, the tourist may be aroused from his reverie by the sound of steam whistles, or the rumbling of long trains of freight cars, laden with the barter of modern industry, while as far as the human vision can extend, stretches beautiful meadows and orchards, and nestling among them are seen the homes of the owners. Located between the sites of the former forts stands the beautiful capital city of the prosperous and progressive state of Idaho.

Truly the sword has been turned into the pruning hook, the battle-ground into an orchard or a meadow; the war-whoop of the savage into an anthem of praise. God has been good to this land.

CHAPTER III.

AMONG the important early settlements in Idaho was that made in 1836 by Rev. Henry Spaulding and family on Lapwai, a tributary of the Clearwater river. This first location was at the foot of Thunder Hill near a big spring about two miles above the mouth of the creek, and approximately twelve miles from the confluence of the Snake and Clearwater rivers where the city of Lewiston now stands.

They arrived at the foregoing place on November 29, 1836. Henry Spaulding, assisted by Mr. Gray, who had accompanied him from the Whitman location near Walla Walla, together with such aid as the Indians cheerfully gave, erected the first mission. After a residence at that place of about one year, Spaulding concluded that a better location for his mission would be at the mouth of Lapwai Creek, near the bank of the Clearwater river, (called by the Indians Koos-koos-ki).

He, therefore, erected a larger and more commodious log house at that point, and moved from his original location.

Among the things brought across the Rocky

Mountain Divide by Rev. Spaulding and Dr. Whitman, who accompanied Spaulding, were a few seeds; a few kernels each of corn, wheat and oats; also a few apple and locust seeds. Preparing a small garden patch of fertile ground, he began patiently to plant and cultivate each species in order that he might in time be able to supply the Indians with seeds, hoping to induce them to become tillers of the soil. His efforts in this direction were crowned with a moderate degree of success; the need of a mill to grind the wheat and corn was felt.

The Indians did not realize this need as Mr. Spaulding did, they having their primitive method of grinding seeds and bulbs—the mortar and pestle, both made of stone. But the civilization he hoped to instill among them meant higher and better methods than could be produced by such crude utensils.

To bring the machinery for a flouring mill across the continent at that time was beyond his possibilities, but he was not to be vanquished in his ambition to supply better methods for these people. Proceeding up the Clearwater river with a few Indians to where he found a granite cliff, he quarried out pieces suitable for mill-stones, and constructed a raft of logs, loaded them onto it and brought them down to his mill site near his residence. He then cut them as best he could into the desired form and proceeded to dig a ditch to carry water out of Lapwai Creek to a wheel which he constructed. He was thus able to set his mill-stone into motion and grind the corn and wheat produced by the primitive agricultural methods at their disposal.

Thus first began the civilization of the Nez Perce Indians; and the work accomplished in this direction by Rev. Spaulding, and his devoted Christian wife, was largely responsible for the friendly spirit with which those Indians received the whites when the discovery of placer gold caused such an increase in the population of their country.

A few years since I visited the site of the old mission (1898). As I wandered over the ground which had been the field of their noble endeavor and thought of the hopes and disappointments of the place, I was overwhelmed with the imagination of what that self-immolated man and his wife had borne on that same spot—so many years ago.

The log building that was the work of their hands, still occupied its original site, although the roof had partly fallen in. The apple trees, old and gnarled, had been grown from the seed he had brought across the plains, some of them still living and pointing back to the days that were. A beautiful grove of locust trees, their origin, the seed from which they grew, came from the eastern home of the Spauldings, now towers above and shelters the graves of Rev. Spaulding and his devoted helpmate.

While on my visit there in 1898, I found imbedded in a gravel bar, one of the old granite mill-stones made by Spaulding and used in his primitive mill. Thinking it would be prized as a historical relic at some future time, I caused it to be conveyed to the University campus at Moscow, where it remained for several years. Later it was sent to the State Historical Society's headquarters at Boise to be displayed among the historical relics there preserved. The grooves on the face of the old mill-stone are as well defined today, after being exposed to the elements for seventy years, as if they were but recently made.

The results of the teaching thus begun is traceable in the improved farms and modern houses now occupied by the sons and daughters of the Nez Perces who were once the pupils of Mr. and Mrs. Spaulding before the first immigrant wagon came to Oregon.

No history of Idaho would be complete unless it contains a more exhaustive account of the struggles and accomplishments of the Spaulding Mission than I am capable of writing. But Miss Kate C. McBeth, in a book entitled "The Nez Perce Since Lewis and Clark," has ably performed this work. Miss McBeth came to Lapwai in the fall of 1873, after Mr. Spaulding's death, and took up the work that he laid down. Up to the present writing her life has been devoted to this work, she now being an old woman. She still resides (1912) within a few miles of the former site of the Spaulding Mission, and her work and advice among the Nez Perces is to this day second only to the Book she teaches.

Her publications may be purchased in the book stores in Lewiston and Moscow, Idaho, or by addressing her at Spaulding, Idaho. It is a book that should be read by all, or at least by those who are interested in missionary effort.

The next established settlement within what are now the boundaries of Idaho was made by the Jesuit Fathers in 1853, on Cœur d'Alene river, at, or near, what is now the head of navigation on that stream. The building they erected is still standing, and is within the territory afterwards included in the Cœur d'Alene Indian reservation, which has been recently opened to settlement in accordance with a treaty between the Indians and the United States government. The work which these devoted and self-sacrificing men began in 1853 has been continued without assistance until the present time. A second mission was later established at Desmet. It is situated on the Cœur d'Alene reservation and on land belonging to these Indians.

I first visited Desmet Mission in 1900; my arrival there was during the wheat harvest, and when I approached the reservation from Tekoa, where the O.-W. R. & N. R. R. station is, my first view of the reservation proper was from a ridge to the westward which was crossed by the mission wagon road. My first impression was that I had not yet reached the border of the reservation, for I saw as far as my eyes could reach, fields of golden grain, waving in the autumn sunshine, with harvest crews and steam threshers at work in every direction.

I saw big red barns and spacious farm houses painted white. As I drew near to where the harvest crews were working, I saw that they were made up of white men and Indians in about equal numbers, and was told by my driver that the Indians owned the land and the machinery, and employed the whites as hired men to perform a part of the labor.

As we neared the Mission I found a little village consisting of several large frame buildings, where boarding schools are maintained for boys and girls, they being separately conducted, the Catholic Sisters having charge of the girls' department, while the boys are taught by the Fathers.

The mission has the appearance of a village, owing to the number of small houses and stables owned by the Indians who live on their farms, but come to the mission Saturday evenings, remaining over night in their cottages in order that they might attend church on the Sabbath, returning to their farms the following day. No man or woman having the true conception of the standards taught by Christ can visit the Desmet Mission and observe the self-abnegation, the devotion to duty of these faithful teachers—both men and women—without being benefited by the example they have witnessed.

There is no record of the Cœur d'Alene
Indians, with whom this mission has labored,
ever having violated any treaty made by them
with the government, or of them being at any
time unfriendly with the whites. Their condition today, morally and financially, as well as
their record for good behavior in the past, is
an example of what might have been accomplished with other tribes if similar methods
had been followed.

The work performed at the Spaulding and
Desmet Missions has been, at no time, heralded
by the blare of trumpets; nor has it been adver-
tised in newspapers and magazines, save as
some brief, occasional notice may have appeared;
hence, their establishment did but little to attract immigration to this part of the northwest.
The outbreak of the Cayuse war, involving as
it did many of the Columbia river tribes, caused
the abandonment of the Spaulding Mission approximately ten years after its establishment,
but the moral and industrial lessons taught the
Nex Perces during those ten years have borne
abundant fruit. The Cœur d'Alene mission con-
tinues the work for which it was established,
and to the efforts of that church may justly be
credited the rapid advancement and prosperity
of that tribe.

Prominent among the early pioneers who
penetrated the vast, and then but little known
region drained by the Snake River and its tributaries, and among those whose advent should

be recorded as following the founding of the
Spaulding and Desmet Missions, were the missionaries sent by the Church of Latter Day
Saints, commonly called "Mormons." They
came to what is now Idaho for the purpose of
locating and establishing a settlement among
the Bannock and the Shoshone Indians near
Salmon river, that country then being in the
Territory of Oregon.

The missionaries, of which there were 18,
were "called," as all missionaries have been, in
this church—the majority of them having had
five or six weeks in which to prepare for the
trip. The personnel of the party was as follows:

A. R. Wright, Thos. S. Smith, Ezra J.
Bernard, Isaac Shepherd, of Farmington; Bald-
win H. Watts, of South Weber; Geo. R. Grant,
of Kaysville; Charles Dalton, Israel J. Clark,
of Centerville, Davis County; William H. Bachelor, Ira Ames, Wm. Brundridge of Salt Lake
City; Thomas Butterfield of West Jordan, Salt
Lake County; William Burgess of Provo, Utah
County; Abraham Zundel, Everett Lish, of Wil-
lard, Box Elder County; Francillo Durfee, David
Moore, Benjamin F. Cummins, Geo. W. Hill, Gilbert Belnap, Joseph Parry, Nathaniel Leavitt,
P. G. Taylor, Chas. McGeary, John Galligher,
John W. Browning, Wm. Burch, David Stephens,
of Ogden, Weber County, Utah.

The instructions received by the missionaries were to settle among the Bannock, the

Flathead or the Shoshone Indians, or at any place where the tribes would receive them, and there teach them the principles of civilization. They were instructed to take with them sufficient provisions to last one year, so they would not be a burden to the tribes whom they were to attempt to civilize and to convert, but rather, to be able to feed them, should this necessity arise.

A well known theory of Brigham Young's was "It is cheaper to feed an Indian than it is to fight him."

On May 18th, 1855, these twenty-seven men, having bade good-bye to their families, started into the desert wilderness to make a home among unknown and untutored savages.

Their outfit consisted of thirteen wagons with two yokes of cattle to each wagon, and a few cows. The party was divided into messes, five or six members to a mess, each member having his own particular duties to perform.

Thus organized, they traveled northward through what is now Brigham City, but which was at that time entirely unsettled; thence their course was along the base of the mountains, crossing Bear river a short distance of where Colliston is now located.

When it is remembered that there were no roads or bridges in those days, it will be realized that the progress of the party was attended with difficulties. Their method of camping was that generally adopted by travelers in an Indian country, with one innovation—each morning and evening they gathered in prayer—each taking his turn, according to roll call.

Crossing the Bannock range of mountains, they continued their journey, passing close to a point where Pocatello now stands. Following a northerly direction they crossed Ross Fork and Blackfoot rivers, and arrived safely at Eagle Rock on Snake river. (Eagle Rock is now called "Idaho Falls.")

Continuing up Snake River a distance of several miles, they crossed this stream and headed for the mountains to the west. The trip across the desert that lies between Snake river and Lost river, proved to be the most difficult part of the journey yet encountered, and before reaching Little Lost River some of the stock was overcome by the heat and the lack of water. However, they were finally brought through, water having been sent back to them.

On June 15th, 1855, the thirtieth day of their journey, the missionary party arrived at a place on Lemhi river, about twenty miles above its confluence with Salmon; here they determined to establish their mission.

At the location chosen, the valley is nearly a mile in width, and has an altitude of about five thousand feet. This location enjoyed two distinctions, (1) water for irrigation was plentiful, and easily diverted for this use; (2) the hills on the east were covered with accessible timber.

On their arrival, they found a large number of Indians encamped near the spot they thought best suited for the site of their headquarters. These Indians belonged to the Shoshone and Bannock tribes, together with a delegation of visitors belonging to the Nez Perces. They were catching and drying salmon, which, at that season, ran up the tributaries of the Salmon river in large numbers.

Missionary Geo. W. Hill, having a knowledge of their tongue, acted as interpreter, and through him it was explained to the Indians that the white men had come for the purpose of teaching them their methods. The missionaries were received very kindly and were permitted to occupy the land, and were allowed to cut such timber as they needed for fuel and for buildings.

The season was already late for farm operations, hence, to have delayed sowing until buildings could have been erected, would have been fatal. Therefore all hands were at once employed in cultivating and preparing a tract of land which, it was hoped, would produce enough general farm products for the next winter's supplies. Peas, potatoes and carrots were planted, and a small quantity of grain was sown. While this was being accomplished a part of their number dug a ditch to bring water into the land. A little creek emptying into the Lemhi was tapped for the purpose.

The acreage thus planted and brought under irrigation that year was not great, but owing to their greater numbers and to their better equipment, the Lemhi mission was enabled to bring under cultivation a tract of ground many times larger than that cultivated by the Reverend Mr. Spaulding at his mission established in 1836 among the Nez Perces.

The crops having been planted, the next labor to confront them was the building of a corral for their cattle and horses, and the construction of buildings for their quarters during the winter.

A spot sixteen rods square was laid out and on four sides a trench three feet deep was dug and logs about twelve feet in length were placed close together on end therein, making a palisade nine feet high. Gates were placed in these walls, one on the east side and another on the west. Within this enclosure houses were then built, logs being utilized for the purpose. There being no saw-mills, the lumber for doors and frames were whip-sawed, or sawed by hand.

It was proved later that these precautions were well taken, for the twenty-seven men were but a handful when compared to the hordes of savages who surrounded them. Every night a guard was kept over the fort and the cattle were under the watchful eyes of armed herders during the daytime. These precautions extended to those engaged in bringing timber for the stockade and the buildings, each being heavily armed with a rifle and revolver.

In addition to the embarrassment caused by

the uncertain attitude of the Indians, legions of grasshoppers descended upon the growing crops, completely destroying them.

The labor performed that first summer by those devoted missionaries was of a nature such as none but the physically and mentally strong could have endured—plowing, seeding, digging ditches, cutting and hauling logs for their stockade and buildings. And each in turn was required to face the additional work of standing guard at night. While all the time was gnawing at their hearts the knowledge that their wives and children at home, were none too well provided with the necessities of life.

It must be admitted by all who can comprehend such a situation that the mental as well as the physical strain on those men must have been so great that nothing but the most ardent devotion to duty could have enabled them to endure. The few still living, and to whom access has been had for this narrative, state that the years passed at the Lemhi mission were the most arduous they have ever experienced.

Prior to the loss of their crops by grasshoppers, it was ascertained that their supplies would run short, and especially would there be a shortage of seeds for the planting of the crops the coming year. Consequently, after the stockade and the houses had been completed, it was determined to send teams and wagons to Utah for the purpose of obtaining the necessities for carrying the party through the following spring.

The trip was taken by about half the brethren, among them being Elders Moore, Belnap, Durfee, McGeary, Grant, Clark and Taylor. They returned November 19th of that year, bringing with them their families. Francis Durfee brought his wife and three or four children; David Moore, his wife and daughter Louise; Chas. McGeary brought his wife, and I. J. Clark his wife and three children.

These were the first white families to settle in Idaho after the Spaulding family.

Owing to an early winter that year, and to the assembling of a large number of Indians, who had been told that the white settlers at Lemhi were their friends, which, if true, means that the whites would, naturally, share with them their food. In order to maintain their friendship, the settlers complied with their wishes in this respect, and, as a consequence, soon discovered that they would be short of food themselves.

By the first of December it was seen that their flour would be exhausted before March 1st. A council was held, and it was the consensus of opinion that someone must go to Utah for more supplies. Accordingly, a party of eight volunteers was sent. They left Lemhi on December 4th, and arrived at Odgen December 26th, nearly all of them badly frost-bitten, but otherwise well, though hungry. Their cattle had suffered severely and were reduced to the semblance of living skeletons.

Returning, the party left Ogden March 28th, 1856, in charge of Elder Parry. They brought with them additional supplies, and were accompanied by twenty-two new missionaries. Their destination was reached without serious mishap on May 15th, 1856. The mission was found to be in good condition on their arrival.

Farming operations were at once begun, and a large acreage was prepared and seeded. Unfortunately, the grasshoppers were as bad as they had been the previous season, and the crop was again totally destroyed, making it again necessary to bring supplies from Utah.

Fortunately, the Indians had not been openly hostile during this and the preceding year, although it was necessary to use every precaution to check any outbreak that might occur.

During these years, several Indians had professed Christianity and had been baptised, but in view of events which occurred subsequently, their conversion could not have been permanent.

During May, 1857, President Brigham Young and a large number of the authorities of his church visited the Lemhi settlement, and in a meeting he told the brethren that they had come too far from home; for, in case of trouble, they could not be reached by rescuing parties, when needed, until considerable time had elapsed. They should have stopped and settled at a locality near Blackfoot, so as to be nearer their more numerous brethren. He was other-

wise very much pleased with their accomplishments and with the spirit they had shown in
the face of such heavy odds, and now that they
had settled here and things looked so propitious,
he would see that more aid was given them by
increasing the strength of the mission. This
promise was not forgotten.

The third season, the summer of 1857, the
grasshoppers did not appear in such great numbers, and the mission demonstrated the possibilities of growing and ripening grain and vegetables at that altitude. They raised a fair crop
of vegetables and two thousand five hundred
bushels of wheat.

Thus, after struggling three seasons against
adverse circumstances and poverty, their efforts
were successful and their larders were filled to
overflowing—the result of their perseverance
and industry.

In the meantime, one of the necessary conveniences supplied to the settlement was a grist
mill, by means of which they ground their own
grain into flour.

In the fall of 1857 a large addition was
made to the membership of the Lemhi colony on
October 27th. Arrangements were at once made
for the building of a new fort, or stockade, four
or five miles below Fort Lemhi, thereby increasing the acreage and the strength of the colony,
and also giving room for new arrivals.

A number of log houses were built along

the lines of those erected at the upper fort, although these were more widely scattered.

For some weeks nothing of note occurred, but the air seemed pregnant with coming troubles. At first it was believed that the Indians would attempt nothing more serious than to drive off some of the stock belonging to the settlers. However, this illusion was banished on February 25th, 1858, when it was shown that the plans of the Indians were of a murderous nature, for on that date two men who were herding stock were shot.

On the 28th of February President Smith called the brethren together and asked their advice as to what was the wisest plan to adopt under the circumstances. It was found that many were discouraged and were desirous of abandoning the mission and going home. Others felt it was their duty to remain until released by President Young. It was finally decided to remain, but to send a dispatch to President Young for the purpose of apprising him of the situation. This was done. E. Bernard and B. H. Watts, who undertook and performed that dangerous mission, accomplished a feat unsurpassed in the annals of frontier history. They traveled over three hundred miles of country covered with snow and beset by relentless foes, and arrived safely with their message at Salt Lake City, having been without food for forty-eight hours.

Immediately on receipt of the news, President Young ordered Col. Thomas Cunningham, with about one hundred mounted men and twenty wagons, together with provisions, to go in and escort the missionaries to their homes. A company under Captain Haight started also from Farmington. These were also under Cunningham's command. He sent an express of ten men ahead to notify the mission of the approach of the relief party. On the 21st of March (Sunday) this express rode into the fort, bringing the joyful news of help; in addition they also brought letters from home.

Two days later the company of mounted men arrived. Then there was joy and thanksgiving. Captain Haight's company of fifty men arrived at the fort March 25th, and on March 28th Fort Lemhi was formally abandoned and left for the Indians. The missionaries and their families, escorted by the mounted men who came from Utah for that purpose, started to their homes, arriving at Ogden April 11th, 1858.

Thus ended in failure, even disaster, the first attempt to found a permanent agricultural settlement in what is now south Idaho. But since disaster and hardships did not discourage our Pilgrim Fathers, who were driven by persecution and intolerance to the bleak and inhospitable shores of New England, so it was with the Mormon people who erected their altars in Utah. Saddened by their experience in Lemhi, other missionaries were called, and a settlement was established in Cache Valley in November,

1859.   Franklin was settled in 1860; Malad in
1864.   Other settlements have followed in rapid
succession until the desert places have been
transformed into the most beautiful and fertile
agricultural districts within the intermountain
region.

To the organization known as the "Church
of Latter Day Saints" must be credited this
wonderful development.

CHAPTER IV.

GOLD DISCOVERIES.

PRIOR to the time when placer gold was found in paying quantities, few white men had penetrated the mountainous region now called "North Idaho" and these were engaged principally in trapping for furs.

The first record we have of the discovery of gold in this district was that made by a French Canadian on the Pend d'Oreille river in 1852, which did not prove of sufficient importance to attract much attention.

Two years later gold was discovered by General Lauder, while he was exploring a route for a military road from the Columbia river to Fort Bridger.

From 1852 onward placer mining was conducted in a desultory manner on various streams in what is now Shoshone county, Idaho. But it was not until the discovery of gold in 1860 by a party under the leadership of Captain E. D. Pierce, that a great mining boom began to assume proportions large enough to attract attention. This discovery was made on what was afterward known as "Canal Gulch," a tributary of Orofino Creek, which in turn empties into the

Clearwater river, a stream which, with its tributaries, drains the western slope of the Bitter Root mountains.

During the winter of 1860-61 the accounts of the strikes thus made were published in the Walla Walla and the Portland papers, causing a stampede the following spring to the new Eldorado. The summer of '61 found the banks of Orofino Creek and its branches lined with tents, which were occupied by thousands of miners and prospectors.

Houses had sprung up like magic in the town named "Orofino," and before the end of the summer of 1861, the newly-fledged metropolis was supplied with stores, hotels and saloons, the last outnumbering the others.

The days were enlivened by the arrival of pack-trains, which were laden with all sorts of merchandise required in a large mining camp where all is new and nothing old.

The braying of the pack-mules, and the clatter of the carpenters' and the blacksmiths' hammers gave zest to the hundreds of pedestrians continually moving about the streets from one place to another as fancy or some excitement attracted them. Violin music was heard in most of the saloons, and gambling was an adjunct of them all. New arrivals were almost continuous and departures of prospecting parties were of daily occurrence. These parties usually consisted of from two to six, and up to ten men, all heavily armed and provided with pack animals to carry their supplies. In this manner the surrounding mountains were quite thoroughly explored during the summer of 1861, resulting in the discovery of many rich claims, including the placers adjacent to Pierce City, Elk City, Florence and Warrens.

All of the foregoing towns were located and built after gold was discovered at or near their sites.

As each new discovery became known, a stampede from the first locations resulted, hundreds of men leaving fairly good claims in many instances, to join the mad rush to the new Eldorado. Disappointment in many cases followed, for, while all the camps contained rich placer deposits, yet, as might have been expected, they were limited in area; it therefore happened that of the thousands of gold seekers who followed each excitement many were unable to secure claims. In fact, it mattered not how extensive the field might be, among such a number were always to be found a number of so-called men, who were merely grown-up boys, without sufficient experience or energy to locate a mining claim.

The mining camps of Orofino, Pierce City, Elk City, Florence and Warrens were all located on lands claimed by the Nez Perce Indians, yet, although their game was slaughtered and their streams polluted by prospectors and miners, and notwithstanding that they were a powerful tribe of recognized prowess in war, they quietly submitted to the confiscation of their property, without resort to the only court to which they could have appealed—that of war. That they did not go on the war-path in what would have proved a vain effort to right their wrongs was due, no doubt, to the spirit of friendliness they had entertained for the whites since the Lewis and Clark party had visited them, this spirit of friendship and good will having been fostered and cultivated by Rev. Spaulding and his wife during their missionary work among them. I believe that those who are promoters of missionary efforts among the Indians may claim, with justice, that the forbearance of the Nez Perces was largely, if not entirely, due to the teachings they received at the Christian mission at Lapwai.

While it is no doubt true that opposition on the part of the Indians to the opening and working of the mines on their land would have been eventually overcome, yet, such accomplishment would have been attained only by the sacrifice of many valuable lives, and the delay incident to a long and bloody war. The avoidance of such a conflict at that time was especially fortunate, as the War of the Rebellion was in progress while the mining camps were enjoying their greatest degree of prosperity, and the United States government, struggling for existence, could ill afford to send troops to quell a conflict such as would have followed a general outbreak of the Nez Perce Indians.

That the friendly reception extended to the miners and prospectors in Shoshone and Nez Perce counties was due to the training many of them had received at the Cœur d'Alene and Spaulding missions, seems to be borne out by the fact that no other Indian tribe, at that time, gave up their country without a struggle that saddened many homes where mother, wife or child watched in vain for the return of one whose chair was to be forever vacant at the family fireside.

The influx of the bravo and the criminal classes into Walla Walla, Orofino, and Florence, during the years of 1861 and 1862, before the Territory of Idaho was created, and before the exodus into Boise basin and other camps subsequently discovered, by those who were not hanged or killed, was the fundamental cause of Idaho's gaining such an unenviable reputation for lawlessness during the earlier years of its organization.

These men were, in many instances, fugitives from justice in other states, and Walla Walla being the largest town in what was then eastern Washington, was the first place in which they took refuge, and it was usually but a short time after their arrival when they made their presence felt in a way that was generally followed by a funeral.

The following is a roster of a few of the prominent characters in the drama of murder, robbery and shame enacted during the early

mining days of the northwest, before and after
the organization of Idaho Territory, together
with a brief synopsis of the career of some of
them before coming to Idaho, and the sanguinary
end which terminated their lawless activities:

"Cherokee Bob," Henry Plummer, Bill Bun-
ton, Charley Ridgley, Reeves, Charley Harper,
Mayfield, Ferd Patterson, Hickey, Matt Bledsoe,
David English, William Peoples, Nelson Scott,
Bill Willoughby, Boone Helm and "Dutch Fred."

In addition to this list of notables they had
a large following of minor satellites who seldom
rose above the rank of horse thieves or "bogus"
dust operators, but who were useful to their
superiors as spies, political boosters and jurymen.

"Cherokee Bob" was a native of Georgia,
his mother being a half-blood Cherokee, for which
reason he gained the picturesque sobriquet by
which he was known. He was a bitter partisan
of the south, and upon his arrival at Walla
Walla could talk or think little else than the
great superiority of the southern soldier over
his northern compeer.

Those who have witnessed a theatrical performance in a mining or frontier town are not
likely to forget the boisterous enjoyment with
which the audience fills up the intervals between
acts. A bar where liquor is sold is almost invariably one of the conveniences attached, and
most of the audience during the interims in the
performance visit and patronize this inspiring
adjunct of the entertainment, while others in-

dulge in whistling, caterwauls, stamping feet, and other demonstrations expressive, usually, of good humor and the bubbling over of the surcharged animal spirits of men, who after all are only grown-up boys.

Walla Walla, during the time of the mining excitement, incident to the discoveries of gold in Orofino and Florence, was a typical frontier mining-supply town; here were gathered during the winter of 1861-1862 a heterogeneous population, made up of all the elements which represent the "good" and the "bad" in the human family. The men who sold dry goods and groceries, the men who made and sold what was appropriately called "Lightning whiskey," the men who robbed stages and the unsuspecting wayfarers, the rollicking cow-boy, the faro dealer and his "look-out," the minister of the gospel, the judge who pronounced sentence upon offenders, with a sprinkling of Uncle Sam's soldiers from the garrison near the town. All these, and other kinds, were mingled together on the streets and in the business houses and places of amusement. Such a crowd of cosmopolites is rarely seen in any country.

Fort Walla Walla was situated about half a mile from the town limits, and the troops stationed there were permitted to visit the embryo city on "leave," some of them attending the theaters during nearly all the performances. At the time of which I write, the fort was garrisoned with California volunteers, the regulars

formerly stationed there having been ordered
east to the seat of war.

One of the volunteer companies in the garrison was recruited in Placer county, California,
many of them having enlisted at "Dutch Flat,"
and were personally known to the writer who,
at the time of their enlistment, resided there.
They were all young men of good families, and
most of them had money of their own when
they volunteered. Their enlistment resulted from
their intense patriotism. They were led to believe that in the near future they would be
ordered to go east, there to engage in the struggle then in progress. But, owing to the need
of seasoned troops, the regulars were sent to
the front and the volunteers were substituted to
do garrison duty. Hence the presence of the
Placer county boys at Fort Walla Walla. They
were sober, industrious young men, and though
their uniforms were those of privates in the
ranks, they were as far above the average civilian roysterers who made day and night hideous
and dangerous in the town as could be imagined.

"Cherokee Bob" was consumed with wrath
every time he saw these clean-limbed young
"hirelings of Abe Lincoln," as he called them, on
the streets, and rarely failed to use some insulting epithet within their hearing; but as they
always came to town in little squads of three or
four, and were armed with regulation revolvers,
he hesitated to start a street fight. He was,
nevertheless, determined to show his superiority

over such "hirelings" and merely waited for an opportunity to arrive when he could display his prowess and venom without incurring any great danger to himself.

Choosing a night when a popular play was being performed in the theatre, and a few of the soldier boys were present, he having previously arranged with a deputy sheriff who acted in the capacity of peace officer in the show, and who, like himself, was a rabid Secessionist, to interfere when the usual noisy demonstration began at the end of the first act, and to precipitate a disturbance, if possible, by using insulting language.

The program was successfully carried out. Porter, the deputy sheriff, at the time agreed upon, sprang from his chair and striding in front of them, yelled "Dry up there, you brass-mounted hirelings, or I'll snatch you bald-headed." The insulting maner coupled with the insulting language, produced the desired effect. Smarting under the reproach, one of the young men inquired "Why do you single us out, when there are others who are more boisterous?" Porter waited for no other provocation, but drawing and cocking his revolver with one hand, he seized the soldier nearest to him with the other and jerked him into the aisle, calling on the deputy city marshal, "Cherokee Bob," and several of his associates who were conveniently near, to assist in arresting him. The plan, as prearranged, was carried out without a hitch.

The soldiers, recovering from their first surprise, offered resistance, and a melee resulted. Cherokee Bob was in his element; with a revolver in one hand and a bowie knife in the other, he sprang at his victims. When the smoke had cleared and quiet was restored Bob and his allies had disappeared, but two of the soldiers lay dead on the floor and others were horribly mangled.

The attack was so unexpected, so sudden and deadly, that the soldiers could make but little resistance. Porter and the deputy marshal were both shot through their legs—the latter was crippled for life.

Before daylight the next morning Cherokee took his departure to Lewiston, riding a stolen horse. Reaching his destination, he soon became the owner of a saloon where he was an efficient aid to the band of organized cut-throats who then made Lewiston a rendezvous, finally drifting into Florence with a painted female called Cynthia, whom he had won from the notorious gambler and murderer, Mayfield, of whom I shall make mention later. The woman referred to was finally the cause of his death. There was a ball in Florence some time after their arrival there, and Cynthia insisted that she must attend. Having made known her desire to Bob, he said in reply, "You shall go and be respected as a decent woman ought to be." So he asked Willoughby, who was suspected of being a member of the Plummer gang, to take her, at the same time saying, "If things don't go right, just report to me." She assented to go with Willoughby, and, doubtless as Bob had anticipated, they were met by scowls and evidences of disgust on every hand. The women present were indignant and gathered into groups by themselves; they soon determined to leave the room if Cynthia was allowed to remain. The managing committee, after holding a conference, informed Willoughby that he and his partner must retire, which they accordingly did.

One of the managers was named Williams; he was a saloon keeper and was familiarly called "Jakey" Williams; the other was Orlando Robbins, known to everyone as "Rube" Robbins. Bob was furious when he learned that Cynthia had been expelled from the ball room, and desired to punish someone for the indignity she had suffered. Choosing as his intended victims the members of the committee who had ordered his mistress to leave the ball, Jakey and Rube, Cherokee Bob and Willoughby the next morning determined to wipe out the offenders. Arming themselves to the teeth, they set out on their murderous purpose.

Men like Jakey and Rube were seldom found unprepared, and realizing no doubt that the ball room incident would lead to serious trouble, they were watchful; so when Bob and Willoughby appeared with weapons in their hands hostilities began. In the interchange of shots which followed, Willoughby fell, mortally wounded, dying in a few moments. Bob was punctured by several bullets and died in his saloon, where he was carried, on the third day after the gunfight.

It is told that in speaking of the relative courage of Jakey Williams and Rube Robins, Bob, before he became unconscious, said "They are both brave men, with this difference: Jakey always steps aside to get clear of the smoke of his revolver, while Rube pushes through it and keeps on coming, getting nearer his adversary with each shot." Thus ended the lives of Cherokee Bob and Willoughby. They were buried in the Florence cemetery, among other unmarked graves—the final resting place of companions in crime, who, like them, were murderers. Their victims, in many instances, received the same obsequies, and now repose in unknown, unmarked graves, among the rock-strewn mountains of the northwest.

Next on the list of these notables comes the name of Henry Plummer. In the spring of 1861 Henry Plummer and wife were registered in the leading hotel of Lewiston. They were strangers to everyone in town except, perhaps, a few gamblers who had known Plummer in Nevada or California, and these men, following the usual close-mouthed methods of their calling, said nothing about his antecedents. He was a man of gentlemanly bearing, and being accompanied by a quiet, gentle appearing woman whom he claimed as his wife, no one suspected their illicit relations.

However, it was only a couple of days before he had established his reputation as a gambler which left no doubt as to his true character.

The woman he claimed to be his wife was abandoned in a short time, penniless and alone among strangers; she told how Plummer with professions of undying love had persuaded her to leave her husband and three children to live with him. Not having the courage to return to her family and confess her fault, she abandoned herself to the downward path which always leads onward to untold sorrows—an early and miserable death. Thus was Plummer's entrance into Lewiston marked by her disgrace and degradation.

Being a gambler, his profession brought him in contact with the rough and dissolute characters when they arrived at Lewiston. It is customary in mining and frontier towns for new arrivals to "take in" the town, meaning that they shall visit all the various resorts—such as saloons, dance halls, etc. These tours are generally undertaken as soon as possible after their arrival at a new camp. Since gambling was usually conducted in these places, Plummer, as a member of the "profesh," soon became a "hail fellow well met" with the patrons of the amusements provided in these resorts.

The criminal classes soon began to recognize in him a leader, and flocked to his standard. Being a keen judge of character, he was able to choose from the common herd or "would-be" desperadoes, the most reckless and daring, the ones who combined with these traits the greatest skill in the use of firearms. These he organized into a band of choice cut-throats, who were governed by iron-clad rules, the enforcement of which was left to a committee, Plummer being its chairman, or head; in fact, he was chief of outlaws.

CHAPTER V.

OUTLAWS AND THEIR METHODS.

THE OUTLAW CHIEF remained in Lewiston during the summer of 1862, following his profession—gambling. Owing to his demeanor, which was quiet and gentlemanly, and to the fact that his clothes were, as a rule, tailor-made and neat, a stranger meeting him would not have suspected him to be the depraved character he was.

By making occasional trips, usually in the night, to interior points, he supervised and directed the operations of the band. What purported to be a road house was established by them on the traveled route between Lewiston and Walla Walla, at Pataha Creek; another was started by them between Lewiston and Orofino. Although these resorts which they termed "shebangs," were ostensibly managed by two men, the traveler might observe several other hangers-on, who were supposed to be guests, but who were actually silent partners holding themselves ready for action.

These resorts were surrounded by high hills in all directions. These hills were cut with ravines, while numerous flats and little valleys were inserted between. Bunch grass and water being plentiful, these places were veritable paradises for horse thieves.

It should be remembered that in those days and for many years later there were no railroads in any direction of the country tributary to the Columbia river, even wagon roads outside of the Willamette and Walla Walla valleys were seldom to be expected, hence the early arrivals at the Orofino and Florence mines generally found their way there in small parties, riding saddle horses or mules, bringing with them on pack animals their camp equipage, including mining tools and a quantity of provisions. During the season of high water boats ascended the Columbia and Snake rivers, bringing passengers and merchandise to Lewiston, but after arriving there those whose destination was one of the interior mining camps were compelled to procure saddle and pack animals to continue their journey, therefore those who realized that fact usually brought their own equipment, and were thus prepared to travel in any direction rumor announced a discovery of new diggings. Lewiston was the point of divergence to all the interior mining camps in the Clearwater and Salmon river region during 1861 and 1862, hence all those destined for Orofino, Elk City, Florence or Warrens went first to Lewiston, where it was the almost universal custom for travelers to remain for a day or even longer, to rest themselves and animals, but more especially to gather information concerning any new discoveries which might have been made. Thus as will be readily understood with the arrival and departure each day of so many prospectors and adventurers, the town of Lewiston was all that is implied in the term "typical frontier mining town."

During the stay made by travelers in Lewiston for rest or other purpose during those early mining days, they were carefully "sized up," by Plummer's emissaries, especially those who were on the return journey from the mines, with the object of ascertaining if possible, whether they carried any considerable amount of gold dust; accurate descriptions were also taken of their saddle and pack animals, including color and brands; bills of sale were then made out in conformity with the descriptions conveying title to the animals at some prior date to the keeper of one of the road houses either above or below, dependent upon which direction the travelers were going, the bill of sale was then dispatched by courier to the man in whose name it was drawn so as to reach him before the arrival of the men with the stock.

All being cunningly arranged in advance, as soon as the victims came opposite the house, they were halted and the demand made "Where did you get those animals? Get off, or I'll blow you off." These requests were made emphatic by the display of double-barreled shot guns or revolvers. The astonished travelers could only comply. They were then shown the bills of sale

as a cause for the demand, and if the real
owners of the stock were sensible men they left
their property with the robbers and resumed
their journey on foot. But if, as was sometimes
the case, they offered resistance, their journey
ended in an improvised cemetery, provided for
just such occasions.

In the mining camps and frontier towns,
a style of building much in vogue during their
first establishment, was built by erecting a
frame of poles upon which rafters of the same
kind of material were set up, then sides, ends
and roof were covered with sheeting or common brown muslin. Such buildings require no
windows and even the doors were mere frames
of small poles covered with the same material.

This class of structures was the kind that
largely lined the streets of Lewiston during
the early mining excitement, which followed the
Orofino and the Florence discoveries. There
were no street lamps, none were needed, for the
sunshine lighted the interior of the buildings by
day, without the aid of windows, while the
lamps and candles used at night illumined the
streets. Such buildings, obviously, presented
slight opposition to burglars, and as a protection
against stray bullets they were a failure.

To provide against the last it was customary
to pile sacks of flour or sand around the beds of
those who slept.

Illustrative of the foregoing, a German
named Hildebrandt kept a saloon during the

winter of 1861, and part of January, 1862, in one of these structures. He was a jovial character, and his place was a favorite resort for both Germans and Americans. His saloon was not a gambling house but was conducted in a quiet, orderly manner. He was known to be the possessor of considerable gold dust, which the Plummer gang determined to appropriate. Between twelve and one o'clock one cold January night the door was burst from its hinges and a volley of revolver shots were fired in the direction of the large bed near the door where Hildebrandt and two friends were asleep. Hildebrandt was killed by the first volley; his friends returned the fire, sprang from bed and escaped with the treasure.

His murderers then proceeded to search the place, and being disappointed in their search, uttering oaths and threats, marched out through the crowd of citizens who had assembled. They were known, but no one attempted to arrest them. The following day, however, a meeting of the citizens was held for the purpose of devising means to arrest the further progress of crime, and for punishing the murderers of Hildebrandt.

This was the first effort made in Lewiston looking to the protection of the people, and as the lawless element composed a large percent of the population in Lewiston, the movement was pregnant with serious possibilities. Henry Plummer took a conspicuous part in the proceedings and made an eloquent plea for conservative action. He explained the horrors of anarchy and urged the assembly not to take any action for which they might afterward be sorry. Since Plummer was known only as a gambler, and but few suspected that he had any connection with the robberies and murders which were of such frequent occurrence, his speech had the effect of dispersing the gathering and prevented an organization from being formed.

Among those who kept saloons at that time was a man named Ford. He was a courageous character, and while in the saloon business to make money, yet he never associated with the rough element; nor did he encourage them to frequent his place, but on the contrary he was their avowed enemy.

When the foregoing meeting was disorganized without taking action to punish the murders of Hildebrandt, he denounced those present as cowards, and accused them of "weakening."

The murdered man had a brother in Orofino, who, when he learned of the tragedy, at once announced his determination to visit Lewiston for the purpose of wreaking vengeance upon the assassins. They learned of his intention, had a message conveyed to him, stating that if he started to Lewiston he would not reach there alive. The threat, as was intended, had the effect of intimidating him, causing him to abandon his purpose. Thus the assassins es-

caped justice that time. But they met their
Nemesis later.

Nothing except the possible organization of
a vigilance committee was feared by the Plummer gang, and for any man to advocate the organization of such an instrument of justice was
to mark him for destruction. Hence, Patrick
Ford, who was present at the meeting, and who
insisted on action being taken, was listed for
death. Ford had opened an additional business
in Orofino, and it was known soon after Hildebrandt's murder that he was going up to Orofino with a party of dancing girls to open a
dance hall. This was thought to afford a
favorable opportunity to dispose of him, so word
was sent out to the "shebang" on the road, to
intercept him, and to put a stop to his proposed
vigilante activities. But Ford, suspecting their
intentions, circled around the place and thus
avoided the encounter, which doubtless would
have been fatal to him.

Having heard of his escape, Plummer,
Charlie Ridgley and Reeves mounted horses and
followed on the trail, their route being marked
with several robberies. When within a few
miles of Orofino, two footmen were espied approaching, one being some distance in advance
of the other. As the foremost one came up he
was ordered to hold up his hands, a command
that was readily complied with. He was
searched, but nothing of value was found on his
person. They then informed him that he would

better move along and get out of the country as
soon as possible, for the rough mountains were
a poor place for a man who was broke.

By the time this search and colloquy were
finished, the second pedestrian had arrived; he
also was a Frenchman and proved more profitable than the first, for notwithstanding that he
stoutly asserted he had no money, their search
revealed a well-filled buckskin purse containing
approximately one thousand dollars in gold dust.
Jubilant over their success, they dashed wildly
into Orofino with the impetuosity of a band of
stampeded buffaloes. Reining up in front of
Ford's saloon they dismounted; entering the
saloon they demanded the barkeeper to serve
them with liquor—Ford being out. After they
had sated their thirst they proceeded to demolish
the furniture, including the bar fixtures. During
the confusion Ford arrived, and with a gun in
each hand he ordered them to leave the saloon
and town. They backed out of the place, gained
their horses and rode to a feed-yard, where Ford
soon followed, demanding why they had not
left town. This demand was answered with a
shot, which precipitated a fight in which Ford
was killed and Charley Ridgley was severely
wounded. The latter was carried to a friendly
ranch near by and given such careful treatment
that he eventually recovered.

Plummer now changed his headquarters to
Florence, from whence his associates made fre-

quent incursions along the different lines of travel leading to and from that camp.

New discoveries having been made in other sections, many began leaving the older camps. Among these were Plummer, Reeves and Ridgley, the latter having recovered sufficiently from his wounds to accompany them to Elk City, their new field. Here he met a coterie of his former California pals, but he suddenly disappeared and was next heard of in Deer Lodge. The former field of his activities was immediately occupied by others of his ilk equally unscrupulous, some of whose deeds will be recorded later.

At this time Plummer seems to have parted from nearly all the members of his old Lewiston gang except Jack Cleveland. Becoming more secretive in his movements, he formed a new band of congenial spirits.

He visited nearly all the camps situated along the eastern slope of the Rocky Mountains in Montana, but while the new members of his gang made robbery a business, and practiced the theory that "dead men tell no tales," Plummer concealed his affiliations so well that for a long time he remained unsuspected outside the membership of his organization of freebooters.

The band of which he was chief at that time consisted entirely of new members whom he had enrolled since leaving Elk City save one man, Jack Cleveland, who had crossed the Bitter Root mountains into Montana with him. His greatest fear seemed to be that Cleveland, while in his cups, would reveal some of the murderous enterprises in which they had participated before leaving Lewiston and Florence, Plummer having thus far succeeded in keeping his former record a secret from his new pals. The suspicions he entertained toward Cleveland finally led to an open rupture one day while they were in Bannock. This was settled in a pistol duel in which Cleveland was killed. Plummer then fled to Rattle Snake Creek, where he was captured by a posse from Bannock. In his trial which followed he was acquitted.

CHAPTER VI.

IN the summer of 1862, a party of prospectors entered what was afterward known as "Boise Basin." This party entered the basin via Boise Valley near the point where now stands the town of Centerville. It was there one of their number made the first discovery of gold in that afterwards famous district.

Moving from there up the creek a few miles, a second camp was made at, or near, where the town of Hogem—now called "Pioneer," was subsequently located. Here the party remained two days, prospecting the stream, which was named "Grimes Creek," after a member of the party bearing that name, a name it has borne ever since. On the third day they moved still farther up the stream, going into camp above a point they called Pilot Knob.

While coming in from the Boise Valley they met a party of Indians, one of whom could speak English, and were informed by them that there were plenty of bad Indians in the mountains where they were going. After crossing the divide and dropping down into the basin they found some Indian tepees, or lodges, but up to the time of making their last camp the party had not been molested. Here, however, an attack was made which resulted in the death of Grimes, who was shot while charging upon a bunch of Indians who were concealed in a thicket of bushes from which they were firing on the camp. Fortunately the men rallied to their leader, a man named Splawn, and repulsed the enemy without further loss.

It was apparent to all that they were in a dangerous and desperate predicament; their only hope of safety was retreat, for their provisions and ammunition were both running low. Assembled around the lifeless body of their late companion, a council was held, and it was determined that Grimes should be immediately buried, and then they would at once start to Walla Walla with news of their discovery and with samples of gold dust they had obtained.

Wrapped in a blanket, the body was tenderly laid to rest in one of the recently dug prospect holes. Thus was left under the whispering pines one of the brave pioneers who had endured untold hardships, and finally gave up his life in conflict with savage foes. Those who have been accustomed to witnessing burial ceremonies in our older states and who have listened to the solemn invocation of the pastor, and admired the banks of flowers heaped by loving hands on the new made mounds, can have but faint conception of the details of such a tragic burial as was there conducted by those grim-visaged men—not one but whom realized that a similar ending might be his within the hour. Outnumbered ten, or even twenty to one, by relentless and merciless foes, those brave men performed their last sad duty to their fallen comrade and friend, and then departing, left him alone in the wilderness.

By this and similar acts of heroism were the first discoveries of gold made in Idaho—such were the men who blazed our early trails.

The discovery of placer gold in Boise Basin and the retreat therefrom was made in August, 1862. The discoverers, after many vicissitudes reached Walla Walla in September. There, without trouble, fifty men were persuaded to return with them to their discovery in Boise Basin.

Saddle and pack animals as well as arms and general supplies had to be provided. Considerable time was thus passed in outfitting for the return trip. Thus, together with the time occupied in making the journey back from Walla Walla, brought the season well into October before the vanguard of the first return party reached its destination in Boise Basin. The men were fortunate in this, however, because the Indians never stay in the high mountains after the cold weather begins, usually leaving the higher altitudes for the warmer climate of the valleys when the first snow appears. Hence all was peaceful and quiet when the reinforced party reached the scene of the recent trouble

6 E. H. I.

with the redmen—there were no Indians in the
Basin.

The arrival of this party was followed almost daily by others. Soon along every gulch
and ravine within several miles, miners' log
cabins with shake roofs were erected, and the
mountain streams, heretofore as clear as crystal,
were transformed into muddy rivulets.

Townsites were located, and Placerville, Centerville, Hogem and Bannock were soon thriving
towns. The name of the last was afterwards
changed to Idaho City, and that of Hogem to
Pioneer. The growth, or rather the creation of
these towns, may justly be cited as one of the
marvels of frontier enterprise. When the first
flakes of snow began to fall in November, 1862,
the locations where these mining towns were
subsequently built were an undefiled pine forest
where the foot of civilized man rarely if ever
had trod. Yet unaided by sawmills to cut the
needed lumber, or teams to haul the material,
bustling towns had sprung into existence before
the snow had disappeared from the hillsides.
The following spring Placerville and Bannock
especially, were places of considerable importance, each having one or more hotels, restaurants and stores, while sandwiched in were many
saloons where business was never suspended,
for they ran both day and night shifts. The
winter of 1862-63 was indeed an eventful one
in Boise Basin.

In the history of mining camps, it is doubtful if there was ever its equal. All who came during the first six months experienced but little difficulty in locating rich claims, and gold dust, the only money in circulation, seemed to be found in inexhaustible quantities.

It should be borne in mind that all these discoveries of gold, and all these rapid-fire events occurred while the country now forming the states of Idaho and Montana was still included within the Territory of Washington. The counties of Shoshone, Nez Perce, Idaho and Boise were by legislative enactment of Washington Territory, and, as provided, sent representatives to the territorial assembly which met at Olympia.

The rapid development of the part of Washington Territory now known as Idaho and Montana, due to the incoming of the gold maddened hordes who scattered to the various camps distributed over a vast area of country, made the enforcement of law so far away from Olympia, the then capital and seat of government, almost impossible. Hence it was deemed advisable to create a new territory out of eastern Washington, which was to include all the new mining districts. Congress was petitioned to this effect, and the following act, having been passed, received the approval of Abraham Lincoln on March 3, 1863.

ORGANIC ACT OF THE TERRITORY OF IDAHO.

An Act to Provide a Temporary Government for the Territory of Idaho.

Be it enacted by the Senate and House of

Representatives of the United States of America
in Congress assembled: That all that part of the
territory of the United States included within
the following limits, to-wit: Beginning at a
point in the middle channel of the Snake river
where the northern boundary of Oregon intersects the same; then follow down said channel
of Snake river to a point opposite the mouth of
the Kooskooskia, or Clearwater river; thence due
north to the forty-ninth parallel of latitude;
thence east along said parallel to the twenty-
seventh degree of longitude west of Washington;
thence south along said degree of longitude to
the northern boundary of Colorado Territory;
thence west along said boundary to the twenty-
third degree of longitude west of Washington;
thence north along said degree to the forty-second parallel of latitude; thence west along said
parallel to the eastern boundary of the state of
Oregon; thence north along said boundary to
the place of beginning. And the same is hereby
created into a temporary government, by the
name of the Territory of Idaho; *Provided*: That
nothing in this act contained shall be construed
to inhibit the government of the United States
from dividing said territory or changing its
boundaries in such manner and at such time as
Congress shall deem convenient and proper, or
from attaching any portion of said territory to
any other state or territory of the United States;
Provided further, That nothing in this act contained shall be construed to impair the rights of

person or property now pertaining to the Indians
in said territory, so long as such rights shall remain unextinguished by treaty between the United States and such Indians, or to include any
territory which, by treaty with any Indian tribes,
is not, without the consent of said tribe, to be
included within the territorial limits or jurisdiction of any state or territory; but all such
territory shall be excepted out of the boundaries,
and constitute no part of the Territory of Idaho,
until said tribe shall signify their assent to the
President of the United States to be included
within said Territory, or to affect the authority
of the government of the United States to make
any regulations respecting such Indians, their
lands, property, or other rights, by treaty, law,
or otherwise, which it would have been competent for the government to make if this act
had never passed.

SEC. 2. And be it further enacted, That the
executive power and authority in and over said
Territory of Idaho shall be vested in a governor,
who shall hold his office for four years, and until his successor shall be appointed and qualified,
unless sooner removed by the President of the
United States. The governor shall reside within
said Territory, and shall be commander-in-chief
of the militia, and superintendent of Indian affairs thereof. He may grant pardons and re-
spites for offenses against the laws of said Territory, and reprieve for offences against laws of the
United States until the decision of the President

of the United States can be made known thereon, he shall commission all officers who shall be appointed to office under the laws of said territory, and shall take care that the laws be faithfully executed.

SEC. 3. And be it further enacted, That there shall be a Secretary of said Territory, who shall reside therein, and shall hold his office for four years, unless sooner removed by the President of the United States; he shall record and preserve all laws and proceedings of the legislative assembly hereinafter constituted, and all the acts and proceedings of the governor in his executive department; he shall transmit one copy of the laws and journals of the legislative assembly within thirty days after the end of each session, and one copy of the executive proceedings and official correspondence semi-annually, on the first days of January and July in each year, to the President of the Senate and to the Speaker of the House of Representatives for the use of Congress; and in case of the death, removal, resignation, or absence of the governor from the territory, the secretary shall be, and he is hereby authorized and required to execute and perform all the powers and duties of the governor during such vacancy or absence, or until another governor shall be duly appointed and qualified to fill such vacancy.

SEC. 4. And be it further enacted, That the legislative power and authority of said Territory shall be vested in the governor and a legislative assembly. The legislative assembly shall consist of a council and house of representatives. The council shall consist of seven members having the qualifications of voters as hereinafter prescribed, whose term of service shall continue two years. The house of representatives shall, at its first session, consist of thirteen members possessing the same qualifications as prescribed for members of the council, and whose term of service shall continue one year. The number of representatives may be increased by the legislative assembly, from time to time, to twenty-six, in proportion to the increase of qualified voters, and the council, in like manner, to thirteen. An apportionment shall be made as nearly equal as practicable among the several counties or districts for the election of the council and representatives, giving to each section of the Territory representation in the ratio of its qualified voters as nearly as may be. And the members of the council and of the house of representatives shall reside in, and be inhabitants of the district or county, or counties, for which they may be elected respectively. Previous to the first election, the governor shall cause a census or enumeration of the inhabitants and qualified voters of the several counties and districts of the Territory to be taken by such persons and in such mode as the governor shall designate and appoint, and the persons so appointed shall receive a reasonable compensation therefor. And the first election shall be held at such time and

places, and be conducted in such manner both
as to the persons who shall superintend such
election and the returns thereof, as the governor
shall appoint and direct; and he shall, at the same
time, declare the number of members of the
council and house of representatives to which
each of the counties or district shall be entitled
under this act. The persons having the highest
number of legal votes in each of said council
districts for members of the council shall be declared by the governor to be duly elected to the
council; and the persons having the highest number of legal votes for the house of representatives shall be declared by the governor to be
duly elected members of said house; *Provided*:
That in case two or more persons voted for shall
have an equal number of votes, and in case a
vacancy shall otherwise occur in either branch
of the legislative assembly, the governor shall
order a new election; and the persons thus elected to the legislative assembly shall meet at such
place and on such day as the governor shall appoint; but thereafter the time, place and manner
of holding and conducting all elections by the
people, and the apportioning the representation
in the several counties or districts to the council
and house of representatives, according to the
number of qualified voters, shall be prescribed
by law, as well as the day of the commencement
of the regular sessions of the legislative assembly; *Provided*: That no session in any one year
shall exceed the term of forty days, except the
first session, which may continue sixty days.

SEC. 5. And be it further enacted, that every free white male inhabitant above the age of twenty-one years, who shall have been an actual resident of said territory at the time of the passage of this act, shall be entitled to vote at the first election, and shall be eligible to any office within the said Territory; but the qualification of voters, and of holding office, at all subsequent elections, shall be such as shall be prescribed by the legislative assembly.

SEC. 6. And be it further enacted, that the legislative power of the territory shall extend to all rightful subjects of legislation consistent with the Constitution of the United States and the provisions of this act, but no law shall be passed interfering with the primary disposal of the soil; no tax shall be imposed upon the property of the United States, nor shall the lands or other property of non-residents be taxed higher than the lands or other property of residents. Every bill which shall have passed the council and house of representatives of the said territory shall, before it becomes a law, be presented to the governor of the Territory; if he approve, he shall sign it, but if not, he shall return it, with his objections, to the house in which it originated, who shall enter their objections at large upon their journal and proceed to reconsider it. If, after such reconsideration, two-thirds of that house shall agree to pass the bill, it shall be sent, together with the objections, to the other house, by which it shall likewise be reconsidered;

and if approved by two-thirds of that house, it shall become a law. But in all such cases the votes of both houses shall be determined by yeas and nays, to be entered on the journal of each respectively. If any bill shall not be returned by the governor within three days (Sunday excepted, after it shall have been presented to him, the same shall be a law in like manner as if he had signed it, unless the assembly, by its adjournment, prevent its return, in which case it shall not be a law; *Provided*: That whereas slavery is prohibited in said territory by act of congress of June nineteenth, eighteen hundred and sixty-two, nothing herein contained shall be construed to authorize or permit its existence therein.

Sec. 7. And be it further enacted, that all township, district and county officers, not herein otherwise provided for, shall be appointed or elected, as the case may be, in such manner as shall be provided by the governor and legislative assembly of the Territory of Idaho. The governor shall nominate and, by and with the advice and consent of the legislative council, appoint all officers not herein otherwise provided for; and in the first instance the governor alone may appoint all said officers, who shall hold their offices until the end of the first session of the legislative assembly, and shall lay off the necessary districts for members of the council and house of representatives, and all other officers.

Sec. 8. And be it further enacted, that no

member of the legislative assembly shall hold or
be appointed to any office which shall have been
created, or the salary or emoluments of which
shall have been increased, while he was a member, during the term for which he was elected,
and for one year after the expiration of such
term; but this restriction shall not be applicable to members of the first legislative assembly; and no person holding a commission or appointment under the United States, except post-
masters, shall be a member of the legislative
assembly, or shall hold any office under the government of said territory.

SEC. 9.   And be it further enacted, that the
judicial power of said territory shall be vested in
a supreme court, district courts, probate courts,
and in justices of the peace.   The supreme court
shall consist of a chief justice and two associate
justices, any two of whom shall constitute a quor-
um, and who shall hold a term at the seat of
government of said territory annually; and they
shall hold their offices during the period of four
years, and until their successors shall be appointed and qualified.   The said territory shall be
divided into three judicial districts, and a district court shall be held in each of said districts
by one of the justices of the supreme court at
such times and places as may be prescribed by
law; and the said judges shall, after their appointments, respectively, reside in the districts
which shall be assigned them.   The jurisdiction
of the several courts herein provided for, both

appellate and original, and that of probate
courts and of justices of the peace, shall be limited by law; *Provided,* That justices of the peace
shall not have jurisdiction of any matter in controversy when the title or boundaries of land
may be in dispute, or where the debt or sum
claimed shall exceed one hundred dollars; and
the said supreme and district courts, respectively
shall possess chancery as well as common-law
jurisdiction. Each district court, or the judge
thereof, shall appoint its clerk, who shall also
be the register in chancery, and shall keep his
office at the place where the court may be held.
Writs of error, bills of exceptions, and appeals,
shall be allowed in cases from the final decisions of said district courts to the supreme court,
under such regulations as may be prescribed by
law. The supreme court, or the justices thereof,
shall appoint its own clerk, and every clerk shall
hold his office at the pleasure of the court for
which he shall have been appointed. Writs of
error and appeals from the final decisions of
said supreme court shall be allowed, and may be
taken to the supreme court of the United States,
in the same manner and under the same regulations as from the circuit courts of the United
States, where the value of the property or the
amount in controversy, to be ascertained by the
oath or affirmation of either party, or other
competent witnesses, shall exceed one thousand
dollars, except that a writ of error or appeal

shall be allowed to the supreme court of the
United States from the decision of the said supreme court created by this act, or of any judge
thereof, or of the district courts created by this
act, or of any judge thereof, upon any writs of
habeas corpus involving the question of personal
freedom.   And each of the said district courts
shall have and exercise the same jurisdiction, in
all cases arising under the Constitution and laws
of the United States, as is vested in the circuit
and district courts of the United States; and the
first six days of every term of said courts, or
so much thereof as shall be necessary, shall be
appropriated to the trial of causes arising under
the said Constitution and laws; and writs of
error and appeal in all such cases shall be made
to the supreme court of said territory, the same
as in other cases.   The said clerks shall receive,
in all such cases, the same fees which the clerks
of the district courts of Washington Territory
now receive for similar services.

SEC. 10.   And be it further enacted, that
there shall be appointed an attorney for said
territory, who shall continue in office four years,
and until his successor shall be appointed and
qualified, unless sooner removed by the President
of the United States, and who shall receive the
same fees and salary as the attorney of the
United States for the present Territory of Washington.   There shall also be a marshal for the
territory appointed, who shall hold his office for
four years, and until his successor shall be ap-

pointed and qualified, unless sooner removed by the President of the United States, and who shall execute all processes issuing from the said courts when exercising their jurisdiction as circuit and district courts of the United States; he shall perform the duties, be subject to the same regulations and penalties, and be entitled to the same fees as the marshal of the district court of the United States for the present Territory of Washington, and shall, in addition, be paid two hundred dollars annually as a compensation for extra services.

SEC. 11.   And be it further enacted, that the governor, secretary, chief justice, and associate justices, attorney, and marshal, shall be appointed by the President of the United States, by and with the advice and consent of the senate.   The governor and secretary to be appointed as aforesaid, shall, before they act as such, respectively, take an oath or affirmation before the district judge or some justice of the peace in the limits of said territory duly authorized to administer oaths and affirmations by the laws now in force therein, or before the chief justice or some associate justice of the supreme court of the United States, to support the Constitution of the United States, and faithfully to discharge the duties of their respective offices, which said oaths, when so taken, shall be certified by the person by whom the same shall have been taken; and such certificates shall be received and recorded by the said secretary among the executive proceedings;

and the chief justice and associate justices, and all civil officers in said territory, before they act as such, shall take a like oath or affirmation before the said governor or secretary, or some judge or justice of the peace of the Territory, who may be duly commissioned and qualified, which said oath or affirmation shall be certified and transmitted by the person taking the same to the secretary, to be by him recorded as aforesaid; and afterwards the like oath or affirmation shall be taken, certified and recorded in such manner and form as may be prescribed by law. The governor shall receive an annual salary of two thousand, five hundred dollars, the chief justice and associate justices shall receive an annual salary of two thousand five hundred dollars, the secretary shall receive an annual salary of two thousand dollars; the said salaries shall be paid quarter-yearly, from the dates of the respective appointments, at the treasury of the United States; but no payment shall be made until said officers shall have entered upon the duties of their respective appointments. The members of the legislative assembly shall be entitled to receive four dollars each per day, during their attendance at the sessions thereof, and four dollars each for every twenty miles' travel in going to and returning from said session, estimated according to the nearest usually traveled route, and an additional allowance of four dollars per day shall be paid to the presiding officer of each house for each day he shall so preside.

And a chief clerk, one assistant clerk, one en-
grossing and enrolling clerk, a sergeant-at-arms
and doorkeeper may be chosen for each house;
and the chief clerk shall receive four dollars per
day, and the said other officers three dollars per
day, during the session of the legislative assembly; but no other officers shall be paid by the
United States; *Provided*: That there shall be
but one session of the legislative assembly annually, unless, on an extraordinary occasion, the
governor shall think proper to call the legislative
assembly together. There shall be appropriated
annually the usual sum to be expended by the
governor to defray the contingent expenses of
the Territory, including the salary of the clerk
of the executive department; and there shall
also be appropriated annually a sufficient sum to
be expended by the secretary of the Territory,
and upon an estimate to be made by the Secretary of the Treasury of the United States, to
defray the expenses of the legislative assembly,
the printing of the laws, and other incidental
expenses, and the governor and secretary of the
territory shall, in the disbursement of all moneys
intrusted to them, be governed solely by the
instructions of the Secretary of the Treasury
of the United States, and shall, semi-annually,
account to the said Secretary for the manner in
which the aforesaid moneys shall have been expended; and no expenditure shall be made by
said legislative assembly for objects not specially
authorized by the acts of Congress making the

appropriations, nor beyond the sums thus appropriated for such objects.

SEC. 12.   And be it further enacted, that the legislative assembly of the Territory of Idaho shall hold its first session at such time and place in said Territory as the governor thereof shall appoint and direct; and at said first session, or as soon thereafter as they shall deem expedient, the governor and legislative assembly shall proceed to locate and establish the seat of government for said territory at such place as they may deem eligible; *Provided*: That the seat of government fixed by the governor and legislative assembly shall not be changed at any time, except by an act of the said assembly duly passed, and which shall be approved, after due notice, at the first general election, by a majority of the legal votes cast on that question.

SEC. 13.   And be it further enacted, that a delegate to the House of Representatives of the United States, to serve for the term of two years, who shall be a citizen of the United States, may be elected by the voters qualified to elect members of the legislative assembly, who shall be entitled to the same rights and privileges as are exercised and enjoyed by the delegates from the several other territories of the United States to the said House of Representatives; but the delegate first elected shall hold his seat only during the term of the congress to which he shall be elected.   The first election shall be held at such time and places, and be conducted in such man-

7 E. H. I.

ner as the governor shall appoint and direct; and
at all subsequent elections the times, places, and
manner of holding the elections shall be prescribed by law. The person having the greatest
number of legal votes shall be declared by the
governor to be duly elected, and a certificate
thereof shall be given accordingly. That the
Constitution and all laws of the United States
which are not locally inapplicable shall have the
same force and effect within the said Territory of
Idaho as elsewhere within the United States.

SEC. 14. And be it further enacted, that
when the lands in the said Territory shall be
surveyed, under the direction of the government
of the United States, preparatory to bringing
the same into market, sections numbered sixteen
and thirty-six in each township in said Territory
shall be, and the same are hereby, reserved for
the purpose of being applied to schools in said
Territory, and in the states and territories hereafter to be erected out of the same.

SEC. 15. And be it further enacted, that,
until otherwise provided by law, the governor of
said Territory may define the judicial districts
of said Territory, and assign the judges who
may be appointed for said Territory to the several districts, and also appoint the times and
places for holding courts in the several counties
or subdivisions in each of said judicial districts,
by proclamation to be issued by him; but the
legislative assembly, at their first **or any** subsequent session, may organize, alter, or modify

such judicial districts, and assign the judges, and alter the times and places of holding the courts, as to them shall seem proper and convenient.

SEC. 16. And be it further enacted, that all officers to be appointed by the President of the United States, by and with the advice and consent of the senate for the Territory of Idaho, by virtue of the provisions of any law now existing, or which may be enacted by congress, are required to give security for moneys that may be intrusted with them for disbursement, shall give such security at such time and in such manner as the Secretary of the Treasury may prescribe.

SEC. 17. And be it further enacted, that all treaties, laws and other engagements made by the Government of the United States with the Indian tribes inhabiting the territory embraced within the provisions of this act, shall be faithfully and rigidly observed, anything contained in this act to the contrary notwithstanding; and that the existing agencies and superintendencies of said Indians be continued with the same powers and duties which are now prescribed by law, except that the President of the United States may, at his discretion, change the location of the office of said agencies or superintendents.

Approved March 3rd, 1863.

CHAPTER VII.

CRIMINALS ACTIVE IN MINING CAMPS.

AS SOON as the snow disappeared in the spring of 1863, many of the miners and prospectors who had been cooped up in Bannock (now in Montana) all winter, started out on prospecting trips. Other gulches containing rich deposits of placer gold were soon discovered.

The entire district was in the Territory of Washington until April 3rd, 1863, when the Territory of Idaho was created. It embraced all the new gold discoveries in and around Bannock and Helena. (There were two towns, or mining camps, named Bannock in Idaho during 1863).

Since the country at that time was not equipped with the machinery of government, the miners depended upon themselves to maintain local government. Each camp elected peace officers, and laws were enacted to secure the rights, peace and safety of the inhabitants. It having been determined to elect one sheriff for all the camps east of the Bitter Root mountains, Plummer, the outlaw, became an active candidate for the nomination on the Democratic ticket. With the support of the members of his gang, and with that of the sporting elements in the towns, he triumphed. Thus with the aid of hundreds of good men who voted the Democratic ticket on account of "principle," the vilest and most cold-blooded murderer who ever polluted the mining camps of the northwest was made sheriff—a man whose trail for years had been marked by the graves of his victims.

His position as sheriff enlarged his opportunities for evil until a long-suffering and forbearing public was aroused, which resulted in the forming of a vigilance committee, at whose hand he, and a dozen others of his partners in crime, expiated their sins on the gallows.

Nearly all of those who were Plummer's associates in Lewiston, Florence and Elk City, including Charlie Ridgley, who was wounded while assisting in murdering Ford, found their way to Boise Basin, where we shall refer to them later.

The next name on the roster of the lawless men who came to Lewiston in the early 60's is Bunton—stool-pigeon, horse and cattle thief, and murderer. He had killed a man at a ball near Walla Walla, was tried for murder, and acquitted for want of sufficient evidence. Next, he killed his brother-in-law, escaping the officers by flight. He then located a ranch on Pataha creek, where he lived with an Indian woman. It was soon ascertained that his business consisted of hiding and selling stolen stock.

The officers raided his ranch, but he had doubtless been warned of their intentions and made his escape, disguised as an Indian wrapped in a blanket. It was at this time that he entered Lewiston and soon became a member of the Plummer gang. As long as Plummer remained there, Bunton proved a valuable aid in all of his nefarious ventures, but when his chief took wing, he too became alarmed and fled to Rattle Snake Creek, where he was soon captured and hanged by the Montana vigilance committee.

Next on the roster is Charles Ridgley, who took a prominent part in the murder of Ford at Orofino. Before this, however, he shot a man named Gilchrist in Walla Walla, and thinking that he had killed him, said "That takes a load off my shoulders." Gilchrist was badly wounded but he recovered. Ridgley escaped arrest by flight. Going to Lewiston, he joined the Plummer gang. After recovering from the wounds received at the time of the Ford murder, he went with Plummer to Elk City and later drifted to Idaho City and South Boise, where he distinguished himself as a friend of Ferd Patterson, a gambler, gun-man and political henchman of E. D. Holbrook. He finally disappeared from the eyes of the writer. Charley was a good fellow of his kind when the cards broke his way; his value as a political henchman consisted solely in his reputation of being a "gun-fighter," and a "bad man."

The next undesirable citizen is Charley Reeves, who accompanied Plummer and Ridgley to Elk City, whence he went to Bannock. While

among the Bannocks in January, 1863, he bought
from them a squaw, but she was so cruelly
abused by him that she fled to her own people.
Reeves and a friend named Moore tracked her to
a tepee where she had taken refuge, and on her
refusal to return with him, he resorted to violence, whereupon an old Indian chief forcibly
ejected him from the tepee.   Reeves and Moore,
joined by a man named Wm. Mitchell, marched
and countermarched by the place, firing volley after volley into it. The brave old chief was killed,
together with a lame Indian, a papoose, and a
Frenchman, named Cazette, who had entered the
tepee to discover the cause of the disturbance.
Two other curious individuals were badly
wounded.

After the dastardly deed had been perpetrated the performers fled, but were captured the
following day, brought back and tried by a jury,
who brought in a verdict of "not guilty."   While
the prisoners *were* guilty, and everyone knew it,
the jury was afraid to bring in a verdict in accordance with the facts, they being intimidated
by the criminal class, who were in the majority,
and who crowded the room where the trial was
being held, brandishing revolvers and threatening to take life for life.

This trial proved disastrous to the community, for it encouraged the lawless element, far
and near, convincing them that they held the
upper hand and had the business and law-abiding citizen cowed.

Emboldened by the foregoing result, and feeling that disguise was no longer necessary, the country was soon startled by a series of murders and robberies more brazen and shocking than any of the others that had preceded them.

The difficulties heretofore encountered by those who would have gladly pursued drastic measures in order to secure a reasonable degree of safety for life and property, were chiefly found in the newness of the country, which precluded the people, who were gathered there from almost every quarter of the globe, from becoming acquainted with one another.

Neighbors did not know one another, hence, as was wise, they hesitated to suggest an organization designed to oppose lawless methods, lest the man approached might be a member of the banditti. There being no church nor society organization with which the better classes could affiliate, it was every man for himself. The road-agents had the only perfect organization, and it shielded its own. But a time came when conditions were altered.

An old man who had come alone to the camp secured a claim. After building a cabin, he begun to work his ground. The hardships he was obliged to undergo were more than his enfeebled frame could withstand. Overcome by sickness, he abandoned his efforts when it was too late. Confined to his cabin and bed, he was given such treatment and care as the rough,

kind-hearted men of the mountains are ever
ready to bestow on the needy. It soon became
apparent, however, that the end was near, and
many of the young men who had left fathers at
home when they came west, felt kindly disposed
toward the suffering old man who had always
been so gentle and kind to them when he was
able to move around. He, too, realizing that the
final summons had come, made known to his at-
tendants that in his home village he belonged to
the society of Free and Accepted Masons, and
expressed a wish that if any of that Brotherhood
could be found, he desired to be buried with
Masonic rites. A notice was accordingly posted,
calling for a meeting that evening at the humble
cabin of the dying miner; all Masons who could
conveniently attend were invited. When the
time arrived, so large was the attendance that
an adjournment to a larger building was necessary.

The funeral of the deceased brother was
conducted in due and ancient form, and as the
members present, amid profound silence,
marched forward, and one by one cast the sprig
of evergreen upon the coffin in that open grave,
each felt a degree of safety such as he had not
known since coming to the place.

All felt that at last they had found those
to whom they could safely talk, and with whom
they could safely act. Though the cemetery con-
tiguous to Bannock had already assumed proportions surprising in such a comparatively small

community, yet the foregoing death was said to be the first to come from purely natural causes.

The subsequent organization of the citizens, followed by the uprooting of the outlaws and the restoration of order and safety, was no doubt primarily due to the meeting of the members of the Masonic Fraternity at the deathbed and grave of their departed brother. Had the conditions that existed up to this time been allowed to continue, the human mind is horrified at the contemplation of what might have resulted; but the departure of a lonely old man on that mysterious journey which we must all, inevitably take, was the means of bringing an end to the era of crime.

"God moves in a mysterious way
His wonders to perform."

The sudden departure of Plummer from the scenes of his former activities, Lewiston, Florence and Elk City, was no doubt accelerated by the untimely but well-merited fate of three members of his gang whose names appear in the roster of notables heretofore given—Dave English, Nelson Scott and William Peebles.

In October, 1863, a packer in charge of a pack train belonging to Neal McClinchey, after delivering a load to Florence, started on his return to Walla Walla, but before reaching Lewiston he was held up and relieved of fourteen pounds of gold dust, it being the amount received for packing in the load he had just delivered. As he transferred the dust to the hands of one of the robbers the latter remarked "That's right and sensible; if every man was as reasonable as you, things would go along smoother." A few days later, Joseph and John Berry having delivered a load at Florence, were returning to Lewiston, driving their loose pack animals ahead. When two days along on their journey they too, were held up by three masked highwaymen, who were doubtless the same ones that robbed McClinchey's packer on the former occasion.

The Berry boys recognized the voices of two of the men who held them up—Dave English and William Peebles; and they ascertained from persons who had met the trio that the third member was Nelson Scott.

The victims made haste to reach Lewiston, and when once there they lost no time in relating the particulars of their loss. Plummer and his leading lieutenants being absent, the members of his band remaining in Lewiston were too few to check the indignant citizens who immediately proceeded to organize for the capture of the road agents. The posse having satisfied itself that the wanted men had not passed through Lewiston, a search was begun up the river which established the fact that the fleeing men had crossed Snake river above town, and had traveled in the direction of Walla Walla.

Public   sentiment   was   now   thoroughly aroused, and clamored for the capture and punishment of the offenders. In the meantime, several determined men who believed in action rather than consultation, had started in pursuit of the lawbreakers. The efforts of these men proved successful, the capture being made in detail—Peebles was captured in Walla Walla; Scott on Dry Creek, and English at Wallula, where he was ready to take the steamer for The Dalles. The prisoners were apparently much surprised at the temerity of their captors. The community had so long held them in fear, and had permitted them to pursue their unlawful trade to such an extent without hindrance, that they felt very much aggrieved and plainly showed that they thought interference by outsiders an outrage.

Recognizing the futility of attempting to escape, they quietly accompanied their captors on the homeward journey to Lewiston, fully expecting to be liberated by their friends when they arrived there. But public sentiment had crystalized while the pursuit was in progress, and a citizens' committee had been organized. The better classes of Lewiston's citizens had been worked up to a high pitch over the repeated crimes occurring at such regular intervals, and they now being at last in the majority, it was determined to try the prisoners by the committee.

The captured men were accordingly taken in charge by the people and confined in an unfinished building standing on the south bank of the

Clearwater river—the building being strongly guarded. In order to complete the good work so auspiciously begun, and for the further purpose of ridding the town of a number of toughs hanging around the saloons, a committee was appointed to bring in for trial all suspicious characters found. News of this movement was designedly circulated, with the result that before daybreak the following morning, all the birds of doubtful color had flown.

As was to be expected, intense excitement prevailed. Business was suspended and men were seen in groups on the streets and in the alleys conversing in low, earnest tones. Everyone was heavily armed, all wearing revolvers, while many in addition carried rifles or shotguns.

The final disposition of the jailed bandits was postponed until another day, a strong guard of well armed men being kept around the building in which they were confined. The town was thrown into a fever of excitement by hearing a fusilade of shots during the midnight hours. The shots coming from the direction where the guards were stationed, it was immediately surmised that a rescue was being attempted, and men, some of them only half dressed, came running from every direction to reinforce the ,ailers. The streets were filled as if by magic. The firing ceased as suddenly as it begun, and it was learned that a friend of Peebles, who was then keeping a hotel in Lewiston, had attempted his rescue, firing upon the guard and getting shot through the arm in return. When this was understood the people returned to their beds, leaving the guards to their dangerous vigil.

The next morning almost the entire populace visited the building where the prisoners had been confined, but no guards halted their approach. Drawing closer, they discovered that the guards had departed, leaving the doors ajar. Timidly pushing them open, the most venturesome entered. Here they found hanging by their necks from the joists, the rigid corpses of the men who had been, in life, thieves, road agents, murderers, and all-around "bad actors." "The wages of sin is death."

It was told of a very humane attorney whose sympathies were known to favor the oppressed highwaymen and horse thieves, that he appeared at the door of the building where the prisoners were confined, during the afternoon after their incarceration, and asked to see them, but was refused admittance and told to come back in the morning, which he accordingly did. In answer to his second request to see the accused, he was told to step inside, and upon doing so, he came suddenly and without warning upon the bodies of his clients suspended by ropes from the upper joists. It is needless to say that the learned barrister with the sympathetic proclivities, made a speedy exit.

CHAPTER VIII.

TERRITORIAL OFFICES ESTABLISHED.

IN ACCORDANCE with the provisions of the act creating Idaho Territory, on the 10th day of March, 1863, or one week after its approval, the President appointed the following officers: Governor, W. H. Wallace; Secretary, W. B. Daniels; Chief Justice, Sidney Edgerton; Associate Justice, Alex. C. Smith; Associate Justice, Samuel C. Parker. On the thirteenth of the same month he appointed D. S. Payne United States marshal. The position of United States attorney remained vacant until February 29, 1864, on which date C. C. Hough was appointed to that office.

The first territorial offices were established in Lewiston, no territorial capital having been named in the organic act. Some criticism of Governor Wallace has been indulged in for selecting Lewiston as the point from which to conduct the business affairs of the new territory, basing the reason therefor on the fact that Idaho City was a larger town and in the midst of a more dense population.

Political prejudice at that time was quite bitter, and it was but natural that any, and in fact, all acts of the appointees of President Lincoln should be criticised. Idaho City at the time of the establishment of the territorial offices in Lewiston, was a new mining town which could be reached only by saddle and pack animals, there being no wagon road thereto, and no post-office had as yet been established.

Fort Boise was not located until early in July, 1863, and since it was not until after the location of the fort that the site where the city of Boise now stands, was located, the territorial offices could not have been established there. In justice to Governor Wallace, long since deceased, it is but fair to state that when he was commissioned governor of the new Territory of Idaho, he found his duties very onerous, not the least of his burdens being the lack of facilities for communication with the Department and the President in Washington. The fact that Lewiston had a stage line, or lines connecting with steamboats at Wallula for Portland, made it the most easily accessible; hence, on that account its selection by Governor Wallace as the temporary seat of the territorial government seems to have been wise.

As was doubtless anticipated, a great deal of correspondence was necessary between the Territorial Secretary and the seat of government in Washington, before the new territory was in position to conduct its own affairs, and consequently much delay resulted.

On September 22nd, 1863, Governor Wallace issued a proclamation calling for an election to be held throughout the Territory on the 31st day of October of that year (1863), naming the officers to be elected, including a delegate to congress and members of the first Territorial legislature, which afterwards convened by executive order in Lewiston, on December 7th, 1863.

The political campaign preceding the first election in the Territory of Idaho was a spirited contest. The bitterness engendered by the War of the Rebellion, then in progress, had divided the people into two adverse factions, rather than political parties. The names Democrats and Republicans were still retained, but the issues were no longer "tariff" or "free trade." Slavery or its abolition—the one great question, overshadowing and sinking into insignificance all others, was the one for which in the east and south vast armies contended. "Shall the Union of states be dissevered, dismantled, or shall that Union *be* preserved?"

Those who voted the Republican ticket were Union men while, generally speaking, those who supported the Democratic nominees were Secessionists. There were a few Democrats in Idaho who were loyal to the Union and the Flag, but none such could obtain recognition in Democratic nominating conventions.

The first election in Idaho resulted in a victory for the Republicans. They elected a delegate to congress and a majority of both houses of the legislative assembly. Governor Wallace was a candidate of the Republicans for delegate

8 E. H. I.

to congress and was elected, thus causing a vacancy in the Governor's office until his successor, Caleb Lyon, was appointed and qualified. In the interim W. B. Daniels, Secretary of the Territory, became the acting governor, following the resignation of W. H. Wallace.

As will be observed by reference to the enabling act it was within the vested authority of the governor to name the time and place for the meeting of the first legislative body. No place being named in the organic act as the capital of the new territory, the duty of locating the seat of government was left to the legislature, it being provided that the governor should name the place or places where the body should meet until the capital was located.

The first territorial legislature was convened in Lewiston, Idaho, on December 7th, 1863, the council consisting of—First District, E. H. Waterby, Stanford Capps, Lyman Stanford; Second District, Joseph Miller, Ephriam Smith; Third District, William Rheem, A. J. Edwards. President, Joseph Miller.

The Representatives were: Joseph Tufts, Beaverhead District; C. P. Bodfish, M. C. Brown, R. P. Campbell, Milton Kelly, W. F. Keithley, Boise County; L. C. Miller, East Bannock District; Alonzo Leland, John Wood, Idaho County; L. Bacon, Nez Perce County; James A. Orr, Shoshone County. Speaker, James Tufts.

At the time the foregoing session was held, the Territory of Idaho included all the country

within its original boundaries, hence, as will be
noted, Beaverhead district and East Bannock,
now within the state of Montana, were represented at that session. The personnel of the
Idaho Territorial legislature that was assembled
in Lewiston by call of the governor, was in some
respects superior to the average legislative assembly of today. Many of the members came
long distances, requiring days of toilsome travel
over rugged mountain trails such as had formerly been traversed only by Indians. No wagon
roads had at that time been constructed, and
hotels were luxuries seldom enjoyed. Mounted
on saddle horses or mules, armed with rifle and
revolver, and bringing with them on a pack animal their blankets and provisions, these early
statesmen "hit the trail" for the scene of their
legislative endeavors. As there has been no
record of any of them having been robbed by
bandits, it is to be presumed that, like their
successors of today, they carried but little "dust"
and consequently were not worthy of the attention of the toll gatherers of the time.

Those who endeavor to comprehend the circumstances under which that first legislature
met will find their minds bewildered by the
effort. Legislative bodies usually have as a
guide the enactments of former sessions, their
duty being to amend laws already in force or
enact such new ones as experience has suggested. But these men came to a little frontier
town where many of the inhabitants were law-

less and where the accommodations were of the most primitive character, and entered with energy and intelligence upon duties which were new to most of them. The session laws enacted by that first session of the Territorial legislature of Idaho, which was convened in Lewiston on December 7th, 1863, bear official evidence of the industry, loyalty and honesty of. its members. To the laws they enacted is attached the following certificate, bearing the Seal of the Territory of Idaho:

"Secretary's Office, Lewiston.

"I hereby certify that the laws contained in this printed volume are true and literal copies of the enrolled laws passed by the first Legislative Assembly held during the months of December, January and February, eighteen hundred and sixty-three and four.

"On file in my office.

"WILLIAM B. DANIELS,
Secretary of the Territory."

The Organic Act, creating the Territory (Sec. 2) provided that "The Governor shall receive an annual salary of two thousand five hundred dollars;" "the Secretary shall receive an annual salary of two thousand dollars;" "the said salaries shall be paid quarter-yearly from the dates of the respective appointments at the Treasury of the United States. The members of the legislative assembly shall each be entitled to receive four dollars per day during their attendance at the sessions thereof."

At the time when the first session convened, and for several years thereafter, the lowest prices for which a meal could be obtained was one dollar, while one dollar and a quarter was the usual charge, and lodgings of the most primitive character rented from one dollar to one fifty per night. Greenbacks, with which all territorial officers, including members of the legislature, were paid, were, at the time of which I write, worth only about fifty cents on the dollar; hence the members of the first legislative assembly were to receive only the equivalent of one dollar and sixty cents per day. Such was the dilemma confronting them. With even mineral water selling at twenty-five cents a drink, the condition was, to say the least, serious.

Although some of them brought blankets, yet they found it impracticable to live on the equivalent of one dollar and sixty cents per day; hence an act was passed providing an additional compensation to be paid in warrants on the territorial treasury: The governor and justices of the supreme court, each the sum of two thousand dollars; the secretary of the territory, one thousand four hundred dollars; the members of both houses of the legislature, six dollars per day each, and a proportionate increase to all the employes, as neither the members or employes could have subsisted on the compensation paid by the government.

It must be remembered that up to the meeting of the legislature and the subsequent enactment of the revenue laws, no taxes were collected, and as a result there was no money to pay warrants issued as provided in the foregoing act; therefore, while the salaries were raised and the warrants paid to the officers and members, they could be sold or bartered only at a heavy discount, bringing the owner, if obliged to sell, as some of them were, not over sixty cents on the dollar, or the equivalent of $3.60 per diem; add to this $1.60 obtained for their greenbacks and their total per diem was only $5.20. The expense of living at that time was far in excess of that of today, hence the members of the Idaho State Legislature who receive $5.00 per diem are much better paid than those of the first session of the territorial assembly.

I have been thus explicit for the reason that I believe an injustice has been done in this matter by a former historian.

The summer following the creation of the Territory of Idaho was an eventful epoch in its history. Boise Basin developed to a degree that attracted wide attention. The towns of Placerville, Centerville, Hogem and Bannock became marvels of business enterprise and vim. During that summer, 1863, the towns of Boonville and Ruby City were located on what is now called Jordan Creek, in Owyhee County, and as very rich ledges carrying silver and gold were soon discovered, another town was located above Ruby on the same stream, and named Silver City. Al-

though Ruby was the first county seat in that
county, Silver proved to be the best business
point, and eventually secured the county offices,
and the pioneer town of Ruby gradually suc-
cumbed to the inevitable, and today exists only
in the memory of a few old pioneers who are
left to mourn its decadence, and they too will
soon be known no more. They did a great and
good work and were manly and true men. May
they find good "diggings" in the Great Beyond,
is the hope and prayer of all who knew them.

Gold was also discovered the same year in
Boise river, near what is known as Rocky Bar.
The discoveries of placer mines in the eastern
portion of the territory, on the eastern slope of
the Rocky Mountains, caused a large influx of
miners, business men and adventurers into that
country also, so that from the east to the west,
over the vast regions of mountain and plain,
constituting the original area of Idaho, before
the first year of her territorial existence had
closed, the march of industry was noticeable in
widely distributed localities, and a constant
stream of yellow gold began to replenish the
channels of trade, materially strengthening the
credit of the government, then in the hour of
greatest need.

As was to be expected, the Indians did not
surrender their hunting grounds and fisheries
without a struggle. The Nez Perce tribe, as
has been told, were very forbearing, no doubt
owing to the Christianizing efforts of Rev.

Spaulding and wife, but no such influence had been brought to the tribes occupying the Boise, Payette and Snake river valleys. There the Indians had held undisputed sway from time immemorial.

As the crickets and jack rabbits sometimes over-run and destroy the crops in these valleys today, without asking leave, so we of the Anglo-Saxon race in those days over-ran and destroyed the hunting grounds of the original owners, and without asking leave, took forcible possession thereof. Not having the time to spare from our other pursuits to sufficiently punish the Indians for presuming to bar our progress, we appealed to the government to support us in holding the country we had entered. In response to our petition, Major Lugenbeil, on the 28th day of June, 1863, arrived with a company of U. S. cavalry and went into camp on what is now called "Government Island," a mile or more down the river from where Boise now stands, and on the 6th day of July selected the present site of Boise Barracks. A few days later a number of men from Bannock, now Idaho City, came down and located the townsite of Boise City, and with the proverbial enterprise of those days, but little time was required to inaugurate a busy mart.

A cargo of goods owned by Cyrus Jacobs, which was then in transit to Bannock, was diverted to the embryo city of Boise, and a building was speedily erected for its accommodation. Another stock of goods was soon shipped in by "Crawford & Slocum," who established a sutler store. Several saloons, two livery stables, and a couple of hotels were rapidly placed in commission, and the quiet which had heretofore reigned was to be known no more. The town begun in the foregoing manner was the following year made the capital of the territory, and is now the capital of the state. It is a beautiful inland city of about twenty thousand inhabitants, at this writing (1912).

The writer and his then partner, John Porter, located a ranch in April, 1963, on one of the tributaries of the Payette river, about four miles above Horseshoe Bend, and there engaged in gardening and farming for four years, finding a ready market for all our produce in the mining towns and along the gulches in Boise Basin, using pack animals to transport our produce over the mountain, a distance of thirteen miles, to Placerville, and approximately twenty-five miles to Idaho City.

Porter was an English-Canadian, and not having had previous experience in packing, that task was mine, while he ran the ranch and kept the sour-dough can in order. During those days nearly all the goods and supplies used in the Boise country were brought via Portland, up the Columbia river to Umatilla Landing, and from there transported by either pack train or wagons to the distributing points, either Boise Basin or elsewhere. Consequently, the cost of all com-

modities was high. During the first three years
nothing in the line of provisions or hardware
sold for less than twenty-five cents per pound,
and when it is remembered that the art of can-
ning vegetables had not arrived at its present
state of perfection it will be understood that
they who were farmers in those days were engaged in a profitable business. They were the
first monopolists in Idaho, and I am willing to
testify that we enjoyed it. During those three
years there were not enough men engaged in
farming to supply the mining camps, consequently there was always a shortage. When
Porter and I began operations we had only about
two gallons of onion sets; these we planted,
spading up a piece of ground in the bend of the
creek. It was a sunny spot, and the soil being a
rich loam, the young plants grew rapidly, and
four weeks after planting them we pulled them
all and tied them in bunches of one dozen each.
There were one hundred bunches, which we
sold in Placerville as fast as we could pass them
out at one dollar a bunch. These were the first
green vegetables sold in the Basin. Cucumbers
brought two dollars per dozen, green corn the
same price.

I arrived on Buena Vista Bar one Sunday
morning in August, 1863, with the first watermelons ever seen in that camp. An emigrant
family had arrived but a few days before. They
were from Missouri, and there were two beautiful girls among the other eight or ten offspring.

These were the first young ladies to arrive, other than the painted kind, and they were lovely girls, wearing white starched dresses. They were even more attractive than my melons. Two gallant young miners had moved into a tent, leaving their cabin to the family, and by this means had become well acquainted. The girls liked watermelons in Missouri, and were anxious to sample the Idaho product, so they solicited one of the young men to buy one. They had doubtless been accustomend to seeing melons sold in their home town for five or ten cents each, and while they must have known that the price would be greater in Idaho, they hardly expected it would be more than three or four times as much. The young man was delighted to gratify the girls, and coming within hailing distance, with a whoop in volume equal to a Bannock Indian, yelled "Hey, Cap, bring us a melon." I sized up the party and taking a rapid inventory of their number, selected as large a melon as I had, and carried it into the cabin where the young ladies stood ready with knives to determine whether it was ripe. Knowing that they were from Missouri it was understood that I was to "show them." The melon proved to be satisfactory and the young man asked how much he owed me. I told him 25 cents per pound, the weight was marked in the rind. Upon examination, it was found to weigh thirty-two pounds, making the price eight dollars.

In justice to the farmer, it is proper to state

that those melons were transported on pack animals from the garden, a distance of twenty-five miles, over a rough mountain trail, and the loss by breakage was great, no farm product being less profitable at that time. And in extenuation of the investment of the young man, it is also fair to state that he thought she was worth it.

My first visit to Boise Basin was in May, 1863, or approximately nine months after the first discovery there of gold. Yet, although winter was included in that time, and the annual fall of snow at that altitude is usually from three to six feet, beginning in December and remaining until April, four towns had assumed considerable importance. All these being busy hives of industry and enterprise. When it is remembered that up to that time, and many months afterward, all supplies were brought from Walla Walla and the Columbia River on pack horses and mules, and the only conveyance for passengers was saddle animals, it seemed as if the Basin must have been touched with some magician's wand. But it was gold that worked the charm.

On the first trip I entered Placerville, which then, as now, was built with a plaza in the center, and facing it on all sides were stores, saloons, and various other business enterprises; including a bakery and hotel. Although I was twenty-three years old, I was yet a boy, and as I rode down Granite street onto the plaza, which was crowded with men, the impression made on

me will always remain. It was Sunday, and the
miners from the adjacent gulches were in town
purchasing supplies or seeking amusement. In
front of a saloon on the north side a dense
crowd had assembled, and after dismounting and
securing my horse, with the proverbial curiosity
of the tenderfoot, I pushed my way among
them. Gaining the attention of a man who
proved to be the owner of a claim on Wolf
Creek, I asked him what the excitement was.
He replied "Oh, nothing. A man for breakfast,
that's all. They have moved him into the shade
of the saloon," pointing around the corner. Following his direction, I ventured with others to
take a look, and there, sure enough, lying on the
ground, was "Hickey," a former member of the
notorious gang of robbers and murderers who
had so effectively for the two preceding years
terrorized Lewiston, Florence, and other northern camps. Accompanied by several of his former boon companions, they had made their way
into the Basin, and although the quality of
whiskey obtainable at that early period in the
history of Placerville was not so enlivening as
the later brews, it was sufficient to give him the
courage to attempt to run a bluff on an old timer,
known by the euphonious name of "Snapping
Andy," who proved to have too much "snap,"
for, snatching a pickhandle from a barrel conveniently near, he gave Hickey his quietus before the latter could use his revolver. The skull
bone was indented where the blow took effect,

and the blood and brains were oozing out. There the body was permitted to lie all that day, while the sightless eyes seemed fixed upon the beautiful summer sky.

This was the first of many tragedies which came to my notice during the early days in Boise Basin. Boy and tenderfoot that I was, for many months I could not banish from my mind that lifeless form. Even now, as I pen these lines, I can see it all again—the lofty pines, the eternal hills, the bearded men, the roofs, steep-pitched, to shed the snow.

No mail contracts having been let or post-offices established, letters carrying news and urging friends to hasten to the new Eldorado were sent out by all possible conveyances.

As a result of this advertising which was emphasized by reports of the enormous quantities of gold being sent to the United States mints, the country was soon invaded by thousands of gold crazed persons. Stage lines were established and a population estimated as high as forty thousand settled down to their various pursuits. A majority of these were no doubt engaged in mining, yet nearly all the vocations followed in the older communities were in evidence.

From the beginning Bannock City increased in population more rapidly than any other of the mining towns, owing, perhaps, to its fortunate location at the confluence of two mountain streams, the channels of which seemed to be literally lined with gold. So profitable was

mining in these streams and in the bars which formed their banks, that I have witnessed the clean-up of a string of sluices where the gold dust was divided among the owners—share and share alike—by measuring it in a tin cup, using for a strike the back of a sheath-knife.

A short time previous to the Snapping Andy-Hickey tragedy, another group of Florence notables arrived in Placerville, among the number Bill Mayfield, Cherokee Bob's former companion. Mayfield killed Sheriff Blackburn in Nevada, was captured, tried and sentenced to be hanged but made his escape. Coming to Lewiston he joined Plummer, and became prominent among the robbers who pillaged the northern mining camps. Soon after his arrival in Placerville he became involved in a quarrel with a man named Evans over a card game. Mayfield drew his revolver, intending to settle the dispute by killing his adversary, but Evans exclaimed "I'm not heeled"—the mountain expression for "I am not armed." "Then go and heel yourself," said Mayfield, replacing his revolver in its holster at his belt, "and look out the next time you meet me, for I am bound to kill you at sight. One of us must die."

The next day while Mayfield was walking down Granite street in company with friends, Evans, who was in a cabin on the north side of the street, doubtless waiting for Mayfield to pass, fired through a window, using a double barreled shotgun charged with buckshot.

Mayfield, being accustomed to the use of a

revolver, even in the act of falling, reached for his weapon, but the vital spark had flown and his gun-plays were over. He fell in the street, and expired shortly afterward, illustrating once more the truth of the maxim "Those that live by the sword die by it."

Evans was placed under arrest, but made his escape the following night, leaving the country on a horse furnished by some friend. He was never apprehended.

The Boise News, a weekly paper then published in Idaho City every Saturday evening, by T. J. and J. S. Butler, was the first newspaper published in the Boise Basin, and it was eagerly sought and read by everyone, single copies being sold at fifty cents. Its issue of Saturday, February 27, 1864, contained an announcement of the appointment of the first county officers for Boise County; the appointments having been made by the Governor and confirmed by the council:

Sheriff, Sumner Pinkham; Probate Judge, Daniel McLaughlin; County Commissioners, John C. Smith, Frank Moore, Henry Crow; Auditor, Washington R. Underwood; Treasurer, Charles D. Vajin; Assessor, George Woodman; Justices of the Peace for the various precincts, and other officers, all of whom were to hold their positions until their successors were elected and qualified.

The same number of the Boise News also announced the convening of the first term of the district court in and for Boise County, Hon. Samuel C. Parks presiding.

Boise County at this time contained a population equal to, if not greater, than that of all the other counties combined; hence, as there had been no prior term, a great deal of business had accumulated. The first order of the court was the issuance of a venire, returnable on Thursday morning, the 25th, for thirty-six persons possessing the qualifications of jurors. The proceedings during this first term of court were conducted under the laws enacted by the first session of the Idaho Territorial legislature, and the jurors were summoned under the provisions of an act concerning jurors, Page 589, Session Laws, 1st Session, as follows:

"AN ACT CONCERNING JURORS."

"Be it Enacted by the Legislative Assembly of the Territory of Idaho, as follows:

"Section 1. The Probate Judge and the Sheriff of the county in which the term of the district court is or may be authorized by law to be held, shall at least ten days prior to the commencement of said term of court, select the names of one hundred persons, lawfully qualified to serve as jurors, from the assessment roll of such county; Provided: That that number of names are contained on such assessment roll; and the names of the persons so selected, after being written on separate slips of paper, shall be deposited in a box to be provided for such purpose, and from the names so deposited the judge and sheriff aforesaid shall alternately draw.

9 E. H. I.

the names of thirty persons who shall constitute trial jurors, for the next ensuing term of such district court.

"Section 2. The list of names so drawn, certified to by the judge and sheriff as selected by them, shall thereupon be delivered to the clerk of the district court who, upon the receipt of the same, shall immediately issue a venire directed to the sheriff of the county, commanding him to summon the persons so named as trial jurors for such term of court, and the sheriff shall summon such named persons at least three days prior to the commencing of such term of court.

"Sec. 3. The venire as provided for in Section 2 of this act shall be returned to the clerk of such district court, by the sheriff aforesaid, at least two days before the commencement of such term of court, and such venire, after its return, shall be subject to the inspection of any officer or attorney of the court.

"Sec. 4. The box containing the residue of the names of the jury list as aforesaid shall, after such drawing, be locked up, and with the key deposited with the clerk of the district court for such county, and by him safely kept for future use by aforesaid officers, or as further provided in this act.

"Sec. 5. When at any time during a term of the district court, it shall become necessary to summon other jurors than as hereinbefore provided for, the clerk shall in open court, under the direction of the judge thereof, from such box, draw a sufficient number of names to constitute

additional trial jurors during such term of
court; Provided: In case any such jurors so
drawn reside at a great distance from the place
where the court is held, the court may, in its discretion, dispense with the summoning of such
jurors and order another to be drawn instead
thereof, and the clerk shall issue a venire directed to the sheriff, for the summoning of such
persons as trial jurors, and the sheriff shall proceed forthwith to summon the same as such trial
jurors, and with all possible diligence, make
return with his proceedings thereon.

"Sec. 6. When at any term of the district
court for the want of an assessment roll, or sufficient time is not permitted in which to prepare
and draw the list of jurors as provided in this
act, or when from any cause which may appear
satisfactory to such district judge, such list has
not been prepared or drawn, or the sheriff has
not summoned the jurors, or the names selected
as jurors, placed in such box be exhausted, it
shall be lawful for such district judge and sheriff
to prepare a list of names of a sufficient number
of persons, competent to serve as trial jurors,
and deposit such names in a box, and at any
time during a term of court when a jury shall
be required, names of persons shall be drawn
therefrom by the clerk, as provided in Section
Five of this act, and from time to time, other
names may be selected and placed in such box
and drawn therefrom as hereinbefore provided
for and summoned as such trial jurors; Pro-

vided: That in the selection of names to be deposited in such box the name of no person from among the by-standers at such court be chosen and selected."

It will be observed that Section 6 of this act provides a method for summoning a jury in case no assessment roll has been prepared. The second session of the legislature, for reasons best known to the members, repealed that law and enacted as follows:

"Sec. 197.   On or before the first day of the term, the judge shall, by an order to be entered on the minutes, direct the sheriff of the county to summon thirty-six persons from the citizens of the county, to appear forthwith, or at such time as may be named in said order.

"Sec. 198.   The clerk shall issue the summons, and the sheriff shall execute and return it at the time specified, with a list of the names of the persons so summoned. If he has been unable to summon the whole number in the time allowed, he shall return the summons with the list of the names summoned.

"Sec. 199.   The court may, in its discretion, enlarge the time of the return, and direct the sheriff to summon the whole number, or may proceed to empanel a grand jury from the number summoned.

"Sec. 200.   Upon the return of the summons, or upon the expiration of the further time allowed, the names of the persons summoned shall be called, and the court shall proceed to empanel

a grand jury and a trial jury, in like manner as
if such persons had been empaneled upon a regular drawing of a jury."

It will be observed that under the provisions
of the statute, the sheriff and his deputies could,
if desired, secure a jury to either convict or
acquit. The records of Boise county show that
there was only one conviction for murder in the
first degree in that county for several years, and
the accused was found guilty of murdering a
Chinaman, but was reprieved by the governor.
It was said of him at that time that "He should
have been hanged because he would not divide
with his friends, the boys." He, consequently,
had no influence.

The political activity of the criminal class
in securing the right men for sheriffs and deputies in the principal counties can easily be com-
prehended. The sheriffs did not necessarily have
to be bad men. All that was required of them
was that they be "accommodating and friendly"
in appointing their deputies.

The next matter of importance to engage
the attention of the court was the certificates of
the attorneys and the administering of the oath
of allegiance to the government, prescribed by
the law enacted by the first session. The following. named lawyers were found to have the
necessary credentials, and after taking the oath,
were authorized to practice before the courts in
Idaho:

J. K. Shaffer, Edward Nugent, George I.

Gilbert, H. L. Preston, John S. Grey, A Heed, John Cummins, Daniel McLaughlin, Frank Miller, I. N. Smith, R. B. Snelling, George Ainslie, E. D. Holbrook, C. B. Wait, V. S. Anderson, J. S. Hascall, W. C. Rheem, W. R. Kethly, R. A. Pierce, J. J. Morland, H. W. O. Margery, Joseph Miller.

Many of the attorneys admitted at that time were able lawyers, and became distinguished in their profession in after years, some of them being chosen to positions of high honor.

After the foregoing preliminary proceedings had been concluded, Judge Parks stated that he desired to make a few remarks, which he did as follows:

"Gentlemen of the Bar: Before proceeding with the regular business of the term I owe it to myself, to you and to the people of this county to make a few remarks. The position of a Judge of the second judicial district was not sought by me. In saying this I do not say that the position is not an honorable one. On the contrary, it is one of which an abler man than I might well be proud. But it is my desire and expectation, and I believe it was yours, that the Chief Justice of this Territory should be assigned to this district. There is in this part of the Territory far more population and legal business than in either of the other two districts. There are many cases here involving character, liberty and life; there are others here on which depend large pecuniary interest. It is doubtful whether any court in so new a country ever needed more ability and experience.

"This district properly belongs to Judge Edgerton, not only from his position as Chief Justice, but from his high moral and official character, and his large experience. But circumstances rendered it inconvenient, if not impossible, for him to be here; while the pressure of business in your court, the crowded state of your jail, and the natural impatience of your people made it necessary that a court should be held at as early a day as possible. Under these circumstances, Governor Wallace assigned this district to me. I consented to the arrangement reluctantly, and with a deep sense of the responsibility it devolved upon me. To some, and perhaps to a considerable extent, the property, the liberty and the lives of many men depend upon my action in this court. I do not say that any judge can always decide aright; I know that I cannot. All that I promise is that to the best of my ability I will discharge the duties incumbent upon me, and by so doing strive to secure the confidence of the bar and of the people. And from my acquaintance for some months past with some of your number, and the cordial greeting you have extended to me on my arrival among you, and the uniform courtesy with which you have treated me since, I feel confident I shall have your assistance in the effort to make this court a means of suppressing disorder and wrong, and promoting good morals, harmony and peace.

"Whatever popular prejudice there may be against the profession of the law, it is a useful and noble one, calculated, when properly pursued, to expand and elevate the mind and heart, and has furnished many of the loftiest intellects and purest characters that have adorned the history of our race. Associated in fraternal relations with the members of such a profession here, I cannot doubt that I shall find them in the conduct of the business of this court devoted to the real and substantial interest of their clients, and not to technicality and free form; relying for success not upon artifice and fraud, but upon professional knowledge and skill—laboring not to embarrass but to assist the Court.

"Amid the difficulties and embarrassments of an untried position, of an unfamiliar practice, and of heavy responsibility, I rely for success much upon your assistance and generosity. In some degree my reputation depends upon the result of this court; if it shall not succeed, I am sure the fault will not be yours. Hoping that I may not fail, and that the just expectation of the community may not be disappointed, I enter upon the discharge of the duties of the office assigned me."

The term of court thus auspiciously begun made an enviable record as to the amount of work transacted.

Idaho City proper, at the time the first court was held, consisted of two streets running parallel with one of the creeks for a distance of approximately one-half mile, intersected by cross streets. It also had an extensive suburb known as "Buena Vista Bar," together with others of minor importance in close proximity. The buildings which covered the townsite were with but few exceptions of wood, many of logs, hewn on two sides and neatly constructed. The lumber used at first was whipped or whipsawed, which process, with wages from eight to twelve dollars per day, made the erection of buildings an expensive luxury.

Two large and well conducted hotels were in operation for the entertainment of the traveling public, in either of which accommodations consisting of room and board could be had for, approximately, present-day prices at first-class hotels; yet the freight rate on all supplies from Umatilla Landing on the Columbia river, in Oregon, which was the nearest shipping point, was not less than an average of $500 per ton, or 25 cents per pound, while nothing in the line of vegetables sold for less, and generally for much more than that, yet neither of these hotels had bar-rooms or sold liquors.

In addition to the hostelries named, were many restaurants where lodging was not provided. These were patronized, rather than the hotels, by persons who had places to sleep in connection with their business. The restaurants never closed, and were frequented largely during the night, when tin-horn gamblers, the demi-monde, and other doubtful characters are generally in evidence. Saloons were more numerous in all mining towns than any other class of business, and as gambling was usually an adjunct, every effort possible was exerted to make them attractive. Talented musicians were employed at high salaries, and not infrequently girls, called "hurdy-gurdies," were engaged to dance with all comers who desired that kind of amusement at the nominal price of fifty cents per dance, and the drinks for self and partner, which cost fifty cents more, or one dollar net per dance.

The girls were engaged by the proprietors of the "social resorts," in sets of four, with a chaperone, who accompanied them at all times.

They were almost invariably German girls, and although they were brought into contact with rough people and sometimes witnessed even the shedding of human blood, the rude, generous chivalry of the mountain men, some of whom were always found in these resorts, was a guarantee of protection from violence, and strange as it may sound to those of modern times, these girls were pure women, who simply did the work they had bargained to do, and when their contracts expired, most of them married men whose acquaintance they had made while pursuing their vocation, the men who knew them best, and with the money they had earned by dancing with "Wild Bill," "Texas Pete," and others, helped to buy a home for themselves and husbands. The poor girls, and they danced only because they were poor, had kind hearts and wonderful patience and forbearance.

They proved themselves loyal wives and tender, affectionate mothers. Most of them have gone to render their final account, but some of their children remain in Idaho, the land of their mothers' adoption, honored and respected citizens.

Among the many musicians employed as an attraction in the saloons and gambling houses, was a violinist named Kelly, whose proficiency as a "fiddler" was well known through all the mountain regions of the Pacific slope. He commanded a salary second to none and was engaged in the largest gambling resort in the city. The contract under which he played included the installation of a swinging stage, or platform, swung by iron rods from the upper joists, several feet above the heads of those who might stand on the main floor below. This platform was reached by a movable ladder, which, after he had ascended, he pulled up out of reach of those below. The object was two-fold: First, when located upon his ærie, he was removed from the danger of panics which were an almost nightly occurrence, caused from the sportive instincts of some visitor, who, having imbibed too freely of the regulation vest-pocket whiskey, or having suffered some real or imaginary grievance, proceeded to distribute the leaden pellets of a Colt's navy revolver, not only into the anatomy of the offender, but quite as frequently to the serious if not fatal injury of some innocent bystander.

When it is understood that it was not unusual for five hundred men to be present in the room at the time these diversions occurred, it is not difficult to imagine the kind of panic liable to ensue. Hence, the first object of Kelly's lofty perch. His second object was to be above the course of flying missles and thus preserve his violin, which was a valuable one, from the chance of being perforated by stray bullets.

It seemed to be an instinct with Kelly to protect it, for he invariably rose to his feet when the first shot was fired and faced the disturbance, holding his instrument behind him, evidently prefering that any stray bullet should find lodgment in his body rather than in his violin.

As an artist with the bow he had no equal in that day; he could make his pet instrument tell a plaintive tale of home and mother, or of tearful ones who awaited, oft in vain, the return of father, brother or lover; again he would arouse the reckless instincts of his hearers by some rollicking tune which told of wine and song. He was a big-hearted son of the Emerald Isle and although untoward circumstances had made him the leading attraction of a den of iniquity, he loved best to play those tender chords that awakened the memories of other days and sent some of his hearers back to their lonely cabins up the gulch better men for the hour they had spent under the musician's spell, even in that dreadful haunt. On such occasions he seemed to be inspired by his own music and all unconscious of games and men, with eyes closed to his surroundings, he played on and on, such strains as melt the hardest hearts.

CHAPTER IX.

MAGRUDER MURDER—PURSUIT, ARREST AND CONVICTION OF THE MURDERERS.

IN AUGUST, 1863, prior to the meeting of the first session of the Territorial legislature, a prominent packer named Lloyd Magruder, who had been engaged for a couple of years in packing supplies from Lewiston into the various camps in the Clearwater and Salmon river countries, purchased a cargo of supplies suitable for a mining camp, and loading his train of mules, which numbered about sixty, started over the Bitter Root mountains to Virginia City—then in Idaho—a distance of nearly three hundred miles.

During the many trips Magruder had made to Lewiston in the previous two years, he had become well and favorably known to many of the citizens of that town. In those days of danger and uncertainty, the men whom a man like Magruder gathered into his circle of friends were of the class to whom the word "friendship" meant something more than the mere breath of air used to utter the word.

Among these friends was Hill Beachy, the proprietor and landlord of the principal hotel in the town. He and Magruder were old acquaintances, they having known each other before coming to Lewiston.

Having made so many trips into the mountains with his pack train without serious adventure, Magruder appeared to have no apprehension of impending danger when he started off on the long trail to Virginia City. But Beachy, the proprietor of the hotel, was in a position to know the kinds of characters Magruder was likely to encounter, both before and after reaching Virginia City, and therefore he lent him a reliable gun, and warned him of the dangers he might encounter.

The departure of such a big mule-train for such a distant camp was an event in Lewiston at that time, and as the mules strung up the Clearwater along what is now Main street, and were lost to sight near where the railroad station now stands, one of those who witnessed the start and watched until his friend disappeared around a turn in the trail, was Hill Beachy, who from the first had a premonition that his friend Magruder would never return. Among the others who witnessed the departure of the mule-train were three men, D. C. Lowry, David Howard and James Romain, who were disciples of the Plummer school and believers in the piratical doctrine "dead men tell no tales."

These men soon after Magruder left began preparations to follow on his trail, and having secured a few more men who were unsuspicious of the characters of Lowry, Howard and Romain, and all having procured riding animals and additional pack horses to carry their provisions and blankets, after a delay of about ten days, started in pursuit of Magruder. The owner of a heavily laden pack train, having a long trip to make, is necessarily anxious to spare his mules as much as possible; hence his drives were short, usually not more than fifteen miles per day and if camping places with water and grass can be found, the daily journey is more likely to be limited to twelve or fourteen miles. So the pursuing party making double the distance each day, that Magruder made, came up with him before he reached his destination. Magruder knew nothing about the characters of the men who had joined him, and as they appeared to be a jolly lot of mountain men and willing to travel with him and assist him in caring for and packing his mules, asking nothing for their assistance but their board, he willingly accepted their aid.

In loading a pack-train, the packers worked in pairs. The animal, horse or mule, after being saddled up, is led up to the cargo he is to carry and then blindfolded. Each man then picks up a side-pack and with a man working on each side of the animal, it is soon lashed in place. Therefore it is convenient to have plenty of men, so that the mules or horses, as the animals may be, need not be held after being loaded, awaiting the others, so on that account, if for no other, Magruder found the assistance of these additional men quite acceptable.

Finally Virginia City was reached without incident. A large tent was erected in the outskirts of the town, and the goods stored within, ready for sale. The men who accompanied Lowry, Howard and Romain from Lewiston, all except one, immediately started out to find work or look for "diggins," and Magruder saw them no more, but the four, including D. C. Lowry, David Howard, James Romain and one other of the Lewiston party whose name is unknown, hung around Magruder's camp, helping at times in caring for the mules, and always taking great interest in the rapid sale of the cargo and the consequent accumulation of gold dust received in exchange for the goods. It was about the middle of October before the last remnant of the goods was sold, and since Magruder was anxious to return to his family before the winter snow blocked his trail, he knew that he must not delay his departure, as the Bitter Root range, which he was obliged to cross, was liable to be covered at any time after early October. He had a large mule train and their equipment, besides having about thirty thousand dollars in gold dust, the result of his venture. Help must be engaged to assist in bringing the mules over the mountains and guard the treasure. The three men whose acquaintance he had first made on the trail and whom he had no reason to suspect, expressed a willingness to return with him, as did also another one of the original party, William Page, a trapper. So he engaged these four men and in addition hired two others, a man named Phillips, the other named Allen. Two young men who were anxious to get out of the country were also supplied with saddle mules and added to the party, thus making the number nine men. The two young men who were last to join the party were trying to return to their homes in Missouri, having secured about two thousand dollars each in gold dust. If they gave Magruder their names in starting he probably made a memorandum in his diary which was destroyed, so their names are not known.

The start was made under favorable circumstances, the mules having had such a long rest on excellent grass, were in fine condition and everything bespoke a speedy and pleasant trip; and such it proved to be until more than half the distance to Lewiston was covered, when one night in camp a tragedy was enacted.

As near as can be determined by the evidence afterward brought out, it had been planned long before by Lowry, Howard and Romain to appropriate Magruder's effects. It seems probable that their first idea was to murder him and his packers while on their way to Virginia City, and appropriate the mules and cargo, but as they could not assemble enough of their gang to successfully carry out that enterprise, it was thought safer to permit Magruder to sell his cargo and take possession of his effects while on the trail returning to Lewiston. It was resolved by Lowry, Howard and Romain

that they would kill the entire party except the
trapper Page. A night was chosen when they
were encamped on a ridge which broke off on
one side almost perpendicular for several hun-
dren feet into a canyon or mountain gorge. Near
the summit was a spring which furnished men
and animals water. From a confession made by
Page, the trapper, it appears that on the night
selected for the massacre, Page was put on
guard and told what was going to happen, and
ordered to keep still under penalty of death.
Magruder and Lowry were also on guard away
from the camp in an opposite direction, while
Phillips, Allan and the other men were fast
asleep in their blankets near the fire. During the
first watch of the night, Lowry, who was on
guard with Magruder, approached within striking distance, and dealing him a powerful blow
with an axe which he had concealed under his
coat, awaiting the fatal moment, knocked him
senseless to the ground, where he was speedily
dispatched. The killing of the sleeping men in
camp was then quickly accomplished. Page, the
trapper, who was watching the mules near by,
claimed that he saw the murders committed.
As soon as daylight arrived, the mules were
brought up and five of the best were selected,
four for saddle mules for the men to ride and
one to pack their plunder. The other animals
were then driven into a deep canyon and they,
too, were murdered. They tied the murdered
men in blankets and dropped them over the

bluff near camp, into the bottom of the canyon, several hundred feet below, after which, having secured the gold dust, they made a bonfire and burned all the camp equipage, including the aparejos and other paraphernalia of a pack train. The foregoing being accomplished, they started for the lower country, expecting to ford the Clearwater above Lewiston and keep on down the north bank, thus avoiding the town, but when they reached the river, the weather having turned cold, the water was full of running ice, so they were afraid to attempt to ford, and going into camp they remained there until in the night, when they quietly entered Lewiston. They found a stock ranchman with whom they left their mules, and took the early morning stage for Walla Walla, booking themselves under fictitious names.

In those days passengers from Lewiston en route to Portland, Oregon, took passage first on stage to Walla Walla, then on a second stage line from Walla Walla to Wallula; there passage was secured by steamer, including two portages to Portland.

Hill Beachy, who was yet keeping his hotel in Lewiston, upon learning that four men had entered town in the night, disguised, and taken the early stage out in the morning, entertaining the same fears for the safety of his friend Magruder that he had from the day of the latter's departure for Virginia City, seemed intuitively to surmise that the travelers had robbed Magruder. So strong was this intuition, that he made complaint before an officer, and since Governor Wallace was in Lewiston, he obtained requisitions on the governors of Oregon, Washington and California. He intended to start immediately in pursuit, prepared to have them extradited, no matter in which of the foregoing jurisdictions they might be found.

Beachy's friends, however, persuaded him to wait a few days in order to see if something definite could not be learned. Accordingly he postponed his departure, and learning that the men whom he suspected had left mules which were to be sent out to a ranch, he had the animals and saddles brought in for examination. One of the mules was recognized at once as having been Magruder's saddle animal, and one of the saddles was also recognized as formerly belonging to Magruder. This evidence removed the last lingering doubt and satisfied the most skeptical.

Beachy at once began his preparations to start in pursuit of the murderers. A man named Tom Pike was engaged by Beachy to accompany him, and so equipped with the necessary credentials, they started to overtake and capture the fugitives, who now had such an advantageous start. Taking a private conveyance and changing horses several times, they made a rapid drive to Walla Walla, thence took the stage to Wallula, from which point they took passage by steamer to Portland. Arriving

there, they learned that four men answering
the description of those wanted had been in the
city a few days previously, and who while there
seemed to be well provided with money. In fact,
they had made a deposit in a faro bank amounting to several hundred dollars, but they had departed on a steamship bound for San Francisco.
Having learned of their departure, Beachy sent
Pike after them by water route, while he started
overland, not caring to await the steamer, for,
at that time, the sailing days were infrequent.
The overland trip from Portland, Oregon, to
Sacramento, by stage, was one that few men
cared to undertake. The road traveled up the
Willamette and Umpqua Valleys were proverbial for deep, sticky and numerous chuck holes,
and since the stages ran both by night and day,
the passengers, necessarily, had but little opportunity for wooing Morpheus. Beachy was
fully aware of these unpleasant features connected with the proposed trip, yet, without hesi-
tancy, he boarded the Concord coach and started
overland, fixed in his determination to capture
the murderers of his friend. After three days
and nights, cooped up in the stage, he reached
Yreka, then the nearest point from Portland
where telegraphic communication could be had
with San Francisco. From this point he succeeded in wiring a full description of the sus-
pects to the chief of police in San Francisco, and
a brief detail of the murder, and requested that
they be arrested and held, pending his arrival.

The request was carried out, and upon his arrival a few days later, he found the murderers behind prison bars. In addition to the arrest, they had traced the dust the men had brought with them on the steamer to the U. S. mint.

After an embarrassing delay, caused by a writ of habeas corpus, Tom Pike having in the meantime arrived, with his prisoners securely ironed, Beachy and Pike started by steamer to Portland, thence by the usual route to Lewiston, where they arrived on December 7th, 1863, the same day on which convened the first session of the legislative assembly of the Territory of Idaho. Before leaving San Francisco, William Page, the trapper, who admitted having seen the murders committed, confessed to Beachy, and gave all the particulars of the tragedy. Upon his arrival in Lewiston with the four prisoners, had Beachy been a man of less determination, the citizens would have given the accused but short shrift; but he told them that the prisoners were his, and that before leaving San Francisco he had promised them that they should have a fair trial by a jury, and his promise must and should be kept.

Arrangements were made for holding the first term of district court ever held in Idaho, commencing on January 5th, 1864. Accordingly the prisoners were confined in jail and closely guarded until they were brought out and arraigned for trial. During the time they were imprisoned, the legislative assembly effected an organization and began their work in a spirited manner.

The organic act which created the Territory of Idaho failed to provide that the laws of the Territories, from which the new Territory was created, should continue in force, until such time as the legislative assembly of Idaho could enact Civil and Criminal Codes. Hence there was a period during the first year of Idaho's territorial existence, extending from April 3rd, 1863, until the first legislative session had met and enacted laws, when we had neither Civil nor Criminal Acts, and were entirely dependent upon the general laws of the United States, which were inadequate to meet all conditions. Consequently the first legislative assembly was confronted with conditions requiring prompt and speedy measures.

The first district court to be held in the Territory was to be convened on January 5th, 1864, less than one month from the first day of the legislative session. The four men then in custody charged with the atrocious murder of Magruder and his party were to be tried during this term of court—and as yet Idaho had no Criminal Practice Act. Fortunately, however, the members of the first legislature were equal to meeting the occasion. They promptly passed the following act—an act adopting the Common Law of England:

"Be It Enacted by the Legislative Assembly of the Territory of Idaho, as Follows:

"Section 1. The common law of England, so far as the same is not inconsistent with the provisions of the Constitution of the United States, the Organic Act and laws of this territory, shall be the law of the land in this territory.

"Sec. 2. This act to take effect and be in force from and after its approval by the governor. Approved January 4, 1864."

Thus, one day in advance of the coming trial, the district court was provided with authority to cover any void existing, heretofore, in the statute.

Judge Samuel C. Parks was assigned to hold the first term of district court in Lewiston, beginning on the 5th day of January, 1864. Of the four men held for the murder of the Magruder party, Lowry, Howard and Romain were indicted for murder in the first degree, and were at once placed on trial and promptly convicted, as the chain of evidence was complete.

William Page, the trapper, having turned state's evidence, was permitted to depart after the trial. Rumor has it that he was killed soon afterwards, but by whom it is not definitely known. The three convicted men were sentenced by Judge Parks on January 26 to be hanged on March 4th, 1864, by the neck until dead.

The sentence was duly executed, and thus miserably perished a trio of human fiends— their execution striking terror to the hearts of

their kind, and causing a prompt reinforcement
to the troop of scoundrels who had already transferred their activities to Boise Basin and other
congenial camps. The territorial legislature being in session during the progress of the trial,
upon the recommendation of Judge Parks, it
made an appropriation to pay Hill Beachy for
the pursuit and capture of the Magruder murderers, including expenses incident thereto,
$6,244.00. (See page 625, First Session Laws
1865. (1863).

The money found on the prisoners, together
with that they had deposited in the U. S. mint
at San Francisco, was paid to the family of
Magruder after the necessary formalities had
been complied with. The loyalty of Hill Beachy
to his friend, combined with his native fearless-
ness and determination, was the leading factor
in bringing the episode to a successful ending.

The following spring Hill Beachy, with a
party of six others, visited the scene of the
tragedy and buried the remains of the victims.
The particulars of the gruesome find, together
with the details of their trip, after being written and signed by all the party, were printed in
a Lewiston paper. This removed every doubt of
the correctness of the testimony of Page, upon
whose evidence the men were convicted.

The punishment meted to the men who murdered Magruder and his party was justly merited; and their conviction and subsequent execution was endorsed by all who were familiar with

the tragedy. Yet, had an appeal been taken to the supreme court of the territory, the red-handed fiends might have escaped execution by the officers of the law. But the public was so thoroughly aroused that no technicalities would have been permitted to prevent their punishment.

The following decision of the Idaho territorial supreme court is of interest, as it shows the utter helplessness of those who by their instincts and training were believers in a government by law during these terrible months when there was no law:

APPEAL FROM THE SECOND DISTRICT, BOISE COUNTY.

C. B. Waite, District Attorney, for the People. S. A. Merritt, for the Respondent.

C. J. McBride delivered the opinion of the Court, Cummin, J., concurring, Kelly, J., dissenting.

This case comes up on appeal from a decision of the district court, quashing the indictment.

The following are the facts: The defendant, John Williams, was charged by the indictment with the crime of highway robbery, committed in the month of September, 1863, in the county of Boise, Territory of Idaho. The indictment was found at the July term, 1865, and the defendant, being in custody, pleaded not guilty. Subsequent to this plea, but before trial, the defendant, by his counsel, moved to set aside the indictment. The motion was sustained, and the

prisoner ordered to be discharged. This ruling
was excepted to by the attorney for the people,
and the case stands for decision upon this motion, and the alleged error of the court below
in granting the same. Preliminary to the investigation of the main question which is involved in the decision below, it will be necessary
to refer to some points raised by the district
attorney in the brief by the appellants.

It is claimed by the appellants that though
the indictment charges the offense to have been
committed in September, 1863, the time is no
material ingredient of the offense charged, and
that the indictment would be supported if the
proof should show that the crime was committed
within the statutory time, although not upon the
day charged, and as there was no proof—there
having been no trial—that the offense was committed in September, 1863, when it was claimed
no law existed for its punishment, that the court
erred in granting the motion, as it might have
appeared that it was committed after that time,
and when no such objection would lie. This is
an error. For the purpose of the motion the
court must take the facts as stated in the indictment to be true. Time is material in this
offense, and though it need not be proved as
laid strictly, still where the time becomes a question of materiality the court must assume that
it is stated according to the fact, and if there
was no law defining this crime, and inflicting
a penalty at the time when it was alleged to

have been committed, then the indictment should have been set aside, and there is no error.

The second point of the appellant is that the defendant having been set at liberty under the order of the court below, the court should not take cognizance of this appeal. This appeal is taken by the people, and the district attorney has the right, if he chooses, to dismiss the appeal; but to prosecute the appeal, and deny the effect of its design, is certainly not allowable.

A third point assigned is that the motion was made to set aside the indictment after the defendant had entered his plea of not guilty, and that the motion came too late, and, therefore, the order should have been refused, and now reversed. The statute settles this question —and reason as well; the objection going to the merits of the prosecution could be raised at any time before or after judgment. It would have been the duty of the court to consider it any time during the progress of the trial, and to have arrested the judgment after verdict. It would be the height of absurdity to say that a court might be fully convinced that it had no authority to pass sentence upon a case, yet must proceed to try a criminal because it had begun the proceedings.

Having disposed of these preliminary questions, it remains to be decided whether there was any law for the punishment of defendant for the offense charged in the indictment. On the third day of March, 1863, Congress organized the Territory of Idaho, by cutting off certain territory from the already organized territories of Washington, Dakota, Nebraska and Utah. The Territory of Idaho then became a separate political community, and the power of government, of making and enforcing statutes, of preserving the rights of the people and punishing wrong-doers, was vested in the citizens of the territory in the manner prescribed by the organic act. Did this segregation of the territory of Idaho from the other territories named leave it without any criminal code? It undoubtedly was a repeal of the several organic acts named—they no longer had any form or validity, had been superseded and become nullities. How they could cease to exist, and yet laws remain in force, deriving their validity from authority conferred by them, we cannot understand. It would be to extinguish the fountain and insist upon the rivulet continuing its flow —cutting off the source of life and affirming continued vitality. To provide against any such hiatus in the criminal code, it is always provided that the remedies shall subsist in full force. Thus in organizing a state government the universal practice is to continue, by special provision, the pre-existing laws; so in organizing new territories the usual provision is to continue the laws of the old political division until the enactment of new ones.

In organizing the territory of Oregon, in 1848, Congress affirmed and continued the laws of the former provisional government until they should be altered or repealed. The uniform practice in this respect conclusively establishes, we think, the principle that the laws of the old organization have no force in the new political community unless by special provision. We are now speaking only of criminal laws. In civil matters the question of rights and remedies are so different that the same rules do not necessarily apply.

In the act organizing this territory no provision is contained recognizing the former laws. Indeed, to have done so would have given vitality to four different codes of law in different parts of the new territory. Confusion would have followed inevitably, and the fact of this difficulty sufficiently accounts for the omission on the part of Congress to provide for their continuance until the new legislature should provide for the wants of the country.

There is no similarity between this case and that of a conquered or ceded territory whose sovereignty is transferred from one authority to another. Then the laws pass with the people and the soil—but not so when the sovereign authority dismembers a piece of territory and makes no provision for the new community.

We are therefore of opinion that there was no statute punishing the offense charged in this indictment at the time it was alleged to have been committed, and that even if the facts alleged be true no sentence could be pronounced. The judgment of the court below will therefore be affirmed. Judgment affirmed.

As will be understood, the effect of the foregoing decision was that it released from confinement all prisoners serving sentence for the commission of crimes committed during the period between the creation of Idaho Territory March 3rd, 1863, and the passage and approval of statutes defining such crimes and providing penalties therefor; or, an interim of approximately nine months during which time there was no law within the borders of the new Territory to protect either life or property.

CHAPTER X.

A T THE TIME when the first discoveries of gold were made in Orofino, Elk City, Warrens, Florence, Boise Basin and Owyhee, those districts were within the Territory of Washington, which was created by act of Congress March 2nd, 1853, and the counties of Shoshone, Nez Perce, Idaho and Boise had been created by act of the Washington legislature.

Prior to the foregoing subdivisions being created, all that portion of what is now Idaho, lying south of the most southerly boundary of what is now Latah county, was incorporated in Skamania county by an act of the Washington legislature, passed in 1854, as follows:

"An Act to Create and Organize the County of Skamania."

"Section 1. Be it enacted by the Legislative Assembly of the Territory of Washington: That all that portion of Clarke County lying east of Cape Horn be, and the same is hereby organized into a county, with all the powers, rights and privileges of other counties in the territory; and that it shall be bounded as follows: Commencing at a point due north of a rock on the

11 E. H. I.

south bank of the Columbia river, called 'Rooster Rock,' running thence north to the parallel of 46 degrees and 30 minutes north latitude; thence along said parallel east to the Rocky mountains; thence south along the base of the Rocky mountains to the southeast corner of Washington; thence down along the line of Oregon and Washington territories to place of beginning.

"Sec. 2. Said County shall be called 'Skamania.' "—[*Session Laws Washington Territory 1854*].

The same session of the Washington legislature created Walla Walla county, including within its boundaries all of that portion of what is now Idaho lying north of the 46th degree of north latitude—as shown by the following copy of the act:

"An Act to Create and Organize the County of Walla Walla."

"Section 1. Be it enacted by the legislative assembly of the Territory of Washington: That all that portion of Skamania County within the following described boundaries, to-wit: Commencing at a point opposite the mouth of Deschutes River, thence running north to the 49th parallel; thence east along said parallel to the summit of Rocky Mountains, thence south along summit of Rocky Mountains to 46th degree of parallel; thence west along said 46th parallel to where it crosses the Columbia river; thence along said Columbia river to place of beginning, be and the same is hereby constituted and organized into a separate county, to be known and called Walla Walla county.

"Sec. 2. That all the territory embraced within said boundaries shall compose a county for civil and military purposes, and shall be under the same laws, rules, restrictions and regulation, as all other counties in this Territory, and entitled to elect the same county officers as other counties are entitled to elect.

"Sec. 3. The said county shall be attached to Skamania county for judicial purposes."—[*Private and Local Laws of 1854, pages 472-73*].

As will be observed, the two counties of the Territory of Washington, Walla Walla and Skamania, embraced the entire area of what is now the state of Idaho, and so continued until after the discoveries of placer gold were made at Orofino and other tributaries of Clearwater river.

The members of early legislative bodies in the northwest were distinguished, among other traits, for the paucity of language used in their enactments. They could embody an area of country equal to an empire into a county, defining its boundaries and naming its officers with remarkable brevity. For instance, the creation of Idaho county by the Washington legislature was as follows:

"An Act to Create and Organize the County of
Idaho.

"Section 1. Be it enacted by the legislative
assembly of the Territory of Washington: That
all that part of Washington Territory south of
Nez Perce County, and east of Snake river, be
organized into a county called 'Idaho.'

"Sec. 2. Be it further enacted that: L.
Lindsey be, and is hereby appointed County
Auditor; Robert Gray, Robert Burns and ———
Sanborn be appointed County Commissioners;
Jefferson Standifer, Sheriff; ——— Parker, Jus-
tice of the Peace for said County until the next
election.

"Passed December 20th, 1861.—Jas. Leo Ferguson, Speaker of House of Representatives, A,
R. Burbank, Pres. of Council.—[*Laws Washing-*
ton Territory, Ninth Session, 1861-62.]

The act creating Nez Perce County, although
a little more verbose, contains no extraneous ver-
biage—the following being a copy:

"An Act Creating and Organizing the County of
Nez Perce."

"Sec. 1. Be it enacted by the legislative assembly of the Territory of Washington: That
all that portion of Washington Territory lying
within the following boundaries be organized
into a county called Nez Perce, to-wit:

"Beginning at the mouth of the Clearwater;
thence up the same to the South Fork of the
Clearwater; thence with the South Fork to the
Lo Lo Creek; thence with the southern boundaries of Shoshone County to the summit of the

Bitter Root Mountains; thence south to the main divide between the waters of the Salmon river and the South Fork of the Clearwater to the Snake river; thence with the Snake river west to the mouth of the Clearwater, to the place of beginning.

"Sec. 2. Be it further enacted, That J. M. Valsah be appointed County Auditor; A. Creacy, Whitfield Kertley and ———— be appointed County Commissioners; Sanford Owens, Sheriff, and ———— Justice of the Peace for said County, until the next general election.

"Passed December 20, 1861. Jas. Leo Fergunson, Speaker House of Representatives; A. R. Burbank, President of the Council.—[*Session Laws, 1861-62, Olympia, Washington*].

The act which created Boise County was also passed by the Washington Territorial legislature at the same session, but not until later in the session, its passage being only a few months after the discovery of gold in Boise Basin.

The legislature either believed the creation and organization of Boise County of more importance than Nez Perce County or Idaho County, or else they had more time for its enactment, hence the "bill" was more lengthy. It is as follows:

"An Act to Create and Organize the County of Boise."

"Sec. 1. Be it enacted by the legislative assembly of the Territory of Washington, That all that portion of Idaho County embraced within the following boundaries, to-wit: Commencing at the mouth of Payette river, and following up said river mid-channel, to the mouth of the middle fork of said river, thence up the mid-channel of said fork to its source, thence in a direct east line to the summit of the Bitter Root mountains, thence along the summit of said mountains to the eastern line of Washington Territory; all that portion of the Territory of Washington lying south of the aforementioned boundaries, the same is hereby constituted and organized into a separate county to be known and called Boise; that said territory shall compose a county for civil and military purposes, and shall be under the same laws, rules, regulations and restrictions as all other counties in the territory of Washington, and entitled to elect the same officers as all other counties are entitled to elect.

Sec. 2. The county seat of said county be, and the same hereby is temporarily located at the mouth of Elk Creek, on Moore's Creek.

"Sec. 3. The following named persons are hereby appointed officers of said county, viz: John C. Smith, Dr. Noble and Frank Moore, County Commissioners; —————— Gilbert, Probate Judge; David Mulford, Sheriff; David Alderson, County Treasurer; A. D. Saunders, Auditor; Wm. Baird, J. M. Murphy, Dr. Swan, Justices of the Peace; James Warren, Coroner, who shall hold their respective offices until the next annual election, or until their successors are elected and qualified, before entering upon the discharge of the duties of their offices they shall comply with all existing laws relating to qualifying by giving bond and taking an official oath. Said bonds may be approved by the persons named county commissioners, or a majority of them, and the several persons named herein as officers may administer the oath of office to each other.

"Sec. 4. All vacancies which may occur by the non-acceptance, death, removal or resignation of any of the persons above named, may be filled by the board of county commissioners, and they may also appoint such other officers as may be required for said county, to hold their offices until the next general election, and until their successors are elected or appointed and qualified.

"Sec. 5. At the next general election the qualified voters of said county shall elect their county commissioners, and all other county officers in the same manner as is by law prescribed for other counties.

"Sec. 6. Said County Commissioners, when elected, as in the preceding section provided, shall hold their respective offices, one for one year, one for two years, and one for three years, as shall, at their first meeting after election, be determined by lot.

Sec. 7. The persons appointed county commissioners may, at any time after the passage

of this act, and before the day appointed for
the next general election, upon posting notices
signed by a majority of them, ten days prior to
the time appointed, hold a meeting of the board
of county commissioners at which they may
transact any business that may be done at a
regular meeting of the board.

"Sec. 8. This act to take effect and be in
force from and after its passage.

"Sec. 9. All acts and parts inconsistent herewith are hereby repealed.

"Passed January 12th, 1863."

The following subsequent act is self-explan-
atory:

*"An Act to Amend an Act Entitled 'An Act Cre-
ating and Organizing the County of Nez
Perce."*

"Section 1. Be it enacted by the Legislative
Assembly of the Territory of Washington: That
the boundaries of Nez Perce County shall be as
follows: Beginning mid-channel of the Snake
river at a point opposite the mouth of the Al-
powai Creek, thence due north to the divide between the Palouse and Snake river; thence following said divide in an easterly direction to a
point due north of the forks of Clearwater,
thence due south to the forks of Clearwater;
then following South Fork to Lo Lo Creek,
thence with the southern boundary of Shoshone
County to the summit of the Bitter Root mountains, thence south, following the main divide

between the waters of Salmon Fork of the Clearwater to Snake River, thence following mid-channel of said river to the place of beginning.

"Sec. 2. All acts or parts of acts conflicting with the foregoing be, and the same are hereby repealed.

"Sec. 3. This act to take effect and be in force from and after its passage.

"Passed January 21st, 1863."

"An Act to Create and Organize the County of Shoshone."

"Sec. 1. Specifies the territory and its boundaries constituting the county.

"Sec. 2. Shall compose a county for civil and military purposes. Under the same laws, etc., as all other counties. Entitled to elect officers. Proviso.

"Sec. 3. Precincts, how to be established. Judges and officers of elections.

"Sec. 4. Election of county officers, when. Laws of territory applicable.

"Sec. 5. Under the jurisdiction of Walla Walla until election. Annexed to Walla Walla for judicial purposes.

"Sec. 6. To take effect, when.

"Sec. 1. Be it enacted by the legislative assembly of Washington Territory, That all that portion of the Territory of Washington embraced within the following boundaries, to-wit: Commencing at the mouth of the Clearwater river, thence due east to the 115th degree of west longitude, thence south to the 46th degree parallel of latitude; thence along said 46th degree parallel to the summit of the Rocky Mountains; thence along the line summit of said mountains to the 42nd degree parallel of latitude; thence west along said 42nd degree parallel, to its intersection with the boundary between the State of Oregon and the Territory of Washington, thence north along said boundary, to the point of its intersection with the Snake River, thence down mid-channel of said river, to the place of beginning; the same is hereby constituted a separate county, to be called Shoshone County.

"Sec. 2. All that territory embraced within said boundaries as conforming to the provisions of this act, shall compose a county for civil and military purposes, and shall be under the same laws, rules, restrictions and regulations as all other counties in this Territory, and entitled to elect the same county officers as other counties are entitled to elect; *Provided, nevertheless*, that until the organization of said county by the election of proper county officers, the territory hereinbefore described shall be annexed to and form part of the county of Walla Walla.

"Sec. 3. And for the purpose of carrying the foregoing provisions into effect, it shall be lawful for the county commissioners of the county of Walla Walla, at the next May term (1861) on the petition of ten or more legal voters residing within the county bounded and described in

Section 1st, of this Act, to establish such precincts as may be deemed necessary in the territory now sought to be organized into said Shoshone county, and to appoint judges and officers competent to conduct the election.

"Sec. 4. The legal voters of the territory embraced in the boundaries of said proposed county shall, at the next general election, elect all officers to which by law they are entitled to elect, and the provisions of law now in force in the Territory of Washington in regard to the mode and manner of conducting elections, shall be applicable to any election held in the said territory hereinbefore described.

"Sec. 5. That until the said county officers shall be so elected and qualified, according to law, the territory described in said Section 1, shall be annexed to and be considered under the jurisdiction of the county of Walla Walla, and for judicial purposes, said county of Shoshone, when organized, shall be and is hereby annexed to said county of Walla Walla.

"Sec. 6. This act to take effect and be in force from and after the qualification of such officers as may be elected at the general election of 1861, pursuant to the foregoing provisions.

"Passed January 9th, 1861.—Lyman Shaffer, Speaker House of Representatives; Paul K. Hubbs, President of the Council."

Shoshone County was created by an act of the Washington Territorial legislature, approved January 9th, 1861. Said act being amended by an act passed December 21st of the same year. The latter act was entitled:

"An Act Establishing and Defining the Boundaries of Shoshone County."

The latter act was intended to reconcile some of the incongruities of the former. Today, these acts are of interest only as they show the almost total lack of information, on the part of the members, of the topography of the county.

I give the acts as they passed, and were approved, believing that they will be of interest in the future, for the old legislative landmarks of a new country are always of interest.

"An Act Establishing and Defining the Boundaries of Shoshone County."

"Sec. 1. Be it enacted by the Legislative Assembly of the Territory of Washington, That the boundaries of Shoshone county shall be as follows, to-wit: Beginning at the mouth of the South Fork of the Clearwater; thence south with said river to the Lo Lo Fork of the same; thence east with said Lo Lo stream, in an eastern direction to the summit of the Bitter Root mountains; thence north to the main divide between the Palouse river and the North Fork of the Clearwater; thence in a western direction with said main divide to a point from which, running due south, would strike the mouth of the South Fork of the Clearwater, to the place of beginning.

"Passed December 21st, 1861.—Jas. Leo Ferguson, Speaker of the House of Representatives; A. R. Burbank, President of the Council."

The second session of the Legislative Assembly of the Territory of Idaho passed an Act to establish a common school system for the territory.

The following is a copy of Sections 1, 2 and 3 of Article I. of said act (Session Laws Second Session, pp. 377-8) :

"An Act to Establish a Common School System for the Territory of Idaho.

"Be it enacted by the Legislative Assembly of the Territory of Idaho, as follows:

"Article I.

"Sec. 1. That the principal of all moneys accruing to this territory, from the sale of any land heretofore given, or which may hereafter be given, by the congress of the United States for school purposes, together with any moneys that, by legacy or otherwise, may be appropriated to the general school fund, shall constitute an irreducible fund, the interest accruing from which shall be annually divided among all the school districts in the territory, proportionately to the number of children in each, between the ages of four and twenty-one years, for the purpose of common schools in said districts, and for no other purpose whatever.

"Sec. 2. For the purpose of establishing and

maintaining common schools, it shall be the duty
of the county commissioners of each county to
set apart, annually, five per cent of all moneys
paid into the county treasury, received as taxes
upon the property contained in each county; and
the said money so appropriated shall be paid
over to the county treasurer, to be appropriated
for the support of common schools in the several school districts, to be drawn in the manner
hereinbefore prescribed.

"Sec. 3. For the further support of common
schools, there shall be set apart by the county
treasurer, all moneys arising from fines for a
breach of any of the penal laws of this territory,
if not otherwise appropriated by law. Such
money shall be paid into the county treasury,
and be added to the yearly school fund raised
by tax in each county, and divided in the same
manner."

In addition to these provisions for the maintenance of common schools, the same session
passed an act to levy a tax of one per cent of
the gross proceeds of toll-roads, bridges and ferries, to constitute a general fund.

At the time these measures were enacted,
there were few school children in the Territory,
but the big hearted mountain men who enacted
these statutes did not propose to have their
education neglected. The spirit manifested by
the members of that early session has been fostered by each succeeding one, and of the thousands of children who have been born and reared

in Idaho—with the exception of the Indian children—it is doubtful if there is a single instance where an Idaho child has grown to womanhood or manhood without being able to read and write.

School houses and churches were early adjuncts of civilization in all our western territories, and the tax-payers of Idaho have always cheerfully contributed to the establishment and maintenance of public schools.

The importance of the levy of one per cent on the gross proceeds of toll-roads, bridges and ferries, for school purposes, will be more completely appreciated after reading the following lists of franchises granted by the second session, 1864:

"An Act to Establish a Wagon Road from Elk City, Nez Perce County, to the Western Boundary of Montana Territory.

"Sec. 1. That Thomas Kirkpatrick, Alonzo Leland, James Tufts, S. S. Slater, John Creighton and George Zeigle, their heirs and assigns, are hereby granted the exclusive right and privilege to establish and maintain a toll-road from Elk City, Nez Perce County, along the practicable route, eastward to the western line of Montana Territory.

"Sec. 2. The said parties shall have the right to charge and collect toll on each twenty miles of said road so soon as completed, at the following rates, in gold or silver coin or its equivalent:

For each wagon with two animals $2.00
For each additional team of two animals.... .75
For each horse or mule, packed .... .75
For each loose horse or mule .... .50
For each loose cattle, each .... .25
For each sheep or hog, each .... .10
    "Approved December 22nd, 1864."

"AN ACT

"To authorize David Watson, David McCullum and Asa Moore to establish a bridge across Boise River."

"AN ACT

"To authorize J. B. McLaughlin, John Duvall, and Jonathan Keeney to establish a Ferry on Snake River in Boise County."

"AN ACT

"To authorize Charles DeLanine, A. George and associates to establish and maintain a toll-road from Placerville to Pioneer City, in Boise County."

"AN ACT

"To authorize J. L. Roberts, and others, to establish and maintain a Ferry on Kootenai River, in Idaho Territory."

"AN ACT

"To authorize Charles H. Campfield, and his associates to establish a Ferry across the Pend d'Oreille river, or Clark's Fork of the Columbia river." (Approved December 22nd, 1864).

"AN ACT

"Authorizing John W. Heillin to establish a ferry on the Spokane river."

This ferry was to be located at, or near, a point known as the "Indian Crossing." The act provided for the following rates of toll, or ferriage:

For each wagon and two animals $2.00
For each additional span of horses or
    yoke of oxen 1.00
For each man and horse 1.50
For each pack animal 1.00
For each loose animal other than sheep
    or hogs .... .25
For each sheep or hog .... .10
For each footman .... .50

Approved December 22nd, 1864.

"AN ACT

"Authorizing Peter Sholl to maintain a tollbridge across Clearwater river in Nez Perce County, on the road from Lewiston to Elk City.

"Approved December 22nd, 1864."

"AN ACT

"Authorizing Leonard Guion and his associates to establish a Bridge and Ferry on Pack River.

"Approved December 22nd, 1864."

12 E. H. I.

"AN ACT

"Supplemental to an Act to establish and maintain a Toll-Road from Clearwater to Elk City.

"Approved December 22nd, 1864."

"AN ACT

"To authorize R. A. Eddy, E. L. Bonner and John W. Walton to establish and maintain a Ferry across the Kootenai River at a point known as Bonner's Ferry, or 'Chulintah.'

"Approved December 22nd, 1864."

"AN ACT

"To authorize S. A. Woodward and L. P. Brown to construct and maintain a Toll-trail from Brown's Mountain House, in Nez Perce County, to Florence, in Idaho County.

"Approved December 17, 1864."

"AN ACT

"To incorporate the Oneida Road, Bridge and Ferry Company, with capital stock of Thirty Thousand Dollars, which may be increased to Fifty Thousand.

"Approved December 10, 1864."

"AN ACT

"To authorize Martin Newcomb to construct and maintain a ferry across the Kootenai river at a point four miles above Bonner's Ferry. The territory attached to Nez Perce County for judicial purposes.

"Approved December 20, 1864."

"AN ACT

"To authorize Julius Newburg to construct and maintain a Bridge in Ada County (at Boise).

"Approved December 22nd, 1864."

The laws enacted and the resolutions adopted by the second session of the Idaho legislature were generally approved by the people, and the members who enacted them were undoubtedly impelled by upright motives.

The session adjourned on the 23rd day of December, 1864, after a full session of forty days.

CHAPTER XI.

EARLY EVENTS.

A COMPANY of volunteers under the leadership of Jeff Standifer, during the early months of 1863, crossed Snake river at Washoe Ferry, to levy reprisals on a band of Piute Indians, who, having raided lower Boise and Payette Valleys, had returned with their plunder to the Malheur Valley. A battle ensued with the result that all the Indians were killed with the exception of one squaw and two boys, aged approximately six and twelve years. After the firing ceased, they were discovered and brought back with the returning party. The squaw was given employment by Ira Worden, a restaurant keeper in Centerville, and the older boy was given a home by the writer, and was named Dick.

The smaller boy was adopted by John Kelly, the violinist, who had a little gray suit, representing a Confederate uniform, made for him. When first captured the child was as wild as a young coyote. With a well knit frame and jet-black eyes which fairly sparkled, his looks proclaimed him what he was, a full-blooded aborigine.

Kelly at once became both father and mother to the little waif. He kept him in his presence continually, and began at once a course of physical training to fit the boy for the future which he had conceived for him. In a few months he had developed into a contortionist of no mean ability, and nightly occupied a place with his adopted father, giving occasional exhibitions to vary the performance, thus adding interest to the attraction. The boy eventually, either from inherent talent, or from having no other associate than Kelly, developed wonderful skill as a violinist. When eighteen years old he equalled his instructor, while on a visit to Ireland with his inseparable companion, he was taken with a congestive chill and died. Kelly had no children of his own, and while he related to the writer the story of the boy's life and death, his furrowed face was deluged with tears.

Wagon roads, from Boise City to Bannock, were early constructed, and from Horseshoe Bend on the Payette river to Placerville, thence to other towns. This was the shortest and best route from Umatilla to Walla Walla. Consequently most of the supplies distributed in the Basin came over that road. After these wagon-roads were completed, stage-lines were quickly started, and big Concord coaches, with four or six horses attached, arrived and departed daily, carrying passengers from each of the towns. These stages also carried the mail and express and other things, including an important indi-

vidual occupying an outside seat next to the
driver, and at all times carrying across his knees
a short, double-barreled shot-gun of large cali-
ber, heavily loaded with buck-shot.

These men were employed by the express
company, and one of them accompanied every
coach which carried treasure. Owing to the
expense of such precautions, and the losses which
at time occurred, the charges made by the express company for the transfer of treasure were
so heavy that the miners, packers and teamsters
usually devised means of their own to accomplish
the transfer.

A favorite ruse was to remove part of the
filling of an aparejo and drop a sack of gold
dust into each side of it; thus each mule would
carry one hundred ounces of dust on a side without attracting attention. Two hundred ounces of
gold dust, worth sixteen dollars an ounce, was
the equivalent of $3,200.00. The larger trains of
forty or fifty mules were selected, on account of
the number of packers employed, all of whom
being heavily armed, made an efficient guard.
There is no record of highwaymen capturing
treasure shipped in this manner. Sometimes
large freight wagons were loaded with dry hides
from the slaughter houses and bags of gold were
stored underneath the skins. Shipments made in
the foregoing manner were for safety, and
necessarily were *sub rosa,* hence no record of
their value was kept. Consequently all estimates
of the gold output of the mines of the Boise

Basin district, during the time of their greatest
prosperity, are largely based upon conjecture.

In those days the nation was in the throes
of civil war, and, though the infant territory
sent no troops to battle for the flag, her mountain streams gave up their hoarded wealth when
gold was needed most.   Thus, all thoughtless of
the good they did, her toiling miners, far removed from battle smoke and shrieking shell,
did well their part.   There is grim humor in the
thought that during the darkest days of the
rebellion, when to be a Union man in Boise
Basin meant danger, sometimes death, yet the
energies of Union men and Secessionists alike
were directed to amassing gold, which was sent
to the United States mints, and became the basis
of credit which enabled the nation to maintain
its integrity and carry on the war to a successful conclusion.

In those days partisan feeling ran high;
political parties then, as now, Democrats and
Republicans, maintained their organizations.
But the issue on which they divided was not
tariff nor free coinage of silver, but simply
Union versus Dis-union.   While there were many
Democrats in Idaho who were as loyal to the
flag as any Republican, they were seldom in
evidence, for they soon discovered that silence,
on political questions, was conducive to long-
evity.   There were also many civil, quiet southern gentlemen whose sympathies were with the
Confederacy, but their conservatism and respect

for law and order made them unpopular in party
caucuses and conventions, which were largely
controlled by the lawless element. It was notic-
able in those days that the most violent and bitter Secessionists were not the southern men
whose homes were being overrun and property
confiscated by the Union armies, but northern
copperheads, or barroom politicians.

E. D. Holbrook, who was elected Territorial
Delegate to Congress in 1864 and again in 1866,
was a fitting representative of the ruling class.
Born in Elgin, Ohio, and educated in the public
schools of that state, his political preferment
was based on his violent hatred of the American
flag, and his desire to perpetually enslave the
African race. He was an able lawyer, a fluent
and logical speaker, and had he lived even a
quarter of a century later, would doubtless have
been a valuable citizen, but as conditions were
then, his influence did much to foster lawlessness.

His highly strung nervous system could not
endure the many kinds of stimulants sold by
his constituents; he simply went wrong, like
many others, from the same or similar cause,
and finally, posing as a gun-fighter, his life went
out in blood—Charlie Douglas, a gambler and
one-time friend, being a quicker or better shot.

There was no railroad across the continent
in those days, and no telegraph lines in Idaho.
Hence news of events transpiring in the outside
world was slow in reaching us. Our main de-
pendence was the *Sacramento Union*, a daily

newspaper published in Sacramento, California, and usually it did not reach us until about two weeks after its publication. When we consider that almost every American citizen in the mining camps had friends or relatives in some one of the armies in the field, engaged in the fearful contest then being waged, it can be understood how anxiously the stage bringing these papers was awaited—and how quickly they were sold for a dollar each. There was never copies enough to supply the demand, and groups would form around the fortunate ones and listen with bated breath, while he read the story of, mayhap, the Battle of the Wilderness, of Gettysburg, or Lookout Mountain. It was noticeable, on such occasions, that, if the narrative was of a rebel victory, the air was at once rent with cheers for Jeff Davis, and the barrooms were soon filled with jubilant men, clamoring for "booze," and predicting the speedy recognition of the Southern Confederacy by foreign nations. On the contrary, if the Union army was victorious, the cheers were for Abe Lincoln, or some favorite Union general; then they usually gravitated, like the others, to some saloon and teased their opponents by sandwiching in between drinks, such songs as "We'll Rally Round the Flag, Boys," or "My Country, 'Tis of Thee, Sweet Land of Liberty, of Thee I Sing." On such occasions the partisans of the cause that had suffered defeat were usually discreet enough to keep out of sight of the roisterers; but not infrequently hostilities were precipitated, the results of which were communicated to the patrons of the eating houses the following morning by the waiters, in the stereotyped phrase, "A man for breakfast this morning," or men, as the case might be, naming the place or places, almost invariably a saloon.

It was understood in early mining days that a camp was not fully equipped until a graveyard was started, and the number of sodless mounds that it contained within a given time was considered an index of the life of the place. It is a strange analogy that life should mean death. Yet it was true. For the life or the liveliness of such places was guaged by the number of saloons, dance halls, etc., and their number determined the amount of liquor sold and that was, almost invariably, what regulated the growth of the cemeteries. In older countries the process is generally slow, but in mining camps, especially in war-times, strong drink such as was sold over the bars aroused the passions of men and led to violence, often death.

Idaho City easily led the other camps in the number of interments. Much has been said and written of the formulas used in the manufacture of a large part of the whiskey sold in mining towns and at the road-houses leading thereto, which, if true, may account for some of the violence it engendered. An anecdote is related of a man who was the keeper of a house of entertainment on the road leading from The

Dalles, Oregon, to the Canyon City mines. It is
stated that being dissatisfied with the prices
charged by the Portland liquor dealers, he concluded to manufacture his own whiskey, and
after trying numerous formulas, he made a brew
containing several ingredients, among them al-
cohol, plug tobacco, strychnia and prune juice.
As soon as the mixture had settled he tried it
on the first man who came along the road—a Jew
peddler, carrying his little stock of merchandise
on his back—with the result that he stole his
own pack and hid it in the willows up the creek.
The next customer was a sheep-herder, who,
after taking his first drink, went out in front of
the house, and throwing his hat in the air, gave
a yell of delight which was ample evidence of
the quality of the "goods." So the liquor was at
once named "Sheep-herder's Delight." It mattered not, however, what the quality happened
to be, it all went, for, while there were a few
who had epicurean tastes, the average tippler
seemed to have the same opinion as the Irishman
who, when told that a certain blend of whiskey
was bad, indignantly exclaimed, "Bad! There
is no bad whiskey; some is a little better than
others, but there is none bad."

While history was being made in the Basin,
and its hitherto silent glades were being transformed into busy hives of industry, each sending
forth a glittering stream of gold, the march of
progress was no less apparent in the valleys
adjacent thereto—both Boise and Payette. The

latter awakened into life earlier than the former, because the road leading from Walla Walla and Umatilla landing followed up the Payette river from near its confluence with the Snake to Horseshoe Bend, where it diverged up Shafer Creek, thence to Placerville. Prior to the construction of the Shafer Creek road, the travel continued on up the river to "Jack-ass Gulch" and Porter Creek, up both of which were trails leading to Placerville and the other camps.

It was over these two trails, before the wagon roads were completed, that most of the influx of travel found its way to the mines. And during that time the population almost, if not quite, reached its highest limits. Many thousands of people were added after the roads were built, but it must be conceded that nearly as many took their departure before this time, some of them being satisfied with what they had accumulated, while others, failing to obtain claims, sought different fields. A few left the country for the country's good—and their own safety.

With hundreds of men passing over the Payette Valley road, road-houses were quickly provided. Of these, Shafer's, Horseshoe Bend, Burner's Ranch, now called Marsh, the Black House, Payette Ranch, Thompson's Ranch, and the "Bug Hay Press," were noted places during the summer of 1863. They all served meals consisting usually of bread and meat, generally bacon, with brown bread and black coffee, all for the nominal sum of one dollar each. These houses were invariably kept by unmarried men, and most of them were orderly and well conducted.

When we consider the difficulty experienced in obtaining even the ordinary necessities of life, it is marvelous how they succeeded as well as they did.

Some stretches of the bottom land which the Payette road traversed was covered with alkali, which, when disturbed by passing horsemen or footmen rose in clouds of dust, filling the eyes, nostrils and ears of the traveler, causing an excessive thirst, which, in many instances, nothing but some kind of alcoholic beverage seemed to assuage, and even that relief was a temporary one, hardly lasting from one house to another. But the proprietors, with few exceptions, were familiar with the malady, and were prepared to promptly relieve the sufferings of all comers. These prescriptions were administered for "two bits," or twenty-five cents each.

During the summer of 1863 large wagon trains of emigrants from Missouri and Arkansas arrived in Idaho. They consisted of entire families of men, women and children, and would have been a desirable acquisition to the population of any country. They had abandoned their former homes to escape the terrors of guerrilla warfare, which was epidemic in those states at that time. As a rule they brought with them good teams and wagons and such household

goods as were portable. Their advent marked
the arrival of the first feather-beds into the
territory. They also brought a new element
into the country—an element which made the
mountains look more attractive. It was immediately noted by the young men that the rivers
and the brooks which had heretofore gone silent-
ly on their way, made sweet music as they
traveled over their pebbly beds; the birds sang
more sweetly; even the clouds which swept the
summer skies bore laughter on their wings.
The magic which wrought such marvelous
changes was a bevy of girls. When the train
of wagons on which they traveled reached Boise
City and stopped on the main street to permit
some of the families to purchase articles from
the stores, the card games, billiard halls and
saloons were quickly deserted, even the "bar-
keep" and the "lookout" for the "faro" games,
with their hair parted in the middle, were soon
in the front row along the sidewalks, craning
their necks to get a peep. "Goo-goo" eyes were
seen on the Boise streets for the first time that
day. Whether they were an importation from
Missouri or Arkansas matters not—they did effective work. Other trains quickly followed the
first, and a camp was established on the river-
bank near the outskirts of the town, where
acquaintances were formed, and during the
evenings which followed, sitting around their
smouldering camp fires, plans for the future were
made by the older people, while the girls and

their visitors from town formed groups of two beneath the blinking stars. Each mountain swain had wondrous tales to tell—of dreary days and nights alone. Of course they had never loved before, and never could again. 'Twas thus the stories ran, while mothers, argus-eyed, looked on.

These fathers grim had guns; some had been tried at Wilson Creek, and others on the plains. So every vow made on that river bank was kept. There was dearth of wedding-gowns, dearth of wedding-bells; but "eyes spoke love to eyes that spoke again" and ere the slim young moon that first had listened to their sighs had grown to full, many a young bachelor had been bound in hymeneal ties, and was enjoying for the first time, since leaving home and mother, the comforts of a feather-bed. Of the marriages resulting from these speedy courtships, I have yet to learn of a divorce. Many of the immigrants of that year located in Boise valley, while a few crossed the divide to Payette. Among the latter may be named the Flourneys, the Burges family, and others.

All of these early settlers enacted a prominent and honorable part in the development of the then new territory. Many of their children are still residents of Idaho, and have reason to be proud of the record they inherited from their ancestors who, having crossed the continent during those turbulent days, devoted their lives

to honest industry, and finally went to their
rest respected and loved by all.

For three years the market price for all
kinds of farm produce, except hay, was never
less than twenty-five cents a pound, and during
that time, ten cents a pound for hay was the
lowest price it reached in the mining towns.
Hence the farmer shared with the miner and
others the general prosperity. There was one
embarrassment, however, which seriously ham-
pered their operations. This was the loss of
horses stolen by horse thieves, this loss falling
most heavily on the settlers in the upper sections
of the valleys, those nearest the mines, and increased, rather than diminished, for two years.

To accommodate those who rode their own
animals to the mines, and who had no place to
keep them after their arrival, what were termed
horse ranches were established in the valleys.
The owners of these so-called ranches had an
office and a corral in Placerville, or one of the
other towns, where horses were received to be
sent out to the ranch, where a pasturage charge
of three dollars a month was made, and an
agreement entered into that the animal, or
animals, would be brought in and delivered to
the owner when desired. The horse ranch consisted of a corral and a tent or cabin, to shelter
the owner, or herder, to whom no financial
responsibility could attach, since the land upon
which they were located, and that upon which
they ranged the horses and mules, belonged to

the public domain, but, in spite of this fact, thousands of animals were delivered into the care of these people. It is needless to say that only a small number of them were ever returned to the lawful owners. It is doubtful if such a harvest was ever reaped by horse thieves since America was discovered, because no such favorable conditions had heretofore existed in any country.

Thousands of saddle and pack animals, many of them very valuable, were turned loose to range over the hills lying east, north and south of Horseshoe Bend. Thus the stock was entirely removed from their owners, and, for that matter, from anyone else who knew them, as it was impossible for the owners of the horse-ranches to familiarize themselves with such a diversity of brands, and, in fact, many were not branded at all. Horses or mules, reduced in flesh by a long trip made perhaps before feed had started in the spring, will, when turned loose on such bunch-grass as then grew on Payette hills and valleys, change so much in appearance in a short time that the owners frequently failed to recognize their animals. Hence the risk of driving off and appropriating this class of stock was not considered great, owing to the lax methods by which the laws were administered, methods which had a tendency to make the business of stock stealing a favorite vocation among those who had received training along this line in other regions.

Three former citizens of New Mexico who had graduated in that territory as stage robbers, horse thieves and cattle rustlers, arrived on the river early in the spring of 1863, and after sizing up the situation, established headquarters in the Payette valley, near the entrance of the canyon, above where is now located the prosperous town of Emmett.

They built a strong log house and corral, which was planned for defense, should necessity arise, and named the place "Picket Corral," by which sobriquet it soon gained repute, the residents thereof being known as the "Picket Corral gang." After getting established, they proceded to organize the business, one of their number locating a ranch and building a cabin and corral across the river from Boise City, on the site of what is now South Boise.

They were all fine specimens of physical manhood, good horsemen and companionable fellows, ready to relieve an unfortunate by sharing a blanket, or dividing with him, what might be their last dollar. Hence they soon acquired well merited popularity among men of of their class, which enabled them to manipulate the first Democratic nominating convention in Ada County, and secure the election of their choice for sheriff, a nomination on the Democratic ticket being equivalent to an election in those days. At that time few men came to Idaho to engage in politics, hence the number who participated in the primaries and the nom-

inating convention was usually small. Aside
from the few who had personal ends to gain,
those who voted at the primaries did so in a
desultory manner—accepting and depositing the
ballots prepared for them by the agents of the
night-riders.

If some of those sturdy, honest farmers who
crossed the plains from Missouri to settle in
Boise or Payette valleys, and who rode, sometimes many miles, to take part in an election,
had been told of the manner in which the political machine was run in Ada and Boise counties
in those days, they would have doubted the
statement if made by their own fathers.

The tickets were all voted, whether Republican or Democratic, under the then territorial
form of government, and carried no political
significance other than they gave expression as
to whether we were in favor of maintaining the
Union. The real issue was not political—only
in the sense applying to whether the lives and
the property of the people within our borders
should be protected. Yet, honest men, as was
said, sometimes rode many miles to vote what
they believed was the same ticket their fathers
voted during the days of Andrew Jackson.

These voters wanted to do what they believed was right. They believed they did right,
hence they were right, and their hearts were in
the right place. Unfortunately, the first sheriff
they elected in Ada county—the first Monday
in March, 1865—was Dave Opdyke, who sub-

sequently resigned his position for cause, and was afterward hanged, as was another sheriff in Bannock, in what is now Montana. The laws of men may be repealed or suspended, but the laws of God are eternally operative. It has been truly written "Those who live by the sword, die by it."

One of the peculiar characteristics of the people in all frontier countries is their hatred of horse thieves, and their belief that nothing less than capital punishment is adequate to suppress them. This sentiment was no doubt prompted in Idaho by the well known fact that those who were entrusted with the enforcement of the law—the sheriff and his deputies—were nominated and elected to their positions through the influence of the admirers of horse-flesh. I was once told by a former resident of Arkansas that "when a man was killed in his state, the authorities empaneled a jury, not for the purpose of determining whether the accused was guilty of killing the man, but to ascertain whether it had been a fair fight." If the latter was shown by the evidence, the verdict of the jury was "Bully for the boy with the glass eye." Yet these same men would hang a horse thief without compunction.

It is well known that Arkansas contributed generously to the population of Idaho during those years, and no doubt many of those who sat on the juries named, were among the number. It was a notorious fact that while many murders were committed in Boise County during the five years when its population was the greatest, not one of the men who committed them suffered the extreme penalty of the law.

After the first stampede to the Basin was ended the business of the horse ranchers was practically at an end. Hence the professional horse-thieves were compelled to cover a wider field to make their operations profitable. They often extended their enterprises into Nevada and eastern Oregon and Washington, returning with their spoils to one of their home ranches—usually on or near the Payette river. If the fruits of their depredations consisted of horses or mules, they were held until sold. But if pursuit was feared, they were moved during the night to some other cache. The favorite place of concealment during such emergencies was the ranch across the river from Boise—now South Boise.

On the occasion of such transfer the stock was driven across the hills to Dry Creek, thence to Crane's Gulch, and, following it down to the valley, a detour was made through some of the back streets of the city, so as to strike the river above the Davis ranch. Here the animals were driven in and made to swim across, where they were cared for by the man, or men, in charge of the ranch.

Boise river in those days had but one channel for a long distance above and below town, and the water was so deep as to preclude fording, a ferry being maintained below town to transfer traffic, and as the trees and bushes along the bank obscured the view from one side to the other, horses, when over, were safe from discovery.

Sometimes relentless persons would continue the chase into the city, and visiting the sheriff's office, would appeal to that officer for assistance, which was invariably promised.

Whereupon, the weary riders would ask him and his deputies to take a drink, an invitation which would be considerately accepted, and the party would at once adjourn to the sheriff's own saloon, and in this social and friendly manner the incident would close.

There is no record of more than one stolen horse being recovered by the owner during the three first years of the mining furore, and the incidents to that event, though attracting little attention at the time, were to be of widespread influence in the near future.

The following synopsis will convey an idea, of the peculiar conditions which existed in our frontier at that time, which was during the month of August, 1864:

A man who was engaged in truck-gardening on one of the tributaries of the Payette river, after delivering a cargo of vegetables to the hotels and restaurants in Centerville, proceeded with his pack train down Grimes' Creek and camped for the night. Although the Basin was then nearly all covered with a growth of fine timber, at the place chosen for his camp there was a large spot of open ground covered with good grass. He had but one packer, or assistant, with him, and after supper, before retiring, they caught and picketed their favorite saddlehorse within a short distance of where they spread their blankets. Fatigued as they were, and anticipating no danger to themselves or animals, they retired early, and were soon in a sound slumber, from which they awakened in the morning to find that in the night some one had slipped into the camp and stolen the picketed horse. Search was made during the following day which disclosed that two men, who were in Centerville during the previous day, and were noticed admiring the missing animal while it was standing hitched in the street, had disappeared, and a party coming into Boise over the Shaffer Creek road had passed them during the forenoon and upon inquiry, were told that they were headed for Boise Valley.

The pack-train was at once started for the home ranch, arriving there in the night after the farm hands had gone to bed. Arousing them, fresh horses were saddled, and accompanied by one man, the owner started for Boise City, where they arrived at eight o'clock the following morning, having rested themselves and their horses two hours on the trail between Dry Creek and Crane's Gulch. A search of the feed corrals and livery stables was immediately made, with the result that, while no trace of the stolen horse was discovered, another one was found in the livery and feed stable which was owned by Opdyke, who was later elected sheriff. The animal, a mare, had been stolen about two months before. She was claimed by a restaurant keeper named Gilkie, who said she had been given to him by John Kelly, the violinist. Everyone knowing Kelly knew he never stole a horse, as he was too lazy, too big and fat to go out on the range and catch one. They refused to surrender the property, so the owner was obliged to secure the services of a lawyer to recover his horse. Fortunately, A. G. Cook, an attorney whom he had known in Lafayette, Oregon, had located in Boise a short time before, and he kindly volunteered to take the case and make no charge. He and John Deisenroth, a blacksmith owning a shop in town, qualified as bondsmen for the required amount; but notwithstanding the validity of the surety, which was unquestioned, the justice of the peace before whom the case was brought, required the complainant to weigh out gold dust enough to pay the estimated costs before he would issue the writ, the result being that it cost the owner seventy dollars, including a back stable bill which he was obliged to pay to recover the animal which everyone, including the justice and the sheriff, knew was his before any evidence was offered.

This was the culmination of what might have been forseen—the breaking down of the barrier of loyalty to law and order which is an instance of all pastoral people. The evidence was no longer lacking that the farmers and traveling public could expect no protection from the ordinary sources through which justice is administered.

The owner of the horse entered the court-room of that Boise City justice, little more than a boy in years and experience, but he came out when the case was decided and he had paid the costs, amounting to nearly the full value of the animal, a grim-visaged man. With no word to anyone, except to thank the two men who had gone on his bond, he and his helper led their horses down the street and stopped in front of the stable where a group of tin-horn gamblers and horse-thieves had preceded them from the court-room, announcing that he would like to make a speech to them before leaving. One of their number told him to "fire ahead"—meaning for him to begin—which he did, stating that he was an American citizen, that he recognized "no chiefs," and that he could catch any man who ever marked those prairies and that the next one who stole a horse from him would be "his Indian"—there would be no law-suit. Waiting a few moments for a reply and none coming, he mounted his saddle-horse and rode away, leading the recovered animal.

Had the members of the gang who were present when the foregoing remarks were made been less confident of their power, and given more attention to the glint of the eyes and the set of the jaws of the man who uttered them, they might have taken warning, but in a spirit of bravado, they resolved to teach the "rutabaga peddler" to take a joke.

A few nights later that part of the Payette Valley which lies above Jackass Creek, and is now called Jerusalem, was raided, and nine animals stolen—five horses and four large mules. There were at that time four gardens, or miniature farms, being cultivated in that neighborhood and the stolen stock belonged to the owners of these gardens. These people had been "long-suffering and slow to wrath," but the recent experience of one of their number in trying to obtain justice in a Boise court, had thoroughly aroused their fighting instincts.

A posse of four men was organized, and after ascertaining that the thieves had started to the lower country with their booty, pursuit was begun. Well mounted and well armed, each riding a horse and leading another, these men, fewer in number than the pursued, took the Brown Lew trail—determined to recover what they had lost or lose their lives in the attempt.

They were gone about three weeks when all returned, bringing with them the lost animals, jaded and worn almost to skin and bones. The story of that pursuit and the recovery of the stolen stock would add many thrilling pages to the history of those stirring days; but it has never been written, and it probably never will be, for the men who make the history of a new country are seldom historical writers.

It is known, however, that the recovery was made in Oregon, on the Grand Ronde river below the valley of that name; and also that the transfer was not a friendly one—but if any casulties occurred they were all on one side.

On their return trip a stop was made at the road-house along their route, and open war was declared against horse-thieves and stage-robbers.

A few days after their arrival home a meeting which included all the residents in their locality was held on Porter Creek, and while no permanent organization was effected, resolutions were unanimously adopted pledging themselves as follows:

1st, to stand as a unit on all matters affecting the personal safety or the property rights of any individual resident.

2nd, to pursue and capture, regardless of expense, all horse-thieves who thereafter appropriated any horses, cattle or mules belonging to any individual resident or traveler passing through that section. Provided, that after the capture was made, the posse effecting it should administer such condign punishment as in their judgment the circumstances merited—always bearing in mind that farmers were not prepared to hold prisoners.

A pronunciamento in accordance with these resolutions was promulgated, and in a few days news of the action which had been taken was widely disseminated, causing a meeting to be called in the "Block House" in the lower Payette Valley. The "Block House," so called because it was built of hewed logs, was two stories high, the upper story being in one room, or hall, made a suitable place to hold public gatherings; in fact, it was then the only suitable place in the valley.

When the meeting assembled, it was called to order. The chairman, Henry Paddock, of the "Hay-press Ranch," stated that the object of the meeting was to devise and consider plans for the better protection of life and property—not alone that of the settlers, but those who traveled through the valley on the public highway. He enumerated the robberies that had occurred within the year and told of the futile efforts made to suppress lawlessness. He related the histories of other countries where the lawless and vicious classes had succeeded in gaining control of the sheriff's office, who, after his election, permitted similar conditions to exist until the people, driven by desperation, organized vigilance committees and proceeded to punish offenders according to their deserts. Citing San Francisco as an example, and referring to the action recently taken by the settlers living above Horseshoe Bend.

After a long discussion in which the concensus of opinion favored the plan of organizing some kind of a committee of safety, it was finally deemed best to adjourn the meeting for a week, in order that a conference might be had with those who, as before stated, had already taken matters into their own hands.

Accordingly a committee was appointed and instructed to visit all the residents in that region with a view to forming an organization that would include all the law-abiding settlers in the Payette Valley—from Brainard Creek to the Snake.

The committee carried out the instructions given to them so faithfully that on the second day after receiving them the people came together and were invited to co-operate in a movement having for its object the suppression of crime in the form of horse-stealing, murders, robberies, etc. As a result of the meeting, a committee consisting of two men was sent to meet the men who had already taken action, as explained above. One of the two men chosen to act as a representative in this matter was he who recovered the horse in Boise, and who had also taken an active part in the Grand Ronde affair.

When the adjourned meeting at the Block House was again called to order, the gathering consisted of nearly every man in the valley living below the Berner ranch. There were probably a score of absentees, a few of whom had families that they could not leave, and the others were so notoriously connected with the lawless organization that they did not have the audacity to attend—although they were aware that such a meeting was to be held.

The man who had presided at the former

meeting was named chairman, and after a secretary had been chosen the chairman announced
that the meeting had been called for the purpose
of organizing a committee of safety, or vigilance
committee, and asked all present who had sug-
gestions to make, to arise. Accordingly, several
short speeches were made by men who had suffered losses, which were explained by the speak-
ers. These discussions disclosed that the losses
suffered by farmers and others were undoubtedly
caused by residents of the valley, it having been
conclusively shown that within a distance of
fifty miles the occupants of no less than four
ranches had no visible means of support other
than that afforded by their dealings in horses
and mules, and it was shown that their trans-
actions in this line were conducted by preference
in the night. These ranches each supported from
two to five men, or about a dozen men all told,
yet their organization was so perfect and their
energy so untiring that up to the time this meeting was called they had kept the entire southern
part of Idaho, outside the towns, terrorized.

A motion having been made and adopted to
this effect, a committee of three was appointed
by the chair to draft a constitution and by-laws,
and a recess was taken to enable the committee-
men to prepare their report.

The name finally chosen for the organization
was the "Payette Vigilance Committee." Its
existence was to be continued until the indus-
tries of horse-stealing, highway robbery and the
passing of "bogus" gold dust were suppressed.

CHAPTER XII.

ALL ACCUSED persons were entitled to a trial by jury, composed of seven members, a majority of whom were permitted to render a verdict—which was final. Three forms of punishment were adopted, as follows:

1st. Banishment, in which case twenty-four hours were allowed for preparation.

2nd. Horse-whipping, to be publicly administered.

3rd. Capital punishment. The meeting which perfected the foregoing organization was composed of earnest, determined men, most of whom attended because they realized that a crisis had been reached. They were not law-breakers, nor had they any intention of interfering with the execution of the laws; but as no effort was being made by those whose duties it was to enforce the law—the sheriff and his deputies—there seemed but one course open, and that they adopted. This was the first organization of its kind in south Idaho, and it met its requirements to the entire satisfaction of its promoters. Within a few months the night-riders had all disappeared, doubtless having found other cli-

mates more congenial, and within one year the
reputation of Payette valley was restored to what
it is today, no stable need be locked. This reformation was not brought about, however, without
strenuous and persistent effort. It must not be
thought that those daring and desperate men
who had for an ally the sheriff of the county,
would at once surrender the prestige they had
gained. The first action taken by the vigilance
committee after perfecting its organization was
to empanel a jury, by whom testimony was tak-
en, relating to the operations of a band of coun-
terfeiters, who made a specialty of "bogus" gold
dust, it having been shown that an extensive organization existed, with headquarters for Idaho
at Placerville and with agents in various places,
and especially in the valley settlements. In the
last places mentioned, the population was largely
made up from immigrants who had recently
crossed the plains.

The possibilities of this unlawful traffic will
be better understood when it is explained that
the medium of exchange at that time was almost
invariably gold dust, or that which passed for
gold dust; and since the recent arrivals were necessarily inexperienced in handling this new
medium of exchange and barter, they were easily
defrauded.

The bogus article most in circulation was
manufactured in San Francisco by simply cutting
bars of lead into small particles which resembled
gold dust in size; these were then galvanized

with gold by means of a special process, and so
perfect was the deception that nitric acid, as
usually applied, would not reveal the fraud.
But if the so-called gold dust was allowed to
remain in the acid for a longer time than was
usual, discovery would follow, for in the process
of galvanization defects too small to be noticed
by the naked eye would inevitably be searched
out and revealed by the acid. This bogus dust
had one fatal defect which could not be overcome and which made its detection easy by both
old timers and by close observers; the angles
were too perfect; while the size of the granules
might and did vary, the general contour was
always the same, which is never true of placer
gold—it being invariably irregular in form.
Large quantities of the counterfeit article were
"worked off" by mixing it with genuine gold dust
and then using the mixture for the payment of
freight bills to packers and teamsters engaged in
hauling supplies. Local agents adopted various
expedients. Along the Payette valley road one
method which usually proved successful was for
the agent to ride up to a road-house or to a place
where supplies were sold and tell the unsuspecting proprietor that he wanted to leave a deposit
of dust for some one, naming the individual.

Then, as now, a deposit was seldom refused
and as deposits are now merged into, and become
a part of the funds of the individual or bank receiving them, so were they then, the difference
being that vaults and safes are now used, while

14 E. H. I.

in those days a yeast powder can was the usual depository. The horseman would be invited to alight, and the proprietor, after weighing the deposit, would dump it into the can where he kept his own dust, and where it was mixed and became a part of the whole. Often weeks elapsed before the dust was claimed, during which time, by the process of adding and withdrawing in the regular course of business, but little if any of the dust which was deposited originally remained, and the claimant received good dust, or nearly so, for a deposit of galvanized lead. The inquiry made by the jury led to the disclosure that a man named Conklin who made his headquarters with the Pickett Corral gang, was the local, or Payette agent of the bogus dust syndicate and it was ordered that he be given twenty-four hours to leave the country. A committee of one was appointed to serve on him a written notice to that effect. Accordingly, on the following day, an escort of five men were detailed to accompany him. It was arranged that they should assemble at 12 o'clock noon at a road house located where the town of Emmett now stands, and from there proceed in a body to Pickett Corral, where it was expected they would find the individual sought. After the adjournment the man who was to serve the notice proceeded to the rendezvous, arriving there at 2 o'clock a. m.

After a few attempts he succeeded in arousing the sleepy landlord, who assigned him to a

well-furnished room containing a comfortable
feather-bed. Retiring immediately, he was soon
wrapped in a sound, refreshing sleep. The next
morning after breakfast he entered the lounging
room, where he found several of the Pickett Corral gang, one of the number being the bogus gold
dust operator upon whom he was authorized to
serve notice to leave the country.

They had probably come down to the road-
house, which was on the main traveled route to
Placerville, in order to obtain news, if possible,
of the decision reached at the meeting held the
previous night at the Block House. Their leader
having arrived, they held a protracted out-door
discussion among themselves. Finally, one of the
men left the others and entered the room where
the representative of the vigilance committee was
standing, and asked him to accompany him outside. He at once complied with the request,
slipping his two Colt's revolvers forward on the
belt, where they could be quickly reached, he
walked out into the midst of the party of desperadoes, which now consisted of four men. They
all started towards a small corral, and he went
with them.

Nothing was said until they were inside the
enclosure. This had been built by digging a
two-foot trench around the area it was designed
to enclose; logs of about twelve inches in dia-
meter and eight feet long were set closely together on their ends therein. The interview that
followed was a stormy one. The move to get

him out of sight of the house was understood by
the committee's agent—another murder was to
be committed, and no witnesses were to be present, save the friends and associates of the murderer—but they had signally failed to correctly
"size up" their prospective victim, who, upon
entering the inclosure, immediately backed into
a corner against the logs facing his enemies, and
said "Well, show your colors; I am no immigrant, I will make the biggest funeral ever held
in this valley. I know you; I understand what
this means. You are here to murder me, but I
don't think you can do it." The men were dumb-
founded; they did not expect such a reception,
and knowing that a movement on their part to
draw a weapon meant death to at least one, and
possibly to all, they hesitated to open the fracas
and finally weakened. A circumstance had happened in La Grande a short time before, which
perhaps had a deterring influence in this case.
An Irishman, enroute from Boise to Portland,
who had considerable gold with him, stopped off
the stage in La Grande, Oregon, intending to
remain over one day to meet some friends. He
was soon marked for a victim by the light-fin-
ered gentlemen of suave manners who hang
around frontier towns, and after he had taken
a few drinks a game of poker was proposed and
he was invited to make a fourth man. It was a
case of three pluck one. The table at which they
played was in the open bar room. Of course, the
stranger was loser from the beginning, as it was

intended he should be. But after a time the influence of the liquor he had drank wore away
and as one of the gamblers who had won the
"pot" began drawing it in, he noticed that the
hand was foul. It then dawned upon his befud-
dled brain that he was being robbed, and reaching over, he attempted to prevent the money
from being removed from the table, whereupon
the gambler drew a pistol and shot the Irishman,
who toppled out of his chair and fell full length
upon the floor, but immediately rose upon one
elbow and drawing a revolver, shot all three of
the gamblers dead before they could escape from
the room and when the last one fell, his arm
collapsed and he turned on his back and expired
without a groan. He not only relieved the country of three characters that could well be spared,
but in doing so he set an example which was
a salutatory lesson to the fraternity of black-
legs. Had not this incident so recently happened, the meeting in the corral might have
ended in a similar tragedy, for the main character has since stated that when he went out to
those men he expected to be killed, all he hoped
to do was to leave a record that his friends
would be proud of. He went into the corral with
them because there they would be out of sight
of the women in the house, realizing how unpleasant for them it would be to see a lot of
men killed. But the moment he succeeded in
getting his back into a corner against the logs,
his muscles became like steel stretched to full

tension, and he knew that unless they punctured his spinal column and paralyzed him the first shot, he would kill them all. After normal conditions were restored and the tension somewhat relaxed, he concluded not to wait for the escort, which was to accompany him to Pickett Corral to serve notice of banishment on the bogus dust man, but inasmuch as that individual was present, he concluded to deliver it to him at once, which he proceeded to do, and as the accused refused to receive the written notice, he read it to him. Another stormy scene resulted but no casualties resulted. Thus was ended a dangerous and annoying traffic in less than twenty-four hours after its existence had been considered by the self-appointed judges. No costs were incurred, no imprisonment followed. The agency simply suspended its operations in that line. The agent did what he was told to do, arranged his affairs within the time given him and disappeared from the scene of his former activities. As was anticipated by the originators, the news of the organization of a vigilance committee and its prompt action in suppressing the traffic in bogus gold dust created consternation in some quarters and indignation in others; among the latter were the owners of the Washoe ferry, on Snake river, near its confluence with the Payette.

The ferry was owned by two brothers who had gained an unenviable reputation by harboring desperate characters who were known to be engaged in unlawful pursuits, one or more of

whom were at the ferry almost continuously.
The ferry-house which they occupied was in
Oregon, the river being the state line. It was
a strong log structure with a dirt roof, about
twenty feet in length by sixteen in width, and
being in a locality that was open to attack by Indians, it was constructed and equipped to resist
assault or withstand a siege should occasion
arise. At one end it had a fireplace and chim-
ney on the inside, a strong door at the other.
Instead of windows, small port-holes for rifle
practice were cut in the walls. The owners and
occupants of this miniature fortress at the time
the news of the recent action taken by the committee, and its proclaimed intentions of taking
more drastic measures in the future if it deemed
such steps necessary, were not merely indignant,
but were enraged, and feeling confident in their
numbers, as well as in their location and the
strength of their building, wrote an insulting
letter, or proclamation, sending it not only to
the president of the vigilance committee, but
copies were also distributed at Boise City and in
the mining towns throughout southern Idaho and
eastern Oregon.

They derided their efforts and challenged
them to attempt the capture of the fortress,
declaring there were not enough vigilantes in
Payette valley to capture them. The challenge
was brought up for discussion at the next regular meeting, which convened a few days later,
and as the crimes said to have been committed by

some of the denizens of the ferry had already attracted wide attention, it was resolved to accept the invitation extended, and to settle the problem respecting their ability to capture the place. The result of the contest that was thought to be inevitable would determine the future status of the country for an indefinite period, so far as property rights were concerned. A captain, with authority to appoint a lieutenant, and to call for volunteers, was appointed to lead the enterprise. A company of twenty men, including the captain and lieutenant, was immediately organized out of the members present at the meeting, and the "Hay-press Ranch" was chosen as the place of rendezvous from which to advance to the attack on the ferry, which was approximately twenty-five miles distant. The time for the meeting was set a few days before the contemplated attack, in order to give the volunteers an opportunity for preparation. When the time for departure arrived, there were no laggards. The roll being called, every man responded "present." They were not only present in person, but were fully equipped with horses and arms, prepared to engage in what they expected would be a desperate enterprise.

The captain was given entire control and his plans were not known to even his lieutenant until the time arrived for their execution. The advance was ordered during the afternoon of a winter day, the ground being covered with snow to a depth of perhaps one foot; the sky was free from clouds, with the mercury hovering near the zero mark. The march was uninterrupted until nearly half the distance was covered, when a point was reached where a branch road diverged from the main line, which at that time crossed the Payette River at the Bluff Station, the branch being the road to Washoe Ferry, the objective point of the expedition. Here a halt was made, and the captain, advancing to a hostelry near the junction, asked the proprietress if she could entertain sixteen men over night and give them their breakfast at four o'clock the following morning. Without awaiting her reply and smiling at her astonishment, he said "Oh, I know you can, so I will leave them with you," and turning to his lieutenant said, "I will leave you here with all the men but three, whom I will take with me"—naming them. I want you to breakfast at 4 a. m., and immediately afterwards start for the ferry with your men, guaging your movements so as to arrive on the bank of the river precisely at sunrise," stating that he would go down the road with the men named, and during the night cross at Central Ferry, and then march back up the river on the Oregon side to the Washoe Ferry—arriving in time to co-operate with the main body.

The men selected fell into line, leaving the main body as directed, and followed their leader down the main or stage road to Central Ferry, where they arrived at eight o'clock p. m.

This ferry at that time was operated by a

man named Eply, who had a woman employed as
housekeeper who was a famous cook. The supper she prepared that night was long afterward
a pleasant memory to those who partook of it;
the horses were as well provided for as were the
men, and after a rest of two hours, the captain
called his men outside and told them that his
plan was to capture the Washoe Ferry that night
before the arrival of the lieutenant and his
force. He called Epley, the Central ferryman,
into the conference and inquired if he could
transfer the party, including their horses, to the
opposite bank of the river that night. Upon his
expressing a willingness to make the attempt,
despite the fact that the river was covered with
floating, or anchor ice, the horses were saddled
and the transfer made without accident. The
distance to be traversed between the ferry landing and their objective point, was only about
three miles, and although there was no moon,
the starlight was sufficient to permit of good
progress along the river bank. Hence they were
but a short time in sighting the ferry house,
which gave out no glimmer of light. A halt was
called and the riders approached as near to one
another as practicable, whereupon the captain
asked all the men whether they knew the owners
or the occupants of the ferry house; and one of
them answering in the negative, he told him to
approach the house alone, after the others had
ridden along the road leading to the ferry to a
point opposite the house. He was to dismount,

and to divert suspicion, the others were to ride
a few rods ahead, as if to approach the ferry-
landing. The man chosen to arouse the inmates
was to call to them that there was a party with
him, desiring to be ferried across, so that they
might pursue their way as far as possible that
night. He was also to say that they had traveled up the river from Old's Ferry, on the Central Ferry road, but owing to anchor ice, the
ferryman there had refused to cross the river
hence their appearance at that time. He was to
state that they were willing to pay double ferriage on account of the ice, and was instructed to
say further that he was nearly frozen. If the
door was opened to him, he was at once to
approach the fireplace and stir up the embers,
throwing onto them any kindling or light material convenient, and as soon as it flared up, or
blazed, to look sharply, for the posse would immediately charge. The plan worked as smoothly as
if it had been rehearsed. There were six men
in the house, all in bed asleep. One of them
when awakened, arose and after lighting a can-
dle and partially dressing himself, proceeded to
open the door, which was fastened by passing a
chain through an auger-hole in the door and
around the jamb, the ends being fastened with a
padlock. As soon as the door was open the supposed traveler went stamping the length of the
room to the fire-place, his heavy Mexican spurs
ringing over the earthen floor. By this time the
entire party had dismounted and were stamping

along the frozen road between the house and ferry, as if endeavoring to restore circulation while waiting for the ferryman. The spurs had, however, been removed from every heel, and all was in readiness for the signal which was momentarily expected. They had but a short wait, as the fireplace was a bed of coals, which upon being stirred, and having a handful of dry willows added, at once flashed up like powder, and in an instant the door was filled with barrels of shotguns covering the inmates. Resistance would have been suicidal, hence none was made, and so without a shot being fired or a blow struck, the capture was effected. Of the six men in the house, only one had arisen and he was not armed.

The beds with which the house was furnished were of the usual frontier pattern, permanently fastened to the logs composing the wall. There were three of these bunks or beds ranging along the sides of the room, each being wide enough to accommodate two men. Above each bed, low enough to be easily reached, were hung the arms of the occupants, rifles and shotguns on the hooks and pistols-in holsters attached to belts. It was plainly evident that had the occupants suspected the character of their midnight callers, no force available could have dislodged them, without the aid of artillery. After taking possession of all the arms and securing the horses in a shed, where hay and grain were found, dispositions were made to spend the remainder of the night. At sunrise, as had been prearranged, the lieutenant arrived with his troop and their surprise at finding the captain and his small posse in possession of the place was no doubt as great as that of the men they had so easily taken.

Two of the prisoners were found to be strangers looking for a place to locate a ranch, and were unconscious of the character of the house in which they had secured a night's lodging. If they are still alive their account of that adventure would be interesting. They were farmers not familiar with strenuous life, never before having been poked out of bed with the muzzle of a double-barreled shotgun, it was doubtless a new and alarming experience. The efforts they made to convince their captors that they were not horse-thieves or stage robbers were pathetic. Upon being told that they were free and given their arms, huge dragoon revolvers, they at once took their back track for their homes in the Willamette Valley, having no longer a desire to own land on Snake river. After the foregoing departure, a jury was selected to try the other men. The trial was not a long drawn-out affair like those of modern times, yet it was conducted with decorum and a degree of fairness seldom surpassed in legally conducted courts of justice.

Technical rules of evidence were not permitted to interfere with the ascertainment of all information bearing on the case. It was disclosed during the hearing that Stewart Bros. were the sole owners of the ferry, together with its appurtenances, and had been since its establishment—a period of approximately two years. That during this time, while not keeping a road-house or hostelry, they had at various times received into their household, for indefinite periods, men of ill-repute who were supposed to be engaged in unlawful pursuits. One instance was shown, relative to a character known as "Black Charley," who was a guest at the ferry for several months during the summer of 1864, and while there, the man who had made the first location on the bottom land near the mouth of the Payette river, sold his claim, and being the nearest neighbor to the Stewart Bros., the circumstance was well known to them, as also was the intention of the man to proceed overland to California, carrying with him the money received for his ranch and driving with him a bunch of valuable horses. Black Charley, learning of the circumstance, became interested, and keeping watch on the ranch knew when the start was made and the following day took his trail in pursuit. No trace of the man was ever found, although his friends in California, upon his failure to arrive, made diligent search. In those days few of the bleaching skeletons on the sage covered deserts of Idaho and Nevada were ever identified.

Black Charlie did not return to his former haunts and the circumstances of his disappear-

ance was known to only a few until the vigilance
committee's jury unearthed the facts. Although
no sufficient evidence was submitted to connect
the Stewart brothers with the supposed crime,
it was shown that they were cognizant of the
character and the intent of Black Charlie and
that, doubtless, had influence with the jury. It
was also shown by conclusive testimony that
while the owners of the ferry had no cattle of
their own and never purchased any, they always
had fresh beef to sell to travelers, as well as for
their own use. One of the men captured with
the brothers was also known to be an undesirable citizen. The other of the four remaining
was considered of no importance.

Juries such as made this investigation, were
vested with more power than that reposed in the
county and district juries of our civil courts.
They not only passed upon the guilt and innocence of the accused, but they also determined
the severity of the sentence. The verdict of the
jury in the foregoing case was acquittal for one
of the men, banishment within twenty-four hours
for another, while the brothers were to suffer
the extreme penalty, which was inflicted at
twelve o'clock meridian the following day, at or
near the Junction House on the stage road, where
a gallows was to be erected.

In the interim before the sentence was executed, the prisoners were to be taken to Cog-
gin's, at Bluff Station Ferry on the Payette, to
be held until the hour set for their final fare-

well. They were accordingly permitted to saddle their horses, then accompanied by their captors, the entire troop crossed the river and proceeded to the point designated, where they arrived late in the afternoon. The condemned brothers were aged approximately 26 and 28 years, and were named respectively Charles and Alexander, but under a custom of the country, their names were abbreviated into Charley and Alex., so they were accordingly recognized as Charley and Alex Stewart. The latter was the younger; as sometimes happens in families, there was but little resemblance between them. Alex was larger and stronger, both mentally and physically, than his brother, though the latter was no weakling. They were born and reared in Canada, on the banks of the St. Lawrence river, and from early boyhood had been trained in the use of water-craft, hence their location on Snake river as ferrymen. When they first established the ferry, the young men were but recently from the home where they were born, and while they were probably no better, it is not likely that they were worse than the average boy reared in the Canadian provinces. Their good-fellowship was the cause of their fall. Living remote from the companionship of neighbors, at a point that was never free from the danger of attack by predatory bands of Indians, they were glad to welcome as guests almost any white men who came to their ferry, and since the gentlemen who sometimes held up stage coaches as a diversion were frequently the most cheerful and companionable men who came over the road, and were seldom in a hurry, they too were made welcome and no questions were asked. Thus the young men, by reason of evil associations, became ambitious of gaining distinction as braves, until finally they identified themselves with the lawless element by issuing a challenge to the vigilance committee, with the results recorded.

The verdict of the jury did not meet the approval of the captain of the vigilantes, so beckoning Alex to follow him, he walked away from the others, down to the bank of the river, and when he had reached a point out of hearing from the house, he waited for him to approach. He then said, "Alex, I am going to let you and Charlie go, or at least I am going to try to do so. These men would hang me as soon as they would you, if they thought I was untrue to them, but I will take the chance. I am going to do so, not because I think you are innocent, for I know you are guilty, but I do not think your crime justifies such severe punishment. I will endeavor to give you your freedom under the promise which I expect you to make, that you will leave this country and try to lead good and honorable lives, and I want you to distinctly understand that if you succeed in effecting your escape, that you must not return at any time in the future with the intention of getting even with the members of the vigilance committee." Alex at this point, for the first time since his arrest, evi-

15 E. H. I.

denced any feeling; his eyes now filled with tears
and in a broken voice he admitted they had
done wrong, claiming they had been used as cat's-
paws by bad, designing men, and promised im-
plicit obedience to all the captain asked.   The
following night, about ten o'clock, the prisoners
were assigned a bed in a log building used as a
store room.   It had a door opening to the street
which was kept locked, and another door opening into another room in which a guard, consisting of two men, was stationed, the night being
divided into two watches.   The men were aroused
to take the second watch, and feeling sleepy, concluded that, as there was no way the prisoners
could effect their escape, except through the door
entering the room where they were expected to
keep their weary watch, they could avoid loss of
sleep and at the same time hold the condemned
by taking the blankets from which they had
recently arisen and making a bed across the
door of the prison room and then retire.   The
prisoners, it was thought, would awaken the
sleepers if they attempted to escape by stepping
over the bed.   But alas, the ingenuity of the
guard was ineffectual.   When day dawned and
the guard awoke, they found a vacant bed in the
prison chamber, and the prisoners had flown.
It was found that the outer door had been un-
locked by some person who had a key, and the
tracks of the escaping men were plainly visible
in the snow.   A consultation was held and the
conclusion reached that pursuit of the fugitives

should be instituted immediately after the horses and men had breakfasted. Accordingly, two hours later, all were in readiness and as the tracks of the fleeing men led in the direction of Snake river, it was concluded that they were aiming for the ferry where their capture had been effected, with the purpose of crossing Snake river and escaping into Oregon. The pursuers, therefore, divided into two parties, one of which, headed by the captain, went by the Central ferry, following the same route traveled by himself and party the night the capture was made, and the other party headed by Lieutenant Paddock followed the tracks of the fugitives. It appeared that the escape must have been made soon after the guard was changed, probably not later than two o'clock, for, instead of going directly to the ferry, the tracks led to a point on the river about two miles above, at which an ice gorge had been lodged for several weeks, their probable intention being to cross there, as it had bridged the river for some distance, but before their arrival it had broken up and the ice had gone on down the river. Disappointed in their object, they turned down to the ferry, where they arrived in time to join Hadley, the man who had been given twenty-four hours to leave the country, and who, at the time of their arrival, had his horses up and was preparing to depart. They, therefore, were able to unite and leave together, taking the trail for the lower country. When the party that had persistently followed their tracks, arrived at the ferry, the objects of their pursuit had disappeared over the hills to the westward. The captain and the men who had gone with him via Central Ferry, arrived soon after the others, and greatly to his discomfiture, found that one of the men belonging to the trailing party had gone on alone after the fugitives, believing that others would follow as soon as the ranking officer arrived. When he arrived the captain was not disappointed to find that the escapes had already left, for he expected such a result, and it had been his intention to call the men together at the ferry and say to them that he believed the real object of the committee, the ridding of the country of a lot of bad men, had been effectually accomplished. The men who escaped were thoroughly frightened, and if permitted to do so, would no doubt keep on going until out of reach. They and all others of their kind would, in the future, have a wholesome dread of the Payette Vigilantes. But the departure of the lone pursuer disarranged his former plans, since he could not permit one lone man to follow three, who, no doubt, were rendered desperate by their recent experience. So he at once rode out in front of the men and expressed his determination to take their trail and recapture the prisoners. Calling for volunteers, he rode rapidly away, while out of all who were present only three men followed his lead, thus showing that nearly all of the company held the same opinions as those the captain had intended to express.

After following the road taken by the Stewarts
for a few miles, the captain's party overtook the
lone rider who had preceded them, and the pursuing force, now consisting of five men, began
the pursuit with renewed vigor. The ground
that their route traversed was covered with
snow to a depth of eighteen inches, and as the
trail had not been traveled during the winter
until its passage was attempted by the fugitives,
the progress made by both parties was necessarily slow. And owing to the distance gained
by the fleeing men, before their pursuers left the
ferry, it was almost night before the latter came
within sight of the camp that had been made by
the escapes, and then the view was not of the
camp proper, but of the smoke from the fire they
had kindled, and of the saddle and pack horses
they had turned loose on the hills adjacent,
where the bunch grass had grown in profusion
the summer previous, much of which was still
above the snow. The men had forced their way
into a dense thicket of willows, growing approximately three-fourths of a mile above Old's Ferry
on the Oregon side of the river, and by cutting
down and bending down a few of the smaller
bushes, they had made a camp which was protected, not only from the wind, but also from the
observation of anyone who chanced to pass along
the Central Ferry road, which followed up the
course of the river near the base of the hill not
far from the camp site chosen.

CHAPTER XIII.

HUMAN LIVES IN THE BALANCE.

FROM the general appearance of things, it was evident to the captain that the intent of the men in camp were to remain there during the night, at least; it being imperative that the horses should have rest and time to feed, and the men were undoubtedly much exhausted after two such strenuous nights and days as they had endured. The captain therefore made a detour to the left, and keeping within the hills out of sight of the camp, passed around it and on down to Old's ferry. Here he crossed both the men and horses on the ice, the boat being frozen in, and they arrived at the comfortable hostelry kept by the proprietor's family, almost as badly in need of rest as the men in camp above in the willows. The following morning smoke was still ascending from the camp in the willows, which was in plain view up the river from Old's, showing that the pursued were still there. After breakfast the men who had passed the night at Old's ferry ordered their horses and mounting, rode out to the middle of the river on the ice, where, after halting the men, the captain said to them that it was his opinion that a body of men *might do*, and sometimes *did do* things that every individual in the party, in his own secret conscience, believed was not right. He simply goes ahead with the crowd and says nothing, for fear that he might be accused of weakening, but for his part he believed moral courage was equally as commendable as physical courage. Hence he desired to state before proceeding further, that it was his opinion that if they could retake the men whom they had followed so far, and disarm them, paying them for their weapons, which would give them some money with which to pay their expenses down the road, it would be better than to kill them where they are. "We can kill them, for we are the stronger party, and are fully as well armed as they, but both as your captain and as an individual, I will not stand for it, and right here and now I want the opinion of every member of this party." Upon which each one gave his views as desired, and of the four men accompanying him, only one differed with the ideas he had expressed; and the one who favored extermination was George Coggan, who was himself killed several years later by the Indians in the Blue Mountains, in Oregon, during the Bannock war. The majority being of the same opinion as the captain, he told them it was not probable that they could advance in a body and retake their late prisoners without precipitating a conflict. But he believed one man might approach their camp and make known the terms of their

proposed surrender without so much probability
of resistance. And as he was responsible for the
suggestion, he volunteered to act as envoy, to
which proposal consent was given, with the proviso that the whole party should be allowed to
accompany him to within pistol shot of a point
in the road opposite the camp-fire where the
conference would probably take place. The carrying out of the foregoing plan was fraught
with serious danger to the envoy, as the bro-
ers might conclude that their escape had been
permitted for the purpose of following them
with a number of picked men and disposing of
them in a more secret manner than was possible in the settlement where all the parties were
known. In case they should conceive such an
idea, it was almost a certainty that they would
resolve to sell their lives as dearly as possible,
in which event they would begin hostilities by
shooting the captain, who, while opposite their
camp-fire, would be at their mercy. These were
the reasons why the men insisted on being allowed to come within pistol-shot. However, the
advance was made as agreed, the men stopping
at a distance of about one hundred yards from
where a thin column of smoke was ascending
from among the willows, but nothing could be
seen or heard around the camp. The captain
kept on until opposite the fire, then halting, he
called, "Boys," twice. No answer was made, so
pausing a moment, he called "Alex." At this
Charlie rose with a double barreled shot-gun and

was leveling it to shoot, when Alex caught his
arm in time to prevent the discharge. The captain then said, "Come out and deliver up your
arms, there is no use in trying to resist." To
which Alex replied, "I will give them up to
you." The captain responded "All right." He
then brought all their guns and pistols out and
delivered them up. An appraisement was made
at once of the weapons, and their value was paid
in cash to the owners; who soon after saddled
their horses and left for Powder River Valley,
while the vigilantes proceeded up the river to
their respective homes, where, upon reciting the
incidents related, they were met with the general acclaim: "Well done, thou good and faithful servant." Stewart brothers were the last
of the Mohicans. The Payette Vigilantes never
met in force again. Like the summer dew which
gently falls even in the darkest night, after refreshing its mother earth, vanishes under the
rays of the rising sun, and is absorbed by the
atmosphere—so vanished, after its duty had been
performed, the Payette Vigilance Committee,
its membership being absorbed by the body
politic of the county. Within three months of
its organization the committee transformed the
Payette Valley, with its hitherto unsavory reputation, into a community of peaceful homes,
where life and property were as safe as in any
of the older states or territories in the Union.
Of the men who enacted the foregoing historical
drama, but few are now alive and they are

widely scattered among friends and kindred, where they as bravely await the Last Call as they once faced their enemies in the '60's. The towns of Emmett, New Plymouth and Payette have sprung up in the valley which was the field of their earlier activities. Troops of eager, laughing girls and boys, on their way to and from school, now pass daily over the same roads that more than forty years ago were traveled by these iron-constitutioned, gun-armed men.

The action of the vigilance committee (1) in driving into banishment the local agent of the bogus gold dust syndicate, and (2) in capturing the stronghold at Washoe Ferry, and thereby scattering its inmates, attracted wide attention, and was the paramount topic of conversation among gamblers, horse-thieves, and stage-robbers for weeks thereafter. It was finally concluded by them that a crisis had arrived, and that unless the vigilance committee was put out of business, their vocations must be abandoned.

The county of Ada having been organized, and Opdyke appointed to the sheriff's office, they appealed to him for protection. A consultation was held and the situation was thoroughly canvassed. It was here determined that the permanency and effectiveness of the committee depended entirely on a few men, who were both the organizers and the leaders. Foremost among this number, they placed the captain who had led the recent movement against the Washoe Ferry gang.

It was decided that an effective method of suppressing the uprising of citizens on the Payette would be to legally remove one or more of the leaders, the captain having been chosen for the first victim of their experiment.

Warrants were issued for the arrests of all those settlers living in the Payette Valley who were supposed to belong to the vigilance committee. A large number of deputy sheriffs were sworn in to make the arrests; some of them were good men, and actually believed that the Vigilantes, as they were called, were a bloodthirsty lot of cut-throats. It was not intended that these deputies should have any part in the execution of the real purpose of those who conceived the plan, which was to strike terror into the hearts of the rank and file of the committee by killing a few of its leaders. Accordingly, the Pickett Corral contingent was appointed special deputies to arrest the captain, who was known to be at his home above Horseshoe Bend.

It was proposed that the Pickett Corral officers should separate from the other deputies at the point where the stage road to Boise City diverged from the Placerville road, the place of divergence being near where is now the city of Emmett, and only a short distance from their own headquarters, Pickett Corral, the plan being for them to remain at the stage-station until the following night, when they were to proceed up the river to make the arrest. Arriving late at night, they were to arouse the cap-

tain and his men after the plan adopted by them
in gaining entrance at Washoe Ferry. No quarter was to be given to either the captain or
those with him. Since no witnesses were to be
left alive to tell a tale differing from that
planned to be told by the posse, who were to
say that resistance having been offered, it was
necessary for them to resort to the use of their
shot-guns. The departure from such a small
place as Boise was, at that time, of so large a
force of men, mounted and armed, could not fail
to excite considerable comment among the population, and soon all kinds of rumors were afloat.
Such an extraordinary procedure as the sheriff's
appointment of deputies belonging to an organization so well and unfavorably known as the
Pickett Corral band caused grave apprehension.

His object was suspected by a party of men
who had assembled at the sutler store soon after
the departure of the sheriff's troop. It was re-
marked by one of the number present that it
was a pity that such a disreputable lot of scoundrels should be dignified by the name of deputy
sheriffs and permitted to advance upon any
man's house in the night, without warning; that
if the captain of the vigilantes knew they were
coming it might be quite different. George W.
Hunt, who in after years became distinguished
as a railroad builder, was present in the store
at the time, and at once announced his willingness to attempt the passage of the trail across
the foothills to Horseshoe Bend, if he could se-

cure a horse. Quartermaster Hughes, who was stationed at Boise Barracks, being present, immediately responded that he had the best saddle horse in the territory at that time, and he would cheerfully place him at Mr. Hunt's disposal. It was soon settled that the attempt should be made, and within an hour the daring rider headed his mount for the unbroken snow on the hill trail, bent on an errand of mercy, without hope of reward, other than the consciousness of being, perhaps, instrumental in saving human life. Only those who have faced the terrible sameness of snow-covered hills, without human habitation, for eighteen miles, can realize the dangers the rider encountered that day. In many places a slip of the horse's feet would have meant precipitation into a gulch, with perhaps broken limbs, without hope of rescue. The horse proved all his owner claimed and the terrible journey was made without accident, in time to give the warning the rider carried. Upon being informed of the intended visit, the captain sent a messenger to a neighboring ranch with the news and asking the early presence of two men prepared to take a ride. The messenger was absent less than an hour when he returned with the information that the men required would follow him as soon as horses could be fed and saddled. During the interim, while awaiting their arrival, preparations were made for departure and in less than two hours from the time the news reached the ranch, a party of four mounted men rode away—the captain observing that it would be a pity to impose on such a distinguished party of deputy sheriffs by requiring them to ride so far to serve papers in such inclement weather, that it would be proper to meet them at least half way. They accordingly proceeded down the river, expecting at any moment they would appear, but a hitch had occurred in the original plan, the special deputies being held until the arrests were made in the lower valley, which caused a delay of twenty-four hours. Consequently the man whom they were detailed to arrest and his friends rode the entire distance before the posse was prepared to start and as they approached the Junction House, seeing a row of guns ranged against the side of the house under the front porch, they realized that the crisis had arrived. The house was but a few feet back from the main road along which they were riding, and there being no windows on that side, the inmates had no warning of their approach until they were immediately in front of the door, when one of the deputies jerked it open and reached for his gun. The movement, however, was anticipated, and the sharp command "drop it," had hardly passed the leader's lips when the hand and arm were withdrawn and the door was as violently closed as it had been opened. No other words were uttered, nothing was said about the warrants or arrests and the horsemen proceeded on their way to the next house, where it was learned that the sheriff's party had returned to Boise with a large number of prisoners, supposed members of the vigilance committee. The special deputies who were supposed to do the deadly work were so crestfallen at their failure that they were ashamed to report to headquarters, and to avoid being gibed, crossed the river to the ranch of an acquaintance and went on a protracted debauch.

The prisoners taken to Boise were promptly arraigned and as promptly discharged, there being no evidence that they had violated any law, and before their arrival it was generally understood that their arrest was to be only an incident of the object to be accomplished. Thus ended a disgraceful fiasco, the expense of which was paid by the taxpayers of Ada County.

But one occurrence ever arose to disturb the tranquility which followed the eventful winter of vigilante reign in Payette and Boise Valleys, and that was brought about by a chance meeting which took place eight months later in Walla Walla, between Alex Stewart and E. D. Holbrook—then delegate to congress from Idaho Territory. The latter, on hearing a recital of the manner in which Washoe Ferry had been captured, and the circumstances relating to the escape of its occupants, insisted that Alex should return with him to Boise, where they would make it hot for the d—d vigilantes.

Stewart finally assented and accompanied Holbrook to Boise City, where a civil action was

promptly begun against a number of men who
had been prominently connected with the movement leading to the breaking up of the Washoe
Ferry gang. Damages to the amount of forty
thousand dollars were claimed.

The sheriff's deputy who was sent to serve
the papers on the defendants, began his work at
the lower end of the valley, and did not arrive
at Horseshoe Bend until the following afternoon,
and it was six o'clock before he completed his
service above that place. The commotion caused
by bringing such an action against the most
prominent ranchers in the valley, may be con-
jectured when it is remembered that the sheriff,
at that time, was so proficient in summoning
and selecting jurors that he was able to secure
almost any verdict desired. The captain was
the last man upon whom the complaint was
served, and upon reading it, he at once directed
one of his men to bring in and saddle a horse,
as he intended to ride to Boise that night. Which
he accordingly did—a distance of twenty-one
miles—arriving in that town the following morning about sun-up; before many people were astir,
proceeding at once to Sheriff Opdyke's office,
which was in a saloon adjoining a livery stable,
also kept by the sheriff, he having learned from
the sheriff's deputy, who served the papers upon
him the previous evening, that Stewart was
staying with the sheriff. Entering the saloon,
which never closed, he found only a porter, who
was cleaning up the aftermath of the previous

night's orgy, and asking him where Stewart could be found, the porter beckoned to a door leading to a back room, opening which, the captain entered and found several men lying on the floor wrapped in blankets, all of whom, except one, were asleep.

The one exception being Stewart, who arose on his elbow and confronted the intruder; for several seconds which were fraught with serious possibilities, not a word was uttered, each looking the other intently in the eye. At last the captain spoke and said, "Alex, I thought you had a little sense, but you have none; you are a fool." To which Stewart replied, "Well, it looks pretty tough; all we received for that ferry was three cayuse horses," To this the captain replied, "That question does not enter into the discussion. When the Payette Vigilantes held you and your brother under sentence of death, I told you that under certain conditions and promises I would assist your escape. One of those promises being that you were to leave the country and try to lead better lives and become good men; telling you at the time, that if you ever returned and attempted to get even on the vigilance committee, or any of its membership, I would go after you and take your scalp, or help hang you sure. Now if from what you know of me, you think I am a man who will keep his promise, you had better withdraw that suit and leave Boise City within twenty-four hours, or the chances are that you will not live forty-eight."

16 E. H. L.

After making this statement the captain turned and left the room without any of the other sleepers being awakened.

The suit was withdrawn, as suggested, and neither of the Stewart brothers were ever seen in Boise after that time. This was the last act in the drama which relieved Boise and Payette valleys of their undesirables.

During the remainder of the year nothing occurred to disturb the tranquility that followed the foregoing events. But when spring arrived, and travel to and from the mines was resumed, the Piute Indians, who occupied the country south and west of Owyhee, made several incursions into the Snake river, Boise and Payette valleys, murdering settlers, killing cattle, and driving off bands of horses. As the small force of infantry, which was then garrisoned at Boise Barracks, was unable to pursue and punish the invaders, a citizens' meeting was called in Boise City to devise measures to meet the emergency. At that meeting it was resolved to issue a call for volunteers and also an appeal to the business men and citizens generally, for contributions to equip a company. A resolution was also adopted, providing that the volunteers should elect their own captain and furthermore, the men who served as volunteers should, on their return from the field, be allowed to retain, as their own, in compensation for their services, the horses and equipment used while in service. After the adoption of the foregoing resolution and the appointment of the necessary committee, an adjournment was taken until eight o'clock the next evening, at which time the committee on volunteers reported the enrollment of sixty names. The committee on finance reported subscriptions amounting to forty-five hundred dollars.

After a thorough canvas of the subject, it was concluded that the money available would be sufficient to outfit and equip forty men, but as only small bands of Indians were usually engaged in the predatory raids, the foregoing number, it was thought, would be able to teach them a salutary lesson. The volunteers assembled the next day and chose Dave Opdyke as their captain, and he at once proceeded to select forty men out of the sixty enrolled. Saddle-horses, pack-animals and all the equipment of frontier warfare were speedily purchased, and four days after the first call for volunteers was issued, a troop of forty well mounted, well armed men crossed Boise river, en route, as was supposed, to the country occupied by the hostiles. Two weeks after their departure a messenger arrived in Boise with dispatches from the officer in command, conveying the information that the company was camped on Snake river about forty miles from Boise City and that the officers and men were in excellent health. They had spent much time in gaining proficiency with fire-arms by shooting at a mark, and having removed the sage brush from a level piece of river bottom,

had prepared a race track and were testing the
speed of their saddle horses. They had, up to
the time the messenger left, escaped being molested by the Indians and expected to return to
Boise soon, as they thought the hostiles learning
of their approach, had abandoned the territory
and gone to Nevada. That such a message was
sent to the expectant citizens of Boise has been
denied, but the fact remains that they spent
most of the time during their absence in camp,
as stated, and returned without having seen an
Indian. Of course, as per agreement, the horses
and equipment furnished by the citizens, had become the property of the returned volunteers
and the war-worn veterans immediately dis-
banded. A few days subsequent, a disagreement
arose between one of the returned men and a
farmer, concerning the ownership of a horse—
the arbitrament of which was submitted to a
justice of the peace. During the taking of testimony which followed, several of the men were
examined under oath, all but one telling the same
story. The one whose evidence differed radically
from the others, was enrolled on the rosters of
the company as Raymond, and was only eighteen
years old, and while he was in size almost a
full grown man, yet he was only a laughing boy,
but recently from a home where his big blue
eyes and curly locks were, no doubt, a mother's
pride. He was a boy in whose defense any man
not a coward would have fought, no matter what
the odds. After the hearing was concluded the

principals and witnesses in the case, leaving the court-room, congregated on the street to discuss the trial and several of those who had testified opposite to young Raymond gathered about him and accused him of swearing falsely; finally one of the number slapped him on the face, whereupon Raymond backed against the wall of a building and drawing his revolver, stood in a position of defense. One of his accusers exclaimed "Shoot, d—n you, shoot," to which he replied: "No, I don't want to shoot, but I am a boy unable to fight men and do not intend to be beaten." After which announcement, a tinhorn gambler named Johnny Clark, who had gone out with the volunteers, drew a revolver and shot Raymond down. A surgeon, Ephriam Smith, who had approached the scene of the shooting in time to hear the conversation and witness the tragedy, made a hasty examination of the wounded boy, and realizing that he had but a few moments to live, turned to the crowd and said, "Gentlemen, this is a d—d outrage." Whereupon Opdyke, who was present, taking the doctor by the arm led him aside and warned him to keep still, as this, meaning the shooting of Raymond, was only a beginning. The young man, after the examination by the surgeon was completed, said to the bystanders, "I did not draw my gun on Johnny Clark, did I?" To which several replied, "No." He then concluded, "I think it was a cowardly act for him to shoot me in this manner; I hate to be shot down like a dog for telling the truth." These were the last words he uttered. The murderer was at once arrested as a matter of form, and as a precaution to prevent the people from taking his punishment into their own hands, a preliminary examination was held during the evening of the same day, at which all the ex-volunteers, who were present, testified that the man who was shot had drawn his pistol first and that the shooting done by Clark was in self-defense. However, the cry for vengeance was so pronounced that the court decided to hold the accused, thinking, no doubt, that many who witnessed the difficulty would soon leave the city and that also public sentiment would undergo a change, as it frequently does in such cases. To protect the prisoner from violence arrangements were made with Major Marshall, who was at that time commandant at Boise Barracks, to confine him in the military guard-house until the storm had blown over. But such forethought came too late. The straw had been added which was to break the camel's back. The good people of Boise were aroused by the pistol-shot that caused the death of poor Raymond.

Word was industriously but secretly circulated during the following day among the business and professional men, announcing that a meeting would be held at a place named, the following night at nine o'clock sharp, for the purpose of considering the advisability of effecting an organization similar to the one which had accomplished such a salutary reformation in the Payette Valley. The proposed meeting convened at the time and place designated and without delay it was unanimously resolved to organize a committee to be known as "The Boise City Vigilance Committee," and they at once proceeded to adopt a constitution and by-laws similar to those of the Payette committee The organization was completed and officers elected at the first meeting, after which the case of the last murder, that committed by Clark, was taken up and discussed.

It being the unanimous opinion of those present that the murder was in cold blood and it being further agreed that, judging by the conduct of the officers and the perjured testimony of the witnesses at the preliminary hearing, it was the intent to give the prisoner his liberty at an early day, a resolution was therefore offered and unanimously adopted, to the effect that the crime committed by Clark entitled its perpetrator to the penalty of death and an executive committee was named to carry the decree into effect, with authority to call out the full membership, if necessary, for the purpose. The military guardhouse in which the prisoner was confined was a stone structure located on the lower side of the square, around which the officers' quarters, commissary buildings and barracks were erected.   In one end of the building was a row of cells, with bunks for the inmates, the remainder of the building being used for a guard-house, where several men were continually stationed, ready to respond to any call from the sentinel, who continuously paced his beat in front. As will be understood, the self-imposed task of the vigilance committee, that of taking from the guard-house the prisoner Clark, was not one easy of accomplishment, since capturing the guard might result in fatalities which must be eliminated.

A sergeant was continually present in charge of the men in the guard room, and as these non-commissioned officers were indignant in consequence of having to guard civilian prisoners, the executive committee experienced but little difficulty in pursuading the officer, who was to be on duty the night chosen, to permit the removal of the prisoner, arrangements were made accordingly. Some months previous, a company of Oregon volunteers, on their way to garrison Fort Hall, had left in the hospital at Boise barracks one of their number who was unable to march.

He had recovered from his illness and was reported fit for duty on the afternoon prior to the proposed capture of the guard-house, and the sergeant not wishing to have a sentinel of his company captured on his post, placed the convalescent volunteer on duty at the time of the expected attack. The volunteer was only about twenty years of age and his illness was caused by homesickness, as much as by malaria. He went on guard duty that night at twelve o'clock, unsuspicious of danger or surprise, and began his tramp within its limits, with mind far removed from Boise City and the Barracks. Only a short time after his watch began and while he was in the act of turning to retrace his steps on his lonely beat, several men darted around the corner of the guard-house and before he could make an alarm he was seized and thrown to the ground, where his captors proceeded to bind his limbs and gag him. They then entered the guard-room, where the inmates being asleep, they had no difficulty in taking possession; opening the cell where Clark was confined they brought him with them outside, locked the door, securing the sergeant and all his men, with the exception of the sentinel on the outside, and then took their way along the foot of the hill to the westward, taking their prisoner with them. Soon after their departure the sentinel succeeded in releasing his hands, and obtaining possession of his musket, sent a bullet after his fleeing captors. The discharge attracted the attention of a sentinel on another beat, who gave an alarm and the entire garrison was soon aroused and under arms, when being deployed in skirmish line, they searched the neighborhood, but without result.

When morning dawned it was discovered that a triangle had been erected on the ground where the old Central school building was subsequently built and on it hung the lifeless body of the murderer.

The prompt and daring action taken by the committee caused great consternation among the so-called sporting class in Boise, and an exodus at once began. The execution of Clark was the only instance in which the organization intervened to punish an offender, although it was generally known that they did not disband for some time afterward and that knowledge doubtless had a salutary influence in preventing further crime.

Some time subsequent to the execution of Clark, Dave Opdyke was hanged on the Overland stage road by three employes of the stage company, and a young man who was, at the time, Clerk of the District Court, was persuaded to accompany them. The hanging was credited to the Boise City Vigilance Committee, owing to a card, or label, with the insignia of the vigilance committee, being attached to the body. However, the committee had no part in the act, and none of its members were present. The word was given out that the hanging grew out of the burning of the stage company's hay, which occurred some time before, and was charged to Opdyke. Consequently the community felt as if another bad man was gone, and no regrets were expressed. The excitement caused by the hanging of Clark did not end with his burial. Seven years after the foregoing events had transpired a transportation company, operating steamboats on the Columbia and Willamette rivers, had what was called an "old horse" auction in Port-

land, Oregon. At such sales the unclaimed cases
and packages are sold without being opened for
examination by the intending purchasers, consequently the sale partook of the nature of a
lottery, and on that account attracted a great
many people, the rival bidders frequently running the bids, on promising packages, up to high
figures. However, it sometimes happened that the
purchaser drew a valuable prize. At the sale,
to which reference is made, a long box, or case,
attracted the cupidity of a groceryman named
Mitchell, who at that time had a store on First
street.   Others besides Mitchell cast covetous
glances at the case, causing the bidding to become spirited, but Mitchell finally won the prize,
and calling a dray, had it conveyed to his store,
where, in the presence of Rachel, his wife, it
was speedily opened and the contents exposed.
To the surprise and horror of them both, the
case was found to contain the mummified body
of a man.   The police were notified and requested to remove the human derelict, but a
question as to the legality of such a procedure
arose.   Learned barristers were consulted, who,
being unable to find any statute covering such
cases, advised that the merchant be required
to bury his own dead, and there being no dispute
as to the ownership of the body, which was but
little more than a skeleton, Mr. Mitchell was
forced to act as funeral conductor in a procession
consisting only of the deceased and himself,
Rachael being so prostrated by grief from the

shock and loss of money paid out at the sale
that she was unable to go to the cemetery.

It was learned some weeks later that the
shrunken body, which caused so many conjec-
tures, was all that remained of the beau ideal
brave, Johnnie Clark, who paid the final penalty
for his crimes in Boise City, Idaho. A woman
claiming to be his sister came to Boise nearly
a year previous to the sale in Portland, and after
having his body exhumed, shipped it by a freight
wagon to Umatilla Landing and the case being
addressed "Portland, Oregon," it was forwarded
there by some unknown person. The sister, if
such she was, never appeared to claim the remains.

Thus, as if pursued by a relentless Nemesis,
it was seven years before the body of the murderer was permitted to rest undisturbed in an
unknown and unmarked grave. Truly "the way
of the transgressor is hard."

A recital of the events which transpired in
Boise and Payette valleys, during the period covered by this narrative, makes it difficult to comprehend that, with the exception of a very small
per cent of the whole, the residents were as good
men and women as could be found in any state
in the Union; yet such was the case. In fact,
the average man was better, for the reason that
there were no drones among the better class of
people; all were workers at some useful employment. The foregoing conditions arose, not from
immorality on the part of the majority, but from

a cause peculiar to new mining countries remote from centers of population. The people were sojourners, rather than citizens; they did not come to stay, only to accumulate enough money to make a comfortable start in the country whence they came—many had left property behind them, when starting west, to which they intended to return. None at that time expected to live to see the desert plains of Idaho transformed into verdant fields dotted with beautiful homes. Consequently, as they considered their residence here but temporary, they had no desire to exercise the rights of citizenship and but few attended the primaries or conventions. Thus, without thought of the harm they were doing themselves and others, they permitted a few dangerous men to gain the offices, with the results heretofore enumerated.

CHAPTER XIV.

PLACERVILLE TRAGEDY.

IF THE first settlers in Idaho had intended to remain and become permanent citizens, as many of them eventually concluded to do, and had directed their energies, not only to making money, but also to public affairs, including the election of good men to fill the offices, life and property might have been as safe from the beginning as in the older and well-regulated states and territories. In even the most desperate and lawless communities, where crime runs riot, it is almost invariably true that the disturbers constitute an insignificant minority of the whole; they simply are possessed of magnetic and physical force sufficient to impress others with the erroneous idea that they are really the "whole thing." Their ability to impress a community with their numerical strength is usually equal, or superior, to that of the timber, or mountain wolf, one of which can start its calliope and in a few seconds convince the novice that the woods are alive with its kind. The ease and celerity with which the citizens of Boise and Payette valleys rid the country of bad men is proof of the analogy.

While the citizens of the valleys and out-
lying districts in southern Idaho were solving
the problems of establishing civil government in
the manner related, Boise Basin, with its large
and incongruous population, had also been engaged in making history. In the mining districts of not only Idaho, but all over the intermountain states, at the time to which this narrative relates, there were a number of men who
were called "chiefs," their right to the distinction
arising from being leaders in such dangerous and
often sanguinary disputes as sometimes occurred
in gambling houses and other disreputable resorts. The rank of these so-called chiefs was
determined by the number of nicks or notches
cut in the handle of their revolvers, the chief,
or bravo, being entitled to add an additional nick
for every man he killed. The following incident
will give the reader a conception of the character of this class of men. One afternoon during
the summer of 1864, a pack-train of mules coming into the town of Placerville over the Centerville road, skirted the north side of the plaza
and passed on and out up Granite street. The
owner of the animals, who was riding behind the
train with one of his helpers, after passing the
Magnolia saloon, turned his mule and rode to a
public well, located in the center of the plaza.
The well was equipped with a bucket and wind-
lass. The packer, after alighting from his mule,
drew a bucket of fresh water and after having
regaled himself, proceeded to tighten the cinch

of his saddle. There were three gamblers sitting in front of the Magnolia saloon when the pack-train passed through the plaza and they had been watching the owner while drawing the water and taking a drink. One of them arose and re-marked, "Watch me and see how I'll fix that fel-low." Saying which he walked to the well and picking up the bucket threw what remained in it after the man had satisfied his thirst, all over him. The packer reached for his holster as if with the intention of drawing his pistol; this action was anticipated by the gambler, who shot and killed his victim before the poor spluttering man with eyes, ears and nose filled with water could draw a weapon, and thus the victor of the drama was entitled to add another nick to its fellows on the butt of his revolver.

The man who had thus distinguished himself immediately surrendered to the officers and on his request, a hearing was at once granted, at which his companions, to whom he had said "Watch me, and see how I will fix that fellow," appeared and testified that the shooting was done in self-defense, the packer having reached for his gun first. Their testimony being considered suf-ficient, the prisoner was discharged. Among the unwritten laws of the Universe is one which pre-scribes that, sooner or later, relentless Justice shall overtake and punish the transgressor who violates the commandment "Thou shalt not kill." Judges may be corrupt, juries may be venal, but a Nemesis pursues and retribution finally overtakes the offender. The next summer after the killing of the packer the man who committed the murder accompanied a party of prospectors into the hills east and south of Boise, now known as the Neal district, and while in camp one day two Indians came in and presented an open letter showing that they were traveling on a permit from the governor of the territory, in search of a band of Bannocks whom the governor desired to come to Boise City and hold council with the purpose of preventing a threatened outbreak. The Indians after a brief halt at the white men's camp took their departure, but a few of those who were there when the Indians left were of the class often met on the frontier in former days, who held that the only good Indian was a dead one, among this number being the hero of the Placerville tragedy. Since the Indians were riding fine horses, they concluded to follow, and after making "good Indians" out of them, appropriate the animals and their equipment. Therefore, as soon as possible, they saddled their own mounts, which were picketed near camp, and started in pursuit.

After a hard ride they came within hailing distance, and the Indians failing to halt when commanded to do so, their pursuers fired upon them, and a running fight ensued, the Indians finally making their escape, but in the excitement a shot-gun loaded with buck-shot was accidentally discharged, the load taking effect at short range in one of the limbs of the Placerville mur-

17 E. H. I.

derer, shattering his thigh bone. He was carried to Boise City, and after many weeks of terrible suffering, was removed to San Francisco. Whether he survived the accident was known to few if any of his former associates.

Among those who posed as bad men in Placerville at the time the foregoing tragedy was enacted, was an ex-colonel, who, it was said, had formerly served in the Confederate army. Seeking for an opportunity to distinguish himself by killing some one, he selected for a victim a man named Brown, commonly known as Butcher Brown, he having a meat-market or what was generally called a butcher shop, on the north side of the plaza. Being a cow-man, or drover, and dealer in cattle, he was interested in not only the Placerville market, but owned another in Centerville, besides supplying beef cattle to other butchers. He was a jovial, manly man, over six feet in height, with the form of an athlete, and having since boyhood followed the business of driving cattle north from Texas, was as familiar with the use of a Colt's revolver as a stock whip. His leading characteristic was an unbending and determined loyalty to the American flag and the army that at that time carried it in the field. His well known prowess had rendered him immune in Idaho for more than a year after his arrival, when the colonel concluded to rid the country of the man, who entertained opinions opposed to those held by his alma mater—the Confederacy. His experience in war

had led the colonel to respect the poet who
wrote "He who fights and runs away lives to
fight another day," so after making arrangements
for a speedy departure in case of need, he walked
deliberately into the market and not finding
Brown in the front room, or stall, he went
through to a back room which was used as an
office, and here he found the object of his
search, who was engaged in posting his books,
using a common kitchen table for a desk, and
sitting with his back turned toward the door.
There being sawdust on the floor, the intruder's
entrance gave no warning sounds, and as no
words were spoken, the first intimation Brown
had of the presence of any one in the room was
the report of the colonel's revolver, instantly
succeeded by two other shots fired at his back.
After firing the last shot, the colonel, with the
gun still smoking in his hand, turned and fled
through the open door by which he entered.

He ran down the street toward the livery
stable where he had arranged for a horse to be
saddled and in waiting. But only one of the
shots fired by the assassin had taken effect, and
the wound it produced proved to be only a flesh-
wound. Though dazed by the suddenness of
the attack and the smoke of the powder, it was
perhaps less than a minute before the wounded
man withdrew his long legs and number ten
boots from under the table, and, straightening to
his full height, he followed the fleeing wretch to
the outer door, but before he reached the outside

the colonel had gained a distance of nearly half a block, and was sprinting down the street between the Magnolia saloon and Higbee's store. Upon reaching the sidewalk, Brown, for the first time since the shooting, began drawing his weapon, and fired. Firing but a single shot at his would-be murderer, he turned into his market, where a surgeon, attracted by the firing, arrived in time to dress his wounds. The shot fired after the retreating colonel had taken effect in his neck, but while his wound bled profusely it caused but temporary annoyance, and not being disabled he soon recovered his equanimity and strutted about the saloons with the assurance of one who had won an honorable victory. A few days later the would-be assassin was arrested and taken before a magistrate, who permitted him to plead to a simple assault for which he was sentenced to serve ninety days in the county jail, the sentence being suspended a few days later.

It must not be thought that such events transpired without more than temporary notice, for they made a permanent and lasting impression on the minds of all the residents who were engaged in legitimate pursuits until, finally, the social fabric in Boise Basin was like a slumbering volcano—liable to erupt at any moment. The manner in which the final eruption came will be told in a succeeding chapter.

CHAPTER XV.

EX-SHERIFF MURDERED.

THE discovery of new placer fields in British Columbia and Oregon caused a large influx of miners and camp followers to flow into those regions during the years 1861-1862, taxing the steamers plying between San Francisco, Portland and Victoria, to their utmost capacity. On one of the regular voyages between the California port and the two last named cities, the passenger list, which was a large one, included a party of so-called sporting men and women, who, after the vessel had cleared the harbor and was fairly out at sea, took possession of the card-room and began to ply their trade, three-card monte and other games being introduced, while in the social saloon orgies were enacted which drove all the other passengers outside. Among these bacchanalians was a man named Patterson, who wore without attempt at concealment a large ivory-handled revolver and a formidable bowie-knife to match.

He seemed to be the recognized leader of the party, and the woman who passed as his wife was equally as proficient as he in dealing three-

card monte—which seemed to be their specialty.
They were a couple to attract attention in any
place. He was in height above six feet, with a
well-knit muscular frame, weighing over two
hundred pounds, without any appearance of being stout or fleshy. He had sandy, or red hair,
and a florid complexion, which bore marks of
dissipation; heavy, bushy eyebrows partially concealed a pair of restless blue eyes, which never
seemed to center on one object, but continually
shifted as if expecting some kind of a hostile
demonstration. He wore a pair of high-heeled
boots, which fitted his shapely feet to perfection,
and a pair of plaid trousers which had been
reinforced, or foxed, with buckskin, after the
manner of similar garments worn by cavalrymen
in our army. He also wore a cassimere shirt, a
fancy silk vest, across the front of which dan-
gled a heavy gold chain, made from specimens of
native California gold. A long frock coat of
heavy pilot-beaver cloth, trimmed with the fur
of the sea-otter completed a wardrobe typical of
the man who wore it. He was about forty years
old, and being destined to play a prominent part
in the then unborn history of Idaho, the foregoing description is given.

The woman who claimed recognition as his
wife was perhaps twenty-eight years of age,
though dissipation and the continued use of cos-
metics had caused her to appear older. She had
a figure to which even the modern mantua-
makers' art could add no line of symmetry, a

brunette in complexion and in form a Venus, tall
and willowy in her movements. Mate to such a
man as Patterson, they were the observed among
the observers. The steamer arrived abreast the
Columbia river bar too late in the evening to
cross in safety and the captain concluded to lie
off and on till morning. Complaint was made to
the officers of the ship during the night, by a
committee of passengers, who demanded that
the boisterous conduct and the profane language
being used in the presence of ladies and children
be stopped. Whereupon the captain visited the
card-room, where he found the sporting fraternity
assembled and addressing them courteously, requested that they retire, as the hour had arrived
when the lights must be extinguished. To this
request Patterson, who had probably been drinking more than was his usual custom, replied in
an insulting manner, causing the captain to
threaten to put him in irons if he did not behave.
The party then dispersed, Patterson saying that
he would see the captain after the ship landed
in Portland.

The vessel crossed the bar the following
morning, and after discharging freight and a
few passengers at Astoria, proceeded on its
way up the river to Portland, arriving there
during the night. After the ship was docked and
secured in her berth, although the hour was late,
the passengers, weary of being confined, went
ashore and were soon distributed throughout the
city. The following morning after the crew,

under the direction of the second and third officers, had begun to discharge the ship's cargo,
the captain proceeded up town to call on some of
his late passengers who had gone to the Cosmopolitan Hotel. That old time hostelry was then
the best in the city of Portland, or for that matter, on the northwest coast, and stood on the
north side of Stark street between Front street
and the river. The main entrance was into the
office, or large reception room, which occupied
the first or ground floor fronting on Stark and
Front streets. There being no hall or elevator,
access to the hotel parlor, which was located on
the second floor, was gained by ascending a
broad spiral stairway which arose from the
office floor; hence no visitor or guest could come
or go without their movements being noted by
the bookkeeper or landlord, one of whom was
always present. The captain, after arriving at
the hotel, sent his cards to those he desired to
see, and was at once shown up to the hotel parlor.
A few minutes later Patterson entered the office
door and proceeding to the clerk's desk inquired
for the captain and upon being told that he had
gone up stairs but would soon come down, he
took a seat directly opposite the stairway, remarking that he would wait. But a short time elapsed
before the captain and the friend he had called
to see, appeared at the upper landing of the
stairway, and after good-bye had been said, he
began to descend. Patterson had been watching
the parting of the friends from where he sat,

and when the captain had descended about half way down the stairs, he arose and shot him dead, the limp body bumping from step to step until it reached the office floor. The murderer surrendered to a policeman, who entered at the moment the shot was fired, but too late to prevent the tragedy. It has often been said that none other than Deity can foretell the verdict of a jury, and such was the case in the trial which followed the death of the captain. He was shot by a ruffian in revenge for an imaginary insult and a jury of "good men and true" exonerated the murderer and turned him loose on society to seek other victims, the first of whom was the woman he had flaunted as his wife on the incoming voyage of the steamer. Suspecting her of disloyalty, he became enraged, and seizing in one hand the coil in which she always wore her hair, drew his bowie-knife, which was as sharp as a razor, with the other, and attempted to cut it off close to her head at one stroke, but aiming too low, when the hair came off in his hand a large piece of scalp clung to it. A policeman, hearing the woman scream, entered the house and placed the offender under arrest. Again Patterson was in the hands of the Portland authorities, and again as quickly released. He then made his final departure from Oregon, vowing vengeance on the officer who had arrested him for scalping the woman. The foregoing biographical sketch is pertinent to this narrative only for the reason that its hero, Patterson, after leaving Oregon went direct to Idaho, where he soon became a prominent luminary among the bravos who controlled the body politic of that territory for years.

One of the characteristics peculiar to all communities alike, is that there are but few men who are willing to take the risk of interfering with the riotous actions of characters such as are sometimes found in frontier towns, not alone in mining districts, but in all others, where the surrounding country is sparsely settled. The men to whom I refer are by nature divided into two classes, both of which believe it to be the acme of human enjoyment to load up with "red liquor" and proceed to terrorize the inhabitants. They generally go on their periodical debauches in parties of three or more, and in towns where, as is often the case, only a city marshal with one assistant is employed, the rioters generally run their course.

The difference which distinguishes the classes mentioned is so pronounced as to be readily recognized, one class being composed of young men of the cow-boy order, whose talent runs to riding wild horses, drinking the before-mentioned "red liquor" and firing off their pistols; using as targets the lamps in saloons, dance-halls and like places. These sportive ones are really not bad men, they simply pose as such; but when they start in to amuse themselves, a cyclone cellar, such as are found in Nebraska and South Dakota, would be a desirable annex to the average residence, as the bullets discharged by these hilarious gentlemen sometimes puncture the walls of houses, greatly to the alarm of the occupants. They do not intend to fatally injure anyone, although accidents on such occasions have sometimes occurred. They are similar to the old-fashioned alarm clock that when it once went off, or started to strike, could not be stopped until it ran down, and the average marshal is powerless to check the festivities of this class of fellows until their steam is exhausted.

The other class is composed of men who, when aroused to a certain pitch by drink, start on a carousal not for fun, not merely to intimidate and drive off the streets and thoroughfares the residents, but generally with the well-digested purpose of using as a target for pistol-practice, not lamps, as do the others, but the anatomy of some one who has become offensive by non-concurrence with their methods. When this class of men start on a rampage, their numbers may not exceed two or three individuals; yet their purpose being usually well known, and the danger of interference so thoroughly understood that seldom does anyone interpose to protect their intended victim—nor is it to be wondered at, as interposition would probably mean death to the intruder. Thus it was and is, even today a few desperate men can terrorize an entire mining camp or frontier town. But their reign is usually short, for emboldened by continued immunity, they at length commit some crowning act

that arouses the indignation of all good men and
most men are good. When such a time arrives
the voice of the people becomes the voice of God
and the agents of the devil had better take notice.

From the time the first county officers were
appointed in Boise county, until after Lee's surrender at Appomatox, civil government presented
a strange anomaly. The territory, for judicial
purposes, was divided into three districts, to
each of which was appointed a judge by the
then president of the United States, Abraham
Lincoln, and for the territory at large was appointed a United States marshal, who in turn
appointed a deputy in each judicial district. The
officers thus appointed were Union men, while
the sheriffs and their deputies, as well as all
other elective officers in the territory, were usually adverse to the government and the laws
which they were expected to enforce. Especially
was this true in Boise county, which embraced
Boise Basin.

To the fact that no fellow-feeling, no community of political and social interest existed between the judge on the bench and the elective officers of his court may be attributed at least in
part the failure in most cases to even bring to
trial those who had taken or attempted to take
the lives of their fellow-men; and in the few
cases where such offenders were brought to trial,
juries were summoned at least a part of whom
considered the offense for which the prisoner was

being tried an act deserving of commendation rather than punishment. As evidence of this condition of affairs, the case of James Pinney, the first postmaster in Idaho City, may be quoted. Pinney was a quiet, unobtrusive young man, considerate of the feelings of others, yet he was shot at his place of business, miraculously escaping death, the would-be assassin escaping the punishment his act justly merited.

There were in Boise county during the foregoing period a few men who were as staunch and loyal to the government as others were disloyal; men who never hesitated to declare themselves and who always were prepared to meet emergencies as they might arise; men who, in fact, courted the danger of conflict. Prominent among this class was a man named Pinkham, who was the first sheriff by appointment in Boise county, serving only until an election was held and his successor qualified. He was one of Nature's noblemen, six feet two inches tall, with the frame of an athlete. Although he was yet in the prime of vigorous manhood, his hair and beard were almost snow-white, while his cheeks were as rosy as a boy's. Not only physically, but mentally, he was a leader among men, and although he had been marked from the first for the bullet of an assassin, the seasons there as elsewhere came and went for more than two years before a man could be found to undertake the desperate enterprise. Finally, Ferd Patterson who had gained notoriety in Portland, Oregon, by killing the cap-

tain of the steamship and scalping his erstwhile
mistress, and who had been a sojourner in Idaho
since that time, expressed a willingness to add
another nick to the handle of his revolver by
killing Pinkham, provided the "boys" would stand
in and secure his acquittal by being present when
the killing occurred and testifying afterward
that Pinkham drew his weapon first, or attempted
to do so, thus showing that Patterson acted in
self-defense.

An arrangement was accordingly made one
Sunday during the forenoon, accompanied by
those who were to appear at the anticipated
trial, Patterson went down to the Warm
Springs, a bathing resort located on the Boise
City stage road about one mile below Idaho City.
Prior to their starting, however, they knew that
Pinkham had been invited to ride down to the
Springs by a Boise City man who was there with
a team and buggy. As he had planned, Patterson and party arrived first at the Springs. At
once they repaired to the bar-room where liquors
were dispensed.

The building in which the bath rooms were
located was erected above the road on ground
which sloped into the gulch, or ravine which
carried into Moore's Creek the overflow from a
large hot spring, which flowed out of the side
of a steep hill above. Along the front of the
house which was the end of the building, ran a
porch, or piazza, and it being elevated above the
ground except at one end, was surrounded

by a railing as a precaution against accidents, while entrance to the house was made via the porch, access to which was gained by means of a short flight of steps at the end where it was near the ground. The room which was entered from the porch was used as a bar-room and a door in the rear of this room opened into a hall which extended the entire length of the building, and on both sides of the hall were bath rooms, while above the house on the hillside was a swimming pond filled with warm water.

The foregoing explanation of the premises is necessary that the future reader who may not have visited this resort will more fully understand the tragedy which was enacted there. When the buggy in which Pinkham rode arrived at the Springs he alighted and entering the bar-room found Patterson and his party there. Having had no previous intimation of their presence, accustomed as he was to the methods of Patterson and his friends, it doubtess flashed on his mind in an instant that the crowd was there to murder him. Patterson began an attempt to start a quarrel, but Pinkham, realizing that he was alone, among unscrupulous enemies would not be drawn into a difficulty and remarking "That's all right, Patterson," brushed past him and entered one of the small bath-rooms and closed the door. Patterson and his friends soon afterwards went out through the hall, and on up to the swimming pond, where they all proceeded to take a swim.

Patterson related the succeeding events to a friend who made the story public after those who were parties to the affair left the country.

Patterson said that he and his companions were so long in the swimming pond that he thought Pinkham would be gone before they returned to the bar-room, and he hoped he was gone, as he knew that if he did not continue his efforts to force a quarrel the men who were with him would think he had weakened, and he said that he knew that if a quarrel was precipitated, he must get Pinkham quickly, or Pinkham would get him; so upon entering the hall he drew his revolver and carried it cocked in his hand as he entered the bar-room, and Pinkham not being there, he walked directly to the open door leading to the porch, and found Pinkham standing waiting for the hack which conveyed passengers to and from the Springs; raising his pistol, he said, "Will you draw, you Abolition son of a b——?" And as Pinkham turned his side toward him he fired. The smoke of his pistol, he said, partially obscured his view, and dropping on one knee, he leveled the pistol across his arm and fired the second shot, both bullets taking effect, although the first shot caused a mortal wound. Pinkham instinctively reached for and drew his weapon, evidently cocking it by the same motion, and as he was falling, it discharged into the ceiling. The murdered man fell to the floor and immediately expired. Thus was completed the mission on which they came.

W. J. McConnell
Captain of Vigilantes.
1864

Arrangements having been made for his speedy departure, Patterson at once mounted a horse and started to leave the country, but Pinkham's former deputy, Rube Robbins, followed by the sheriff, were soon in pursuit, and the murderer was overhauled by Rube who came up on him first before half the distance to Boise valley was covered. His arrest was accomplished without difficulty, when, joined by the sheriff, they started back to Idaho City, and making a detour to avoid difficulty with a large force of miners who had assembled and were threatening to hang Patterson, they arrived at the county jail and succeeded in placing him behind the bars without interference, although at least a thousand men were clamoring for his blood.

But the danger-point had been reached. Meetings were quietly assembled in all the mining towns for several successive nights and couriers were kept continually on the move, carrying news from one point to another. Men gathered in whispering groups on the hillsides and in the miners' cabins. A spirit of mystery and secrecy pervaded the atmosphere, culminating finally in a delegation from all the mining towns being sent to Idaho City for the purpose of holding a conference, looking to the organization of a vigilance committee similar to that which had accomplished such effective work in the Payette valley. The conference was held in a large fire-proof cellar used for storage purposes, and it was concluded that before perfecting an organization a

18 E. H. I.

messenger should be sent to the captain of the Payette Vigilance Committee, and if possible, secure his attendance at a subsequent meeting which would be called in Idaho City at such time as would be convenient for him to attend. Orlando Robbins, or Rube Robbins, as he was generally known, was accordingly dispatched to find the captain and if possible persuade him to come to Idaho City at once. Robbins was successful in his mission and two days afterward returned with his man.

Arrangements were at once made for a meeting consisting of a few reliable men to be held the succeeding night in the fire-proof cellar which had heretofore been used for meetings. As secrecy was to be observed until an organization was perfected the cellar was wisely chosen. Ten o'clock that night was the hour named, and when the time arrived approximately two score of the most prominent men in the Basin were present, to whom was introduced the captain, who upon being informed of the object of the gathering, at the request of the chairman, gave those present an outline of the constitution and by-laws of the Payette committee, stating that it was the fault of the citizens of Boise Basin that conditions such as had heretofore prevailed were allowed to continue. In the aggregate the men who had committed all the crimes in Idaho were few in numbers, and he thought the time had arrived for the people to put a stop to such atrocious murders as had been of frequent occurrence

in the past. He stated that as the first object of
the proposed organization was the punishment of
Patterson, the murderer of Pinkham, he would
like to be present when that event took place,
and assured them that while his own affairs
would prevent him from becoming a member of
their organization, he would come to Idaho City
at any time on receiving notice that they were
ready to act.

The meeting then proceeded to organize on
the same lines as the Payette committee had followed, adopting for its name "The Idaho City
Vigilance Committee." A blacksmith who had a
shop on Buena Vista Bar was chosen as captain,
and an executive committee of five elected who
were to have entire control of the organization,
issuing their orders direct to the captain whose
duty it was made to carry them out. A committee on enrollment was also appointed, the duty
of which was to enroll as members all persons
who would be willing to act with the organization in suppressing crime and punishing murderers and robbers.

At the meeting a Methodist minister presided
and none of those present ever forgot his opening address; and while the average minister is
generally considered out of place in mining
camps where the Sabbath is respected no more
than any other day, his bold stand in favor of
suppressing the lawless class did more to elevate
the churches in the minds of his hearers than
all the sermons they were likely to hear. Among

other things he said "He could fight or he could
pray, as occasion required." The man was Reverend Kingsley, who became a permanent resident of Idaho and lived many years of usefulness
to his fellows and when his final call came took
his departure, loved and respected by all.

Two weeks were consumed in preparation, at
the end of which time a membership of nine
hundred were enrolled. Among the number were
two men who had served in the navy and were
familiar with explosives. They were detailed to
prepare a number of hand-grenades which were
intended to demolish the gates of the prison. It
had been determined by the executive committee
that the entire force would advance to the door
of the jail where Patterson was confined and demand that he be delivered up to them, and if
denial was made then the walls were to be scaled
and the place captured by assault.

For the purpose of carrying out the foregoing plan, the members were notified to appear
fully armed at the city cemetery at two o'clock
on a morning named, it being the object to advance on the jail at daybreak. The cemetery
was located but a short distance above the jail
but it was doubtless chosen as a rendezvous not
solely on account of its contiguity to the object of
their attack. The leaders apparently counted on
the effect which the newly-made graves, and they
were all comparatively new, would have on the
friends of the murdered men who slept beneath
those sodless mounds, as it was well known to

the executive committee that many of those who
slept their last sleep in that hallowed ground had
died from the knife or bullet of an assassin, and
from the hearts of a hundred friends, those who
were assembled in the haze of that star-lit morning, meeting around those silent mounds, arose a
cry for vengeance. At least an hour before the
time named in the call the men, in groups of two,
three or more, began to arrive, and by two o'clock
nine hundred men were on the ground awaiting
the order to advance, while on the side nearest to
the jail, an emergency field hospital was improvised, with two surgeons in attendance, showing
that the serious nature of this enterprise was
fully understood by all.

The assembling of so many men could not be
accomplished secretly even in the night time—in
a place like Idaho City, where many of the inhabitants were night-hawks, men who worked on
the night shift, and, while doing so, worked the
other fellow. Consequently, as so many men
were noticed slipping out in little groups, it was
readily surmised that their object was an attack
on the jail, so the sheriff was at once apprised.
It is more than probable that the news of the
intended movement had leaked, and that he was
informed in advance. Consequently, in line with
his duty, he had garrisoned the jail with practically all the thugs and tin-horn gamblers in the
city, and was prepared to defend his prisoner,
Patterson. Thus a comical side was presented by
even the serious condition that existed at that

moment, and this was, that the majority of the men whom the sheriff had engaged as defenders of the jail, and consequently of the law, were many of them, for the first time in their lives, its defenders. But the sheriff was unquestionably right in employing such help as was at hand, it being clearly his duty, as an officer of the law, to protect his prisoner.

The men who were expected to defend the jail from assault were ensconced behind its walls and were provided with arms, besides, judging by the yells and pistol shots, they were also furnished an ample supply of nerve tonic, "the cup that cheers." Immediately prior to the time set for the advance, a man who had been reclining on the ground, well to the rear of the others, arose, and threading his way carefully toward the center of the cemetery, mounted a log and in a voice that could be distinctly heard by all present, said, "Gentlemen: You all know me— at least by reputation; I am the man whom the Payette Vigilance Committee calls captain; I am here tonight upon invitation of your executive committee. Up to the present time I have taken no part in advising, or managing your affairs, but the time has arrived when human lives are in the balance, and I feel that although there are many older and, doubtless wiser men here than I, yet I feel that at this critical moment that it is due you that I should express my views, and whether you concur with me or not, my duty so far shall have been performed.

"You have assembled here for the purpose of demanding from the sheriff and his deputies in charge of the jail, their prisoner, Patterson, your object being not only to punish him for the murder of Pinkham, but in so doing, impress upon the lawless classes the certainty that, hereafter, no murderer shall escape. The only object you could have in assembling here in the night and advancing on the jail at daybreak was that you might surprise the guard and capture them without resistance, but as is evident, your plans are known and the sheriff has made provisions for the defense of his charge. You can storm the place and take it by assault, but in so doing many lives will be lost, and I cannot see the philosophy of sacrificing perhaps forty or fifty good men's lives to hang one criminal. A mistake has been made in calling out so many men; I can take Idaho City with ten men; I would go through it like a cyclone, and take whomever I wanted."

Some one in the crowd immediately spoke up and said "That is the man for our captain." The words were scarcely uttered when they were repeated by hundreds of voices. The man who had been in charge up to this time was a blacksmith who worked at his trade on Buena Vista Bar. He at once came forward and asked the Payette visitor to take charge, stating that he was "not qualified for such work."

To this he replied: "Gentlemen, under the circumstances I will assume the responsibility and issue my first orders now. They are that

you all go home. When I want any of you, I
shall let you know. Before you separate, however, I desire to say that Patterson killed my
friend, and the earth is not big enough to hide
his murderer."

The crowd at once began to disperse, and
when day dawned there was no evidence that
such a gathering had taken place, except the
trampled weeds and ground in the cemetery.

Thus ended the first crisis in the history of
Idaho. Had an attack been made on the prison many lives would have been lost in the battle
that would have followed, and it would not have
ended until vengeance had been wreaked upon
every man in Boise Basin who had unlawfully
taken human life.

It was Saturday morning when the gathering dispersed. During the day following business
was practically suspended. Men gathered in
groups in the streets and in the miners' cabins,
the one subject of their discussion being what
was likely to occur now that a new leader had
been chosen. It was generally believed that a
way would be found to punish Patterson, but
how was it to be accomplished? No one seemed
to be informed on that subject.

During the day warrants were issued for
the arrest of Rube Robbins, Elder Kingsley and
one other, and they were placed under arrest. It
was generally believed that the arrests were made
under the impression that the new captain would
undertake to rescue the prisoners, in which event

it was probably planned that he would be shot
by some one concealed for the purpose. But he
paid no attention to the matter, in fact did not
appear in the crowd that immediately gathered.
The prisoners were at once paroled by the federal
judge who was in the city. Thus, under high
tension, passed that day and the succeeding night.
That the leader had formulated some plan which
was known to not more than two or three persons, was considered certain. But what was the
plan? All was shrouded in mystery. Sunday
afternoon he and Rube Robbins appeared on the
street, both mounted, and rode across to Buena
Vista Bar and down the road past the warm
springs toward Boise City—the cynosure of all
eyes. Soon afterward a group of miners and
others began to assemble at the blacksmith shop
on Buena Vista Bar, owned by the former captain, and when the assemblage had grown to
such a size as to attract attention, the sheriff
approached and demanded that they disperse
within thirty minutes, or he would arrest them
all.

They were doing nobody any harm, being
merely there on the public road, each one being
intent to learn all he could concerning the probable outcome of the pending difficulty. Some of
those present were doubtless members of the
Idaho City Vigilance Committee, but many were
not, and as the observations of all alike had
caused them to have but little respect for sheriffs
and their deputies as peace officers, they did not

propose to be ordered off the public highway, or
arrested, because they did not see fit to go. So
they at once began the erection of barricades
along ditches that crossed near the shop. John
C. Henly, an attorney, happening along on horse-
back, took in the situation at a glance, and at
once galloped down the road after Robbins and
the captain. Fortunately, he met them on their
way back to town, and spurring up their horses,
they were soon at the scene of the proposed hostilities. From here could be seen the sheriff and
his deputies assembling their forces on a sawdust
pile near the jail, preparatory to making a
descent on the miners. Attracted by the unusual
sight of a large force of men tearing down ricks
of cordwood and building barricades, many persons had congregated, who knew nothing about
the approaching conflict. Among this number
was a company from Payette Valley, consisting
of, approximately, twenty men, all of whom were
members of the Payette Vigilance Committee,
who had come to Idaho City to look for their
captain, fearing something had happened to him.
On their arrival they had placed their saddle animals in a feed-yard and started out in quest of
the object of their search, arriving at Buena
Vista Bar in time to meet him at the barricade.
A hurried conference followed, in which he requested them to take no part in the coming conflict, if one occurred, but to remain where they
were, and they would probably see the prettiest
fight they had ever witnessed. He told them his

plan was to draw his men off to the other side of
Moore Creek and take possession of a large dry
ditch which girdled an ox-bow point, and there
make a stand, since the ditch was a breastwork
already prepared, and, furthermore, if a battle
ensued, it was far enough removed from town or
dwelling houses to insure the safety of non-com-
batants. He would listen to no remonstrance,
but turning from them to the trenches and barricade, sang out, "Boys, this is no place to make
a stand; I will show you a better one; follow
me," and immediately started across the creek
bottom for the ditch on the opposite side. Arriving there he instantly threw his men into
line and dividing them into three squads, placing Rube Robbins in charge of one, and Al Hawk
another, while he took command of the third,
placing them in front at the apex of the bend,
sending Rube to guard one flank with his men
and Hawk the other. By the time these dispositions were made the sheriff had started his
men on the double quick from where they were
assembled, to make an attack. When they
reached Moore Creek they were halted by the
captain, and told "if they had an officer to send
him forward to talk matters over, and if not,
they had best come no nearer." A man who
was mounted on a horse at once rode out and
across to where the captain stood awaiting him,
and on gaining speaking distance, exclaimed,
"The only terms I have to propose to you is that
you stack your arms and disperse, or the last

divvil of you will be kilt." To this salutation the
captain responded: "The h—— you say. What
is your name?" the answer being, "My name is
German; I am under-sheriff." The captain then
said: "Mr. German, you had better return to the
ranks; you and I cannot settle anything—send
your chief up here. I will talk to him." Mr.
German quickly complied with the suggestion,
and within a few minutes the sheriff approached,
exclaiming as he came near, "My God, cannot
this be stopped?" To this the captain replied,
"It is stopped. I've stopped right here. Don't
you think I've got a good place? If you had
wanted to arrest me, or any of my men, we respect your duty as an officer, and would submit
to your authority, as was done yesterday; or, if
you had needed a posse, and had secured one
composed of respectable citizens, I or any of
my men would surrender to you, but instead
of such a posse, you come with all the cut-
throats in the country." To this the sheriff
answered that "when he chose men with a fight
in view, he picked fighting men." The captain
replied that there had always been a doubt in
his mind "as to whether blow-hards and murderers could fight better than decent men. We
have a chance to settle the matter now. The responsibility rests upon you—fire the first gun
and not a man of you will ever cross that bar
alive."

The sheriff then proposed that "they all deliver up their arms to him, and he would pledge

his word of honor that in thirty days they would be returned, and the men could all go home." The captain in reply said, "I have a very pretty gun here; it was sent me by a friend in Center-ville when he learned that these boys had chosen me to be their captain. He thought, when he sent me the gun, that I would not surrender it while I lived, and he was not the least bit mis-taken.

"You have sent Holbrook around with a body of men to get in my rear, and I have sent some boys over there who will hurt him, and we shall be obliged to hold another election. You had better send men to call him off at once, and you go back to town with all your force, and try to make them behave. I am not going to attack your jail. You may rest easy on that score—for I would not sacrifice the life of even one man for the sake of hanging a murderer. You may give Patterson his trial without hindrance, and, since the evidence has been arranged to secure his acquittal, he can go forth into the world, but the world is not big enough to hide him." Thus ended the second crisis. The sheriff withdrew his force and left the captain and his men in undisputed possession of the field.

A calamity was happily averted, for, had a single hostile shot been fired that day, the few decent men who were with the sheriff's party would have paid the penalty for being in bad company, because it would have been impossible, in the battle which would have ensued, to dis-

tinguish them from their allies; and as a force
even larger than that with the captain had assembled on Buena Vista Bar, and joined the
company from the Payette, the sheriff's force
would have been between two fires—meaning
their total extermination. The promise made to
the sheriff, not to attack the jail and allow the
trial to proceed, became generally known during
that and the following day, hence the excitement
subsided and business was resumed.

A short time afterward court convened and
the trial of Patterson began, culminating, as he
had prearranged, in his acquittal. That he would
evenutally receive punishment for his crimes
merited, no one doubted; but when or where he
was to pay the extreme penalty was known only
to the executive officers. He took his departure
from Idaho City soon after his acquittal, going to
Walla Walla, where there happened to be, at the
time of his arrival, the man who was on the
police force in Portland when Patterson scalped
his paramour, and whom he had threatened to
kill for arresting him. The ex-policeman having
faith in Patterson's intent, as well as ability to
keep pledges of that character, was on the lookout for him, and seeing him enter a barber-shop
soon after his arrival in Walla Walla, followed
him in, and finding Patterson seated in a barber-
chair, shot and killed him instantly—after the
same manner he had been in the habit of killing
his victims. Thus ended a career of crime, relieving the Idaho City committee of the task they
had set for themselves.

The writer of the foregoing narrative was the captain of the Payette Vigilance Committee, hence he was in a position to know the details of what transpired during those turbulent days and nights.

CHAPTER XVI.

CALEB LYON, of Lyonsdale, New York, was appointed Governor of Idaho Territory, February 26, 1864, to fill the vacancy caused by the resignation of Governor Wallace, who was elected Delegate to Congress at the preceding election.

Governor Lyon did not arrive in Idaho to assume the duties of his office for several months after his appointment.

He was a man endowed with more than the average intellect, and was possessed of scholarly attainments. But, unfortunately for his own peace of mind, and the success of his administration, he could not appreciate and conform to the American doctrine that "all men are created equal." He insisted on wearing clean linen, taking a bath, and even, on state occasions, wearing a dress suit. In fact, he was the first individual who had the temerity to appear at a society function in Boise City in a swallow-tail coat. It was even hinted that he wore suspenders.

Of course such eccentricities did not meet the approval of the majority of the male population, whose wardrobe consisted of less pretentious but more serviceable garments—men who took a bath only when necessity compelled them to swim a river.

Governor Lyon was a prominent citizen and politician in his home state—New York—but he was not the type of man needed to guide the destinies of a new territory such as Idaho was at the time of his appointment. He doubtless did the best he could, knowing nothing and learning nothing of either the territory or its inhabitants during his incumbency of the governor's office.

The following Thanksgiving proclamation will convey a very good idea of the style of Governor Lyon:

"THANKSGIVING PROCLAMATION."

"Thanksgiving let us give to the King of Kings, and the Lord of Lords, for the foundation, preservation and perpetuation of the government of the United States against the manifold schemes of wicked men, the attacks of open enemies, and the machinations of secret foes.

"Thanksgiving let us give to the God of Battles, who holds the destiny of nations in the hollow of His hand, for victories upon the land, and for victories upon the sea, and for blessings of uninterrupted health, and fruitful harvests, during a time of great national anxiety and trouble.

"Thanksgiving let us give to the God of Mercies for healing the wounded, comforting the sick and imprisoned, consoling the widows and

19 E. H. I.

the fatherless, and delivering those that were in bondage.

"In concord with the recommendation of the President of the United States, I, Caleb Lyon, of Lyonsdale, Governor of the Territory of Idaho, hereby appoint Thursday, November twenty-fourth, as a day of thanksgiving and praise, and truly commend its observance.

"In testimony whereof, I have hereunto set my hand, and caused to be affixed the Great Seal of the Territory of Idaho.

(Seal).   "Done at Lewiston, this fifteenth day of November, A. D. 1864, and in the year of the independence of the United States the eighty-ninth.

"CALEB LYON, OF LYONSDALE.

"By the Governor,

"SILAS D. COCHRAN, *Acting Secretary.*"

The conditions under which Idaho was settled were peculiar. Owing to its isolation, those who came first, in consequence of the discoveries of placer gold, did not intend to remain longer than the short time they thought would be necessary to make what money they needed, a fortune, and the standard by which wealth was guaged, in those days, was not so high as it became later. During the summer of 1864 and 1865, there was a population of perhaps twenty-five thousand people in Boise Basin, and I believe I can safely say that none of them intended to remain as permanent residents. Approximately the same was true of the people in Boise City, and the valleys tributary thereto.

Even the territorial officers and delegates to congress made no secret of their intention to make their sojourn brief.

The two first sessions of the Idaho territorial legislature were held in Lewiston before the capital was located, and then it was fixed in Boise, but it was not until 1885 that a capitol building was erected. Up to that time there was no permanent depository for the records of the different departments. The first records made were kept in Lewiston until the capital was located in Boise and then, what were not lost, were removed to that city. There the territory owned no buildings, and they were, together with those accumulated during a period of many years before the capitol building was built, moved around from one building to another, as quarters could be rented. Take the foregoing into consideration, with the further fact that as soon as one officer, or set of officers, vacated to make place for their successors, those who retired from the office usually retired from the territory, and it is not to be wondered that many of the records of the early proceedings are not to be found among the archives of the state.

Especially are some of the early journals and session laws missing, and at most there are but few copies now in existence. Hence, as a matter of interest, as well as showing the kind of men who composed the early legislative bodies

of Idaho, I will refer briefly to some of the
"bills, memorials and documents."

The exigencies of the times caused Congress
to enact the following:

AN ACT

*To Prescribe an Oath of Office, and for Other
Purposes.*

Section 1. Be it enacted by the Senate and
House of Representatives of the United States of
America in Congress assembled, that hereafter
every person elected or appointed to any office
of honor or profit under the government of the
United States, either in the civil, military or
naval departments of the public service, excepting the President of the United States, shall,
before entering upon the duties of such office,
and before being entitled to any of the salary or
other emoluments thereof, take and subscribe to
the following oath, or affirmation:

"I, A. B., do solemnly swear, or affirm, that
I have never voluntarily borne arms against the
United States since I have been a citizen thereof,
that I have voluntarily given no aid, countenance,
counsel or encouragement to persons engaged in
armed hostility thereto; that I have neither
sought nor accepted, nor attempted to exercise
the functions of any office whatever, under any
authority or pretended authority in hostility to
the United States; that I have not yielded a
voluntary support to any pretended government,
authority, power or constitution within the
United States, hostile or inimical thereto.

"And I further swear (or affirm) that, to the best of my knowledge and ability, I will support and defend the Constitution of the United States against all enemies foreign and domestic, that I will bear true faith and allegiance to the same; that I take this obligation freely, without any mental reservation or purpose of evasion, and that I will well and faithfully discharge the duties of the office which I am about to enter, so help me God," which said oath so taken and signed, shall be preserved among the court, house of congress or departments records, to which the said office may appertain. And any person who shall falsely take the said oath shall be guilty of perjury, and on conviction, in addition to the penalties now prescribed for that offense, shall be deprived of his office and rendered incapable forever after of holding any office or place under the United States.

Approved July 2, 1862.

Not to be outdone in loyalty to the government, the territorial legislature at its first session enacted the following statute:

OFFICIAL OATHS.

An Act to Regulate the Official Oaths. Be It Enacted by the Legislative Assembly of the Territory of Idaho, as follows:

Section 1. That all officers elected, appointed or chosen in this territory, before entering upon the duties of their office, and all attorneys, counsellors and solicitors in chancery, in all the

courts of this territory, before being admitted to
practice, shall take and subscribe to the following oath, before some person competent to administer oaths in this territory, viz.: "I, (here
the name of the person and office to which he
has been elected, appointed or chosen) do solemnly swear (or affirm) that I will support, protect and defend the Constitution and government
of the United States against all enemies, whether
domestic or foreign, and that I will bear true
faith, allegiance and loyalty to the same, any ordinance, resolution or law of any state convention or legislature to the contrary notwithstanding; and further, that I do this with a full determination, pledge and purpose, without any mental reservation or evasion whatever; and further,
that I will well and faithfully perform all the
duties which may be required of me by law, so
help me God."

Sec. 2. All attorneys, counsellors and solicitors in chancery, who have been admitted to the
bar of the courts of this territory, prior to the
passage of this act, shall not be allowed to appear or practice in any court of this territory on
and after the first Monday in February, eighteen hundred and sixty-four, unless he shall take
and subscribe to the foregoing oath.

Sec. 3. This act to take effect and be in force
from and after its approval by the governor.

Approved December 28th, 1863.

Thus not only all the appointive and elective
officers of the territory were required to take

the oath of loyalty to the government, but all attorneys as well.

At the present writing, A. D. 1911, during the Eleventh Session of the Idaho State Legislature, while our wise men are laboring with the great problems of Sunday rest and prohibition, it is interesting to note that at so early a period in the history of this commonwealth as the meeting of the first session of the territorial legislature, the Solons who constituted that body were cognizant of the need of reform in the method of observing the Sabbath. It is to be presumed that coming as many of them did within a recent period, from eastern homes, they were shocked by the click of faro and poker chips, together with the noise of dance halls and other hilarious amusements incident to a frontier town. They submitted to such proceedings for nearly two weeks, when forbearance ceased to be a virtue and they proceeded to devise in an official way, a method to reform the town of Lewiston and the Territory of Idaho, their deliberations resulting in the following act, which was approved January 23rd, 1864:

OBSERVANCE OF THE LORD'S DAY.

An act for the Better Observance of the Lord's Day. Be It Enacted by the Legislative Assembly of the Territory of Idaho, as follows:

Section 1.   No person shall keep open any play house or theatre, race ground, cock pit, or play at any game of chance, for gain, or engage in any noisy amusements, on the first day of the week, commonly called "Lord's Day."

Sec. 2.   No judicial business shall be transacted by any court, except deliberations of a jury, who have received a case on a week day, so-called, and who may receive further instructions from the court, at their request, or deliver their verdict, nor any civil process be served by certifying or attesting officer, nor any record made by any legally appointed or elected officer, upon the first day of the week, commonly called the Lord's Day; Provided: That criminal process may issue for apprehension of any person charged with crime, and criminal examination to be proceeded with.

Sec. 3.   Any person or persons violating the provisions of the two preceding sections of this Act shall be punished, on conviction thereof, by a fine of not less than thirty dollars, nor more than two hundred and fifty dollars for each offense.

Sec. 4.   Justices of the peace may have jurisdiction of all complaints arising under this act.

Sec. 5.   On complaint of any person, before a justice of the peace, the person or persons found guilty of any offense specified in this act shall be fined as aforesaid, to be paid to the treasurer of the territory, for the benefit of the common schools, and the offender shall, in addition to the said fine, and the cost of the prosecution, give bonds with two good and sufficient sureties, in the sum of no less than two hundred dollars, for good behavior during any time within the discretion of the court, and stand committed until the whole order is complied with and the fine be paid.

Sec. 6. This act to take effect and be in force from and after its approval by the governor.

Approved January 23rd, 1864.

That the foregoing act was inoperative need not be stated. Sunday was the day usually chosen by the miners in the mining camps to go to town and purchase supplies, and while there, engage in such amusements as appealed to them. Some indulged in the "social glass," and others tried their luck at the gaming tables, while not a few "tripped the light fantastic toe" in the dance halls. To have attempted to enforce a Sunday rest law, at that period of our territorial history, would have resulted in vacancies in some of the offices. The majority of the men who supported this legislation were not distinguished for their regard for either religion or morality. And all of them knew such a law could not be enforced. Hence it is difficult to understand why they passed it, except that they might send copies of the measure to their former homes.

The first session also granted twenty-six franchises, as follows: To

James Silcott, for ferry.

C. W. Frush, for ferry.

H. D. VanWyck, manufacture gas.

J. Meeks & Co., for ferry.

H. O'Neill & Co., for ferry.

Bannock Water Co.

C. F. Cone, for ferry.

J. Howerton, toll road.

South Boise Wagon Road Co.

E. B. Johnson, toll road.

T. Prather for ferry.

Old, Ridout & Co., for ferry.

J. Herring, for bridge.

Hill Beachy, for toll road.

S. A. Woodward & Co., toll road.

W. B. Knott & Co., for ferry.

J. R. Wiley, toll road.

T. H. Stringham, toll road.

A. G. Turner & Co., toll road.

N. C. Boatman, manufacture gas.

Wright Ditch Co.

C. Addis, for ferry.

A. J. Mallett, for telegraph line.

W. Graham & Co., toll road.

J. S. Wilson & Co., for ferry.

W. Mulkey, for ferry.

The franchise mentioned as having been given to Olds, Ridout & Co., was for what has ever since been known as Old's Ferry, and is one of the historic land-marks of pioneer days. The franchise was approved January 22, 1864, and Section 3 provided that "It shall be lawful for said parties, their heirs or assigns, to collect the following rates of toll for ferrying on said ferry:

For one team with wagon $3.00
For every extra team 1.00
For each loaded pack animal ...... .75
For pack animals returning .... .50
For horse and rider .... .75
For footman .... .25
For loose animals, each .... .25"

The location of the foregoing ferry was, at that time, in Idaho county. The rates of toll collected were, approximately, the same as allowed in other franchises granted and were not exorbitant under the circumstances.

The number of such franchises granted may appear to the reader of today, as well as the future, exceedingly large, but it must be borne in mind that the country was new, and, as in all other new countries, ferries at first supplied the place of bridges, and toll roads came before public highways in all mountainous districts.

During the foregoing session an effort was made to locate the capital, as provided in the Organic Act, but after a somewhat protracted struggle, the bill was indefinitely postponed on the last day of the session, February 4, 1864. Before adjournment of the first session provision was made for "an election to be held in the several election precincts of the territory, on the first Monday of September, in each year, unless otherwise provided for."

No subsequent session of the Idaho Territorial Legislature has been held under more trying circumstances than that of the first. While there were many good law-abiding citizens in Lewiston, the general environment was conducive to such mental activities as would promote the rapid use of defensive weapons rather than the calm consideration of legislative matters.

The Territorial Secretary was the acting

governor, hence the members were without the moral support and advice of the executive head of the territory.

Taking all the conditions into consideration, the enactments of that session are indisputable evidence that its membership was composed of able men; after adjournment they saddled their horses and with their primitive camp outfits, disappeared among the mountains and ravines from whence they came.

CHAPTER XVII.

BOISE CITY CHOSEN CAPITAL.

THE second session of the Idaho Territorial Legislature convened in Lewiston November 14, 1864, for a forty-day session, as limited by the Act of Congress which created the territory.

The House of Representatives was composed of thirteen members, five of whom were elected from Boise county, two from Idaho, two from Nez Perce, two from Owyhee and one from Shoshone county.

The Council consisted of seven members, one from Alturas county, two from Boise county, one from Idaho county, one from Nez Perce, one from Owyhee and one from Shoshone county.

The work of the second session of the Idaho legislature was devoted, largely, to amending and repealing the acts of the first session, but, in addition, several measures were enacted into laws. The act creating Ada county was passed by this session, and approved December 22, 1864.

Another important act was passed providing for taxing foreign miners. It will be remembered that, up to the time of this enactment, no surveys of the public domain had been made by the United States government, and consequently no patents had been issued. Therefore there was no real property to be taxed. Hence the revenue necessary to carry on the government was provided very largely by collecting licenses from all sources possible, and the additional revenue derived from taxing alien miners four dollars a month, was an important item.

Section X. of the act provided that it "should be construed to apply only to such persons as are inhibited from becoming citizens of the United States, by the laws thereof." The fact was that the law was designed to affect Mongolians alone, and prevent or check their influx to the placer mines.

As provided in the Organic Act, the Second session also passed the following act, locating the capital:

AN ACT

To Permanently Locate the Capital of the Territory of Idaho. Be It Enacted by the Legislative Assembly of the Territory of Idaho, as Follows:

Sec. 1. That the capital of the Territory of Idaho be, and the same is hereby permanently located at Boise City, in the county of Boise and said territory of Idaho.

Sec. 2. The capital buildings are hereby located on the grounds known in and described on the plat of said Boise City, as the said Capitol Square. And the Honorables Caleb Lyon, C. B. Waite and J. M. Cannady are hereby appointed commissioners to receive a deed to said Capitol Square, and such other grounds as may be deemed necessary, to hold in trust for the territory, for the purpose of erecting the capitol buildings aforesaid.

Sec. 3. The secretary of said territory is hereby authorized to immediately draw a warrant upon the treasury of the territory, not exceeding the sum of two thousand dollars, as shall be necessary to remove the papers, books, documents and other property belonging to his office, to said Boise City.

Sec. 4. This act to take effect from and after the twenty-fourth day of December, A. D. 1864.

Approved December 7th, A. D. 1864.

The passage of the foregoing act caused strained relations between the counties of the north and those of the south, which resulted in the question being carried to the Supreme Court, and finally, to the Congress of the United States, where a bill returning the five northern counties of Idaho to Washington was introduced, and it passed both houses, but failed to receive the approval of the president. The following is a copy of the act, also a copy of the report from the committee on Territories, as well as other proposed legislation looking to the segregation of Idaho Territory.

IDAHO AND WASHINGTON.

February 3, 1886.— Referred to the House Calendar and ordered to be printed.

MR. SPRINGER, from the committee on Territories, submitted the following

REPORT.

(To accompany Bill H. R. 2889).

The Committee on the Territories, to Whom was Referred the Bill (H. R. 2889,) to Annex a Portion of Idaho to Washington Territory, Make the Following Report:

It appears that that portion of Idaho, the annexation of which to Washington Territory is contemplated, cast a vote of 2,788 on November 4, 1884, indicating, at a ratio of population to vote, 4.7, a population of 13,103. These people are almost wholly isolated from the southern portion of the territory by the Salmon River range of mountains, which are exceedingly rugged and precipitous in their character. The construction of a wagon road across these mountains from north to south has, thus far, been regarded as wholly impracticable, so that at this time the sole direct means of communication between the two sections consist of a primitive Indian trail. During six months of the year this trail affords facilities alone to those who are expert in the use of snow-shoes. Under the most favorable conditions, pack-animals alone furnish any means of direct communication.

Because of the natural barriers indicated, a journey from any portion of northern Idaho to Boise City, the capital, is a very tedious and expensive affair. The distance across the mountains ranges from 200 to 400 miles, while the distance necessary to be traveled ranges from 400 to 600 miles, the route being a very circuitous one, through the Territory of Washington and the State of Oregon. For these reasons there are practically no commercial relations between these sections of Idaho, while on the other hand, the northern section is so situated with reference to Washington Territory as to make their interests—social, political and commercial—identical.

In 1873 the Legislative Assembly of Washington Territory memorialized Congress for the annexation of northern Idaho, as contemplated in the proposed legislation. In the winter of 1884-85, the legislative assembly of Idaho passed a similar memorial, and during the last campaign the platforms of both political parties, in both Territories, declared in favor of said annexation, indicating an almost unanimous sentiment on the part of the people of both Territories favorable to the enactment of the proposed law.

In response to the manifest necessities of the case, and in deference to the clearly expressed wishes of the people of both Washington and Idaho Territories, your committee rec-

20 E. H. I.

ommended the passage of the accompanying bill.
Forty-ninth Congress, 2nd Session, H. R. 2889.

IN THE SENATE OF THE UNITED STATES.
February 25, 1886.

AN ACT

To Annex a Portion of the Territory of Idaho to Washington Territory.

Be it enacted by the Senate and House of Representatives of the United States of America in Congress assembled, That all of that portion of Idaho Territory north of the following boundary line, to-wit: Commencing at a point in the middle of the main channel of Snake River due west of the headwaters of Rabbit Creek; thence due east to the headwaters of Rabbit Creek; thence down the middle of said Rabbit Creek to its junction with Salmon River; thence up the middle of said Salmon river to the junction of Horse Creek; thence up the middle of said Horse Creek to the junction of the East Fork of said creek; thence up the middle of said East Fork of Horse Creek to the crest of the Bitter Root range of mountains, be, and is hereby annexed to Washington Territory; Provided: That the people of that portion of Idaho Territory hereby annexed to Washington Territory shall in no wise be released from the payment of their just portion of the bonded indebtedness of Idaho Territory; and in ascertaining such bonded indebtedness there shall be deducted therefrom the amount of money in the territorial treasury at the time of the passage of this act; And provided further, That the auditor of each county wholly or partially within such' portion shall, as such indebtedness may become due and payable, draw his warrants on the treasurer of his county, in favor of the treasurer of the Territory of Idaho, for such proportion of such indebtedness as the assessed valuation of all property therein shall then bear to the assessed valuation of all the property of said Territory and said detached portion.

Sec. 2. That within sixty days after the passage of this act, the Territorial Auditor of Washington Territory and the Territorial Comptroller and Territorial Treasurer of Idaho Territory shall meet at the offices of the Territorial Comptroller-Treasurer of Idaho Territory, at Boise City, and shall ascertain and determine from the books and records of said offices the exact amount of said bonded indebtedness, and the time the same or any and every portion thereof shall become due, and after deducting therefrom the amount of money found to have been in the treasury at the time of the passage of this act, to fix the several proportions justly due and to become due from the several counties and portions of counties detached from Idaho and attached to Washington Territory as provided in Section One of this act. They shall also in like manner apportion the cost of keeping the Territorial prisoners under sentence and in prison at

the date of the passage of this act, at the present
cost rate of keeping the same, to the expiration
of their several terms of sentence; and the Territorial Comptroller and Territorial Treasurer of
Idaho, on the first day of each month, shall make
out an itemized bill of the cost of keeping said
portion of prisoners, and shall certify to the correctness thereof, and forward the same to the
Auditor of Washington Territory, who shall draw
his warrant on the territorial treasurer of Washington Territory for the amount thereof, not to
exceed the cost rate of maintaining and keeping
said proportion of prisoners at the date of the
passage of this act.

Sec. 3. That all insane persons who at the date
of the passage of this act are accredited to that
portion of Idaho Territory which is hereby annexed to Washington Territory, and who are at
that time being cared for at the expense of Idaho Territory, shall be transferred to the hospital
for the insane of Washington Territory.

Sec. 4. That from and after the passage of
this act the government of the Territory of Idaho
shall continue unimpaired, with the boundaries
of said Territory changed as herein provided;
and preparatory to the holding of the next general election, the governor, secretary, chief justice, president of the council, and speaker of the
House of Representatives of said Territory, or a
majority of them, shall subdivide the Territory
into the requisite number of legislative districts
of convenient size, to be composed of single

counties or of several adjoining counties, so as to
apportion, as nearly as practicable, the representation in each branch of the legislative assembly,
among the different districts according to population; Provided: That until otherwise provided
by law, the legislative districts of that portion
annexed to Washington Territory by this act
shall be and remain as now fixed by law, and the
number of the members composing the legislative
assembly of Washington Territory is hereby increased to fifteen members of the council and
twenty-nine members of the house of representatives.

Sec. 5.   That until otherwise provided by
law, the judges of the supreme court of the Territory of Idaho shall subdivide said Territory
into as many judicial districts as there are judges
of said court, and shall in like manner assign
said judges severally thereto, and designate the
places therein for the holding of courts for the
trial of causes and the transaction of business
arising therein;   Provided: That all that portion of Idaho Territory annexed to Washington
Territory by this act shall form and constitute
the fifth judicial district of Washington Territory until otherwise provided by the legislative
assembly of Washington Territory; and there
shall be appointed therefor, by the President of
the United States, by and with the advice of the
Senate, an additional associate justice of the
supreme court of said Territory of Washington.

Sec. 6.   That all cases of writ of error or

appeal heretofore prosecuted and now pending in
the Supreme Court of the United States upon
any record from the supreme court of the Territory of Idaho, or that may hereafter be lawfully
prosecuted from said court, may be heard and
determined by the supreme court of the United
States; and where the same arose within the
limits by this act annexed to Washington Territory, the mandate of execution or of other and
further proceedings shall be directed by the
supreme court of the United States to the said
district court herein provided, or to the supreme
court of the Territory of Washington, as the
nature of the case may require; and each of
said last mentioned courts shall be the successor
of the supreme court of said Territory of Idaho
as to all such cases, with full power to proceed
with the same and to award mesne or final
process therein.

Sec. 7.   That in respect of all cases, proceedings and matters pending in the supreme or
district courts of Idaho at the time of the passage of this act, arising within the limits hereby
annexed to Washington Territory, the supreme
court of Washington 'Territory and the district
court for the fifth district of said Territory,
shall be the successors of said supreme and district courts of Idaho; and all the files, records.
indictments and proceedings relating thereto
shall be transferred to said supreme and district
courts of Washington Territory, respectively,

and the same shall be proceeded with therein in due course of law.

Sec. 8.   That all justices of the peace, constables, sheriffs, and other officers who shall be in office within the limits of the district hereby annexed shall be, and they are hereby, authorized and required to continue to exercise and perform the duties of their respective offices as officers of said Territory of Washington until they or others shall be duly elected or appointed and qualified to fill their places in the manner provided by the laws in force in Washington Territory, or until their offices shall be abolished; Provided: That from and after the passage of this act the laws of Idaho shall cease to be in force in the district hereby annexed to Washington Territory, and the laws in force in Washington Territory are hereby extended over the same.

In the Forty-ninth Congress, 1885-1887, House Bill 2889, introduced by Mr. Voorhees, passed both houses, a copy herewith.   This bill provided that the government of the Territory of Idaho, being that portion not detached, should continue unimpaired.

The Congressional Record does not show that any debate took place at the time of the passage of the bill in either house.   While under consideration in the senate, Mr. Edmunds offered certain amendments relative to suits then pending, that were agreed to without discussion.

In the same congress three other bills were introduced on the same subject, H. R. 10057 by Mr. Toole, a member from Montana. His Christian name was Joseph Kemp Toole. There was no action taken by the House committee on H. R. 10057.

Section 4 of H. R. 10057 contained the same provisions relative to the remainder of the territory as does H. R. 2889, that is, that the government of the Territory of Idaho should continue unimpaired, with the boundaries of said territory changed as herein provided.

December 8, 1885, Daniel W. Voorhees, a senator from Indiana introduced Senate Bill 39 providing for the annexation of the same portion of Idaho to Washington Territory. Section 4 of this bill contained the same provision relative to the remainder of the territory, that is, that the government of the Territory of Idaho should continue unimpaired, with the boundaries changed as herein provided. No action by the senate committee was taken on this bill.

In the Forty-ninth Congress the other senator from Indiana was Benjamin Harrison, who on March 11, 1886, introduced (by request) Senate Bill 1848. Section 4 of this bill contained the same provision relative to the remainder of the Territory. This bill differed from H. R. 2889 in that it detached all that portion of Idaho north of the 47th parallel of north latitude and provided that this portion should be annexed to Montana. The portion to be annexed to Wash-

ington was the same as in H. R. 2889. This
same provision was contained in H. R. 10057,
introduced by the delegate from Montana, Mr.,
Toole. No action on either bill. So that there
was no action by the committee on the bills that
provided that that portion north of the 47th parallel be annexed to Montana.

The Second Session of the Legislative Assembly of the Territory of Idaho also made provisions for the organization of the counties of
Kootenai and Latah by the following enactment:

AN ACT

*Creating the Counties of Latah and Kootenai. Be
It Enacted by the Legislative Assembly of
the Territory of Idaho, as Follows:*

Sec. 1. That all that portion of Idaho Territory embraced within the following described
boundaries, be, and the same is hereby created
into, and shall be known as the County of
Latah, to-wit: Beginning at a point in the
main channel of Snake River at its junction with
the Clearwater River; thence running due north
along the dividing line between Washington and
Idaho Territories, to the forty-eighth degree of
north latitude, thence east with said degree of
latitude until it intersects the boundary line of
Shoshone County; thence south with the boundary line of said county to the middle channel of
the Clearwater river; thence with the channel of
said river to its junction with Snake river, to
the place of beginning; and the county seat of

said county of Lah-Toh is hereby located at Cœur d'Alene.

Sec. 2.   That all that portion of Idaho Territory embraced within the following described boundaries be, and the same is hereby created into and shall be known as the county of Kootenai, to-wit: Beginning at a point on the forty-eighth degree of north latitude, on the dividing line between Washington and Idaho Territories; thence north with said line of longitude to the forty-ninth degree of north latitude; thence east with said degree of latitude to the northwest corner of the boundary line of Montana Territory; thence southerly with the boundary line of said territory to the forty-eighth degree of north latitude; and thence west along the said degree of latitude to the place of beginning, and the county seat of said county of Kootenai is hereby located at Sin-na-ac-qua-teen.

Sec. 3.   That whenever the inhabitants, to the number of fifty or more, of each or either of said counties of Lah-toh and Kootenai, shall desire to perfect a county organization, they shall apply by petition to the governor, who, if he deem it advisable, shall proceed to designate by appointment three discreet and well qualified citizens of the county or counties so applying, to act as a board of county commissioners of such county.   The board of county commissioners as appointed, after they have qualified in pursuance of law, and enter upon the duties of their office, may proceed to fill, by the appointment of suitable residents of the county, the various county offices, as required by law for other organized counties in this territory.

Sec. 4. The officers appointed in pursuance of Section three of this act, shall hold their offices until their successors are, by law, elected and qualified. At the general election next succeeding the appointment of such county officers as herein mentioned, the qualified voters of the county so organized shall elect their county commissioners and all other officers, in the manner as now prescribed by law for the election of officers of other counties.

Sec. 5. The said counties of Lah-toh and Kootenai shall be attached to and compose a part of the first judicial district, for all judicial purposes, and until such counties, or either of them, shall have completed their organization as in this act provided, they shall be attached to and compose a part of Nez Perce county for all civil and criminal jurisprudence; Provided: That nothing in this act shall be construed as to interfere with any Indian reservation, or any treaty stipulations between the government of the United States and any Indian tribe or tribes, within the limits of either of the said counties hereby created.

Sec. 6. This act to take effect and be in force from and after its approval by the governor.

Approved December 22, A. D. 1864.

At the time the foregoing bill was passed,

there was no such town as Cœur d'Alene, where
the county seat of Lah-toh County was to be
located, nor was there any town at the place
named as the county seat of Kootenai county, the
population of both counties consisting of but a
few prospectors.   Therefore the new counties
could not organize.   Two years later the following act was passed, which repealed the act creating Lah-toh, and extended the boundaries of
Nez Perce and Kootenai counties, wiping Lah-
toh off the map.

AN ACT

*To Amend an Act Entitled An Act Defining the
Boundary Lines of Counties West of the
Rocky Mountains; Repealing the Law Creating the County of Lah-toh, and Defining
the Limits of the County of Kootenai.*

*Be It Enacted by the Legislative Assembly of the
Territory of Idaho, as follows:*

Sec. 1.   That all that portion of Idaho Territory contained within the following boundaries,
to-wit: Beginning at the middle channel of
Snake river, opposite the mouth of Clearwater
river; and thence due north along the westerly
line of Idaho Territory to the main divide between the waters of the Palouse river and Lah-
toh, or Hangman's Creek; thence easterly to the
westerly line of Shoshone county; thence southerly along said line to the Clearwater river;
thence up the South Fork of Clearwater river
to Lolo Creek; thence with Lolo Creek in an
easterly direction to the summit of the Bitter

Root mountains; thence southerly along the summit of said mountains to the juncture of Salmon river and Bitter Root Mountains, thence in a westerly direction along the summit of the Salmon river and Clearwater Mountains to a prominent landmark known as the "Buffalo Hump;" thence westerly along said divide between the water of White Bird Creek and Camas Prairie, to a point where the road leading from Lewiston to Slate Creek crosses said divide, thence in a direct line to the foot of Ponte Bar on Salmon River; thence in a direct line to a point on Snake River known as Pittsburg Landing; thence down the center of the channel of Snake river to the place of beginning, shall comprise the county of Nez Perce.

Sec. 2. All that portion of the Territory of Idaho north of the Counties of Nez Perce and Shoshone shall comprise the County of Kootenai.

Sec. 3. Whenever the county commissioners of Kootenai shall be appointed as provided by law, they shall have the power to locate the county seat of said county.

Sec. 4. The act creating the counties of Latah and Kootenai, approved December 22nd, 1864, so far as the same conflicts with the provisions of this act, and the provisions of all other acts and parts of acts inconsistent herewith, are hereby repealed.

This act is to take effect after its passage.

Approved January 9th, 1867.

A few years later the upland plateau, now

known as the Palouse country, began to attract attention as an agricultural district, and during the years between 1870 and 1880, all the open or prairie land lying north of the Clearwater River, in Nez Perce county, was located by actual settlers, and two prosperous towns, Genesee and Moscow, sprang into existence, the latter soon rivalling Lewiston, the county seat, in population and business enterprise.

A division of Nez Perce, and the founding of a new county, began to be advocated as early as 1880, and a bill was eventually passed by the Territorial Assembly submitting the question of county division to the voters of the County. The division contest was waged in a spirited manner and resulted in a victory for Lewiston, and the defeat of county division.

The citizens of Moscow, however, carried the fight to the United States congress and were successful a few years later. (1888).

The creation of a new county in a territory by act of congress is without a parallel in the history of Congressional legislation.

The following is a copy of the act which created Latah county and established the county seat at Moscow:

*An Act to Create and Organize the County of
     Latah.*

Be it enacted by the Senate and the House of Representatives of the United States of America in Congress assembled, That all that portion of Nez Perce county, in the Territory of Idaho, lying north of the following line, to-wit: Commencing at a point where the middle line of township thirty-eight north intersects the line between Nez Perce and Shoshone Counties in said Territory; thence west to Big Potlatch Creek where it first intersects the said middle line of the township thirty-eight; thence down said creek southwesterly to a point where it intersects the middle line of township thirty-seven; thence due west to the line between the Territories of Idaho and Washington be, and the same is hereby, formed and organized into a county, to be known and designated as the county of Latah, with all rights, power and privileges of counties under the existing laws of the Territory of Idaho.

Sec. 2. That W. W. Langdon, J. L. Nailer, and William Frazier are hereby appointed commissioners of said county of Latah, and their annual compensation shall be the same as now provided by law for the commissioners of Nez Perce county.

Sec. 3. That the county commissioners above named are hereby authorized, within twenty days after the approval of this act, to qualify before a justice of the peace and enter upon the discharge of their duties as such commissioners, and are hereby empowered to appoint all necessary county officers to perfect the organization of said county of Latah under the laws of the Territory of Idaho, and the said county commissioners and other county officers appointed as aforesaid shall hold their offices until the next general election provided by the laws of said Territory, and until their successors are elected and qualified according to law.

Sec. 4.   That the justices of the peace, constables, road supervisors, and other precinct and school officers heretofore elected and qualified and now acting as such, residing in said county of Latah, are hereby continued as such officers in said county of Latah until the next general election aforesaid and until their successors are duly elected and qualified.

Sec. 5.   That the county of Latah shall pay to the county of Nez Perce a just proportion of the net indebtedness of said Nez Perce county, the same to be determined as follows, to-wit: The County Treasurer, Recorder and present County Assessor of Nez Perce County are hereby constituted a board of adjusters, who shall proceed to ascertain the net indebtedness of said county of Nez Perce, which shall be done as follows, namely: Ascertain all the county justly owes in warrants, scrip, or other just debts, which amount shall constitute the gross indebtedness of said county, from which deduct the amount of the unpaid portion of the assessment roll of eighteen hundred and eighty-seven and the amount of all delinquent assessments-rolls which are considered collectable up to that date, and the amount of all moneys, and other credits due the county then, and the balance so found shall constitute the net indebtedness of said county of

Nez Perce; and the net indebtedness of said county of Nez Perce, ascertained as aforesaid, shall be divided equally between the counties of Nez Perce and Latah in proportion to the taxable property of said counties as it legally appears on the assessment roll for the year eighteen hundred and eighty-seven, and the said county of Latah shall cause a warrant or warrants to be drawn upon its treasurer to the county of Nez Perce, which said warrant or warrants shall take priority in payment over all other warrants, scrip, or other indebtedness of the said county of Latah.

Sec. 6. That the county commissioners of Nez Perce county are hereby authorized and required to furnish to the county of Latah transcrips of all records, indexes and documents and other papers on file and of record in the offices of Nez Perce County, which may be necessary to perfect the records of Latah County. They may contract with the auditor of Nez Perce County to make the above-named transcripts, the compensation for which shall be in addition to his regular salary. The necessary books for the aforementioned transcripts shall be furnished by Latah County, and the expense of making the said transcripts shall be paid by the counties of Nez Perce, and Latah equally. Certificates of the correctness of said records, made as aforesaid, shall have the same legal effect as if made by the auditor of Nez Perce county.

Sec. 7. That the County of Latah is hereby

21 E. H. I.

attached to Nez Perce County for judicial purposes until the next meeting of the judges of the supreme court of Idaho Territory, when it shall be the duty of said judges to fix a time for holding court in said county of Latah as provided by the laws of said territory for the other counties thereof. Thirty days after the time of holding said court is fixed as aforesaid, the said county of Latah shall assume and be vested with all the judicial rights, privileges and powers of a county under the laws of the said Territory of Idaho.

Sec. 8.   That the county of Latah shall remain with Nez Perce County for the legislative purposes until otherwise provided by law.

Sec. 9.   That the county seat of Latah county is hereby located at the town of Moscow in said county.

Sec. 10.   That the commissioners of Latah County be, and they are hereby authorized to issue bonds to an amount not exceeding twenty thousand dollars, of denominations not less than one hundred nor more than one thousand dollars, running for a term of not less than ten nor more than twenty years, bearing interest at the rate not exceeding eight per centum per annum, with interest coupons attached, which bonds shall be signed by the chairman of the board of county commissioners and the auditor of said county, and be authenticated by the seal of said county.

Sec. 11.   That the said board of commissioners are hereby authorized to make sale of said bonds and apply the proceeds thereof to the erection of a court house and jail, and such other public buildings as may be necessary; Provided: That no bond shall be sold by said commissioners for less than its par value.

Sec. 12.   That the said board of commissioners and their successors in office are hereby empowered and required to levy such tax as may be necessary to promptly pay the interest on said bonds, and also to levy such tax as may be necessary to pay the principal of said bonds as the same shall become due.

Sec. 13.   That in the event said board of commissioners shall issue bonds as hereinbefore authorized, the interest coupons thereof shall be receivable in payment of the county taxes of said county of Latah.

Sec. 14.   That the commissioners of Nez Perce county be, and they are hereby, authorized to issue bonds to an amount not exceeding thirty thousand dollars, of denominations not less than one hundred nor more than one thousand dollars, running for terms of not less than ten nor more than twenty years, bearing interest at a rate not exceeding eight per centum per annum with interest coupons attached, which bonds shall be signed by the chairman of the said board of commissioners and county auditor, and be authenticated by the seal of said county.

Sec. 15.   That the said board of commissioners are hereby authorized to make sale of said bonds and apply the proceeds thereof to the erection of a court-house, jail, and such other public buildings as may be necessary, and for the building of necessary bridges; Provided: That no bond shall be sold by said board of commissioners for less than its par value.

Sec. 16. That the said board of commissioners and their successors in office are hereby empowered and required to levy such tax as may be necessary to promptly pay the interest on said bonds, and also to levy such tax as may be necessary to pay the principal of said bonds as the same shall become due.

Sec. 17. That in the event said board of commissioners shall issue bonds as hereinbefore authorized, the interest coupons attached to said bonds shall be receivable in payment of the county taxes of said county of Nez Perce.

Sec. 18. That the county of Latah shall not be entitled to any portion of the property, real or personal, of the said county of Nez Perce.

Sec. 19. That all acts in conflict with any of the provisions of this act be, and the same are hereby repealed.

Sec. 20. That this act shall be in force from and after its ratification.

Approved May 14, 1888.

CHAPTER XVIII.

MANY AFFAIRS OF INTEREST.

THE Third Session of the Legislative Assembly of the Territory of Idaho convened in Boise City December 4, 1865. and adjourned January 12, 1866.

The Council consisted of eight members, and the House of nineteen members. The membership of both houses was composed of capable and industrious men.

It is possible that some of the legislation which they enacted was ill-advised, but the members were honest and earnest in their efforts to promote the interests of the Territory.

The following is an excerpt from Governor Lyon's message to the Third Legislative Assembly of the Territory of Idaho:

"Gentlemen of the Council and House of Representatives:

"The Temple of War is closed. No more shall its iron-mouthed and brazen-throated cannon peal forth dread 'miseries' over half a thousand battle-fields, where sleep their last sleep—the victor and the vanquished. No more shall the ear of night be pierced with the echoes of fierce assault and stubborn defense from encompassed and beleaguered cities. The conflict is over, and with it expires the cause.

"They who appealed to the last argument of kings, appealed in vain. The Constitution of our common country has been vindicated and the Union gallantly sustained. The destroyers have become restorers, and those who were last in war have been the first to hail the glorious advent of peace. Each returning state is welcomed with National joy; each renewed tie of the ancient fraternity of feeling is another evidence of the wisdom of the Government in its position —that statehood may be suspended, but can only with annihilation die. I heartily congratulate you as a source of profound gratitude to the God of Nations, that the representatives of thirty-seven sovereignties will assemble this December, as of yore, at the Capitol in Washington, over which the old flag floats with a new splendor, lighted by the stately stars of a perfect constellation. In older communities the many precedents, like lamps, guide the feet of legislators in the beaten way, but here in the paramount interest that presents itself, our legislation has no analogies. Personal security, protection of property; the fostering of moral and material advancement—will give wide scope for your judicious investigation and patient research. To your care, your wisdom and your judgment, have been confined, in part, the welfare of the people of the territory, and under such auspicious circumstances may you, as representatives, prove worthy of their fullest confidence."

The gentlemen who constituted the membership of the Third Session were "jolly" good fellows—very liberal in their disbursement of public funds. As an example of this liberality, the following may be quoted:

AN ACT

For the Relief of James I. Crutcher, Sheriff of Boise County, Idaho Territory.

Be it enacted by the Legislative Assembly of the Territory of Idaho, as follows:

Sec. 1. The sum of eleven thousand five hundred dollars is hereby appropriated for the benefit of James I. Crutcher, Sheriff of Boise County, Idaho Territory, to reimburse that officer for large sums of money by him expended on behalf of the Territory, to-wit: The sum of nine thousand dollars for the maintenance of Territorial prisoners; and the further sum of two thousand five hundred dollars for the protection of Territorial prisoners and property during the late riot in said county.

Sec. 2. That the said Crutcher is hereby authorized to realize the said sum of eleven thousand five hundred dollars by retaining that amount for his own use and benefit, out of any moneys in his hands, which have been collected by him as Tax Collector for Territorial purposes.

Sec. 3. That the said James I. Crutcher be allowed, and he is hereby required to turn over, in his settlement to the officer authorized to receive it for the Territory, Territorial warrants, amounting in the aggregate to the said sum of eleven thousand and five hundred dollars.

Sec. 4. This act to take effect from and after its approval by the Governor.

Approved January 6th, 1864.

It is difficult to account for this liberality under the conditions existing at that time, as explained in "Hailey's History of Idaho," pp. 128-129:

"Condition and Conduct of the People in Idaho in 1865."

"Some writers, who never lived in Idaho, have seen fit to give exaggerated statements in regard to the kind of people who lived in Idaho in the early days, and more especially, to criticise the conduct of brave pioneers who paved the way for others to come.

"From some of these statements, the reader would infer that Idaho was first settled by a band of thieves, robbers, murderers and general law-breakers. We desire in behalf of justice to those brave old pioneers, both men and women, to refute this statement.

"The writer was engaged in the transportation of passengers and freight between the Columbia river and Boise Basin from the spring of 1863 to July, 1870, spending a portion of my time every month in Boise Basin. My business necessarily brought me in contact with men and women of all classes and professions, and I can truthfully say that I never had business dealings with, or met more honest, upright men and women than in the early sixties in Idaho. I do not mean by this that there were no bad men in Idaho. There were a few, as there are in all communities, but they were the exception.

"The courts and officers enforced the law strictly. It may be interesting to the reader to know something of the number of law breakers who were sent to the territorial prison in '64-'65. Under a law passed at the Second Session, 1864, the Territorial Treasurer was made prison commissioner with power to audit the accounts of the prison keeper. In his report to the legislative assembly, under date of December, 1865, he reports for the year 1864 three prisoners—one confined 267 days; one for 160 days; and one for 113 days. From January 1st, 1865, he reports four prisoners. From July, 1865, to December 5th, 1865, the date of the prison commissioner's report, the prisoners confined in the Territorial prison averaged ten. There must have been in Idaho at that time not less than twenty-five thousand people, mostly grown men and women.

"The reader may say that our laws were not enforced, but I desire to state that they were strictly enforced. The people in Idaho were, as a rule, honest, upright, intelligent citizens, kind and generous to a fault. No appeal for aid to anyone in distress was ever unanswered. The pioneers of Idaho were unquestionably a noble class of men and women, and well deserve credit for redeeming this fair 'Gem of the Mountains'

from a land of savages and a barren waste to a
land of beauty, peace and plenty."

It will be noted that there were in the
Territorial prisons, all told, three prisoners during 1864, and from January 1, 1865, to July of
that year, four; and from July to December,
1865, an average of ten in both prisons—one of
which was in Lewiston and the other in Idaho
City. The writer has not the commissioner's
report at hand to determine how many were confined in each prison, but even if all of them
were in the Idaho City penitentiary, it would
seem today as if $9,000.00 was a very liberal
compensation for their keep for the time specified.

Yes, the members were "jolly" good fellows;
two of the Ada county members were elected
from the same saloon in Boise City—thus saving
mileage.

During the Third Session the following
amendment was enacted:

AN ACT

To Amend An Act Relative to Attorneys and
Counselors at Law.

Be it enacted by the Legislative Assembly
of the Territory of Idaho, as follows:

Sec. 1.   That Section Three of said act shall
read as follows: Every applicant for admission
as attorney and counselor, shall produce satisfactory testimonials of good moral character,

and undergo an examination by a committee of attorneys appointed by the Court as to his qualifications.

Sec. 2. All laws in conflict with this act are hereby repealed.

Sec. 3. This act to take effect from and after its approval by the Governor.

Approved January 5th, A. D. 1866.

The act thus amended was passed by the First Session and required attorneys and counsellors at law to take an oath of allegiance to the U. S. Government. Strange as it may appear today, the taking of such an oath was then considered a great hardship.

The Third Session enacted a large number of franchises, providing for the operation of ferries, and the construction of toll roads, as well as much valuable legislation looking to the future welfare and development of the Territory. The session came to an end January 12, 1866.

The year 1866 witnessed the departure of many placer miners from the country and the consequent decline in that industry. But the previous discovery and development of rich silver lodes in Owyhee county together with a number of quartz mines in Boise Basin, served to maintain the output of precious metals, and gave permanence and stability to the business interests of the Territory.

On April 10, 1866, David W. Ballard of Lebanon, Linn county, Oregon, was appointed governor to succeed Governor Lyon. Governor Ballard was a physician by profession and came to his new duties well recommended. He filled the office of chief executive of the Territory for four years, and at the close of his service he returned to his former home, respected by every one. He was a man of tranquil temperament, with a clear conception of duty, and a fixed determination to do whatever he conceived to be right.

PIUTE INDIANS.

From the time of the first discovery of precious metals south and west of Snake river—in what is now Owyhee county—prospecting was retarded by the hostile disposition of the Piute Indians. The discovery of not only placer deposits, but of very rich silver ore in the vicinity of Ruby and Silver Cities, caused an influx of population, which, concentrating as it did within a radius of a few miles, sufficed to hold the Indians in check in the immediate vicinity, but for several years travelers in small parties were in continual danger on all the routes of travel to and from the Owyhee towns and mining camps.

It was not an uncommon experience for the stage that carried passengers and express between Boise City, Ruby and Silver City, to be made a target while crossing the ridge between Reynold's Creek and Snake river, and although a wholesome fear of the express messenger and the passengers, who were always well armed, served to prevent the Indians from coming to close quarters, several passengers were killed or wounded while attempting this trip. These murderous assaults, as in fact were nearly all others at that time, were made by small predatory bands of usually not more than half a dozen warriors, who were generally young men with a consuming ambition to distinguish themselves, and being always well equipped with saddle animals, they, after firing a volley into a stage coach, usually made their escape. The troops stationed at Boise being infantry, were unable to pursue and punish the perpetrators of these attacks. They might pursue, as indeed they sometimes did, 'each man carrying a few days' rations on his back, but such pursuit served only to make the Indians bolder.

It was not until after the close of the war of the Rebellion in 1865 that our government was able to give proper attention to our, at that time, extensive frontier.

As soon as the situation in South Idaho was understood, army posts were established throughout the favorite haunts of the Indians, and thus they were brought under control. But, in the interim, many tragedies were enacted, many sodless mounds marked the trails where later progress and civilization entered the desert wastes of Idaho.

The fact that the United States troops, up to the year 1866, had failed to suppress the hostilities of the Indians in the vicinity of Owyhee, was the cause of much unjust criticism, especially from those whose sympathies were with the Confederate rather than with the Union armies, and it was repeatedly stated until it became a fixed belief that "soldiers were 'no good' for fighting Indians; it required miners and packers to clean them out." This belief, which was very general, culminated during the early summer of 1866, in the organization and equipment of a private company under the leadership of an old Indian fighter and packer named Jennings. This company intended to penetrate the country occupied by the hostiles lying west and south of Silver City. It consisted of forty men, well provided with saddle horses and pack animals to transport their equipage, which included a commissary sufficient to permit them to remain in the field for at least three months.

It must not be thought that all the men who constituted the membership of this troop were impelled to enlist through patriotic motives or a desire to defend the lives and property of their fellow- citizens, for such motives were unknown to many of them. The real object of the enterprise was to enrich themselves by the capture of horses and mules which the Indians were known to possess in large numbers.

It is true that many of those who joined the company were good men who happened at that time to be out of employment, and through that spirit of adventure which permeates all frontiermen, resolved to "take a chance." But among the number, on the other hand, were many of the "bravo" type, whose field of adventure is usually confined to the saloons and dance-halls.

As the company started out on its dangerous mission, its members were the recipients of the well-wishes of everyone.

It is doubtful if a better armed and equipped body of men ever took the field against these or any other tribe of Indians. As their leader was a man of courage and experience, it was confidently expected that a courier would shortly return bringing the news of an encounter in which the Indians were annihilated, and that the volunteers had covered themselves with glory. However, it was not until the expiration of more than three weeks that any news of their activities reached Silver and Ruby Cities, and then it was in an unexpected form.

Court was in session during the interim of their absence, and the famous "Poor Man" mining case was on trial. The town of Ruby, then the county seat of Owyhee county, and its sister town, Silver City, with suburbs merging into each other, were tense with excitement over a trial involving title to what, at that time, had the appearance of being the richest silver mine ever discovered.

The disputed property was claimed by the New York & Owyhee Gold & Silver Mining company, which claim was contested by Put Bradford and associates of Portland, Oregon. Each of the contestants had erected stockades, or miniature forts, adjacent to the disputed ground, and these were garrisoned by professional gun-fighters employed by the contestants.

Rumors were rife that neither party to the contest would peacefully submit to defeat, and, as a consequence, not only was the U. S. marshal's office represented by numerous deputies, but a company of infantry from Boise Barracks were also encamped below town in order to be convenient in case of lawlessness.

Thus, with hostilities imminent, both within and outside of the towns, the atmosphere was tense with expectancy.

One morning between three or four o'clock, some weeks after the departure of the company that went in search of the Indians, and while the mining dispute was at its greatest tension, a general alarm sounded. This was effected by blowing the steam whistles of all the quartz-mills, of which there were several in operation; the beating of gongs and the ringing of bells. In a few minutes the streets were thronged with men, armed with such weapons as they could hastily procure, all ready to repel an assault, the first impression being that the Indians were about to attack; but it was soon learned that the tumult was caused by the arrival of two scouts who had accompanied the party in quest of the Indians.

The scouts reported that thirty-five of the original party of forty men were surrounded about sixty or seventy miles from Silver City by a body of Indians estimated to be five hundred strong. They had been attacked while preparing to cross the Owyhee river at a ford, and had retreated from the place where the attack was made to where they had camped the previous night. This position, which happened to be well adapted for defense, was being held by them when the scouts managed to escape the following night through the Indians' lines. The escape was effected by crawling between the Indian sentinels at night, which, fortunately, happened to be a dark one. The men traveled all that night and lay concealed the next day among the lava rocks, enduring the rays of the July sun without shade and without water. When darkness' fell again, making it safe for them to move, they continued their journey, arriving at their destination, Silver City, at the hour stated.

They brought a note from Captain Jennings, which stated that unless relief was sent as quickly as possible, not a man would be left to tell the tale.

For perhaps twenty minutes chaos reigned in Silver City and Ruby; but the citizens having assembled in front of a store in the former place, a man mounted a box, and, reading the message, he called for volunteers to go to the relief of the endangered men. It was proposed that all who had arms, and who could procure horses to ride should ride at once to Flint, which was several miles on the road to be traveled in attempting the rescue.

In about one hour from the time the first alarm was given, nearly one hundred men were mounted and en route to Flint. There a halt was called and an organization was effected.

22 E. H. I.

The men were divided into three companies, each of which elected its own captain, who named his own lieutenants. No regimental organzation was effected.

As soon as these preliminaries were completed the march began. Company A, of which the writer had been chosen captain, was in the lead, and was closely followed by the other two companies. The scouts, although nearly exhausted, after a few drinks and a hearty meal in Silver, announced themselves able to accompany the relief expedition, and were accordingly given horses and assigned to places in the lead of the cavalcade to pilot the way. They expected to lead the rescuers to the battle ground so as to arrive at daylight the following morning. But owing to darkness the first night, and to the sameness of the lava country over which they were obliged to travel, they became bewildered, and losing their way, did not reach their objective point until late the next afternoon.

The Indians, who had doubtless been warned of the approaching volunteers, made a hasty retreat, carrying with them their dead and wounded. The saddle animals being so jaded and the men so exhausted from fatigue and hunger, immediate pursuit was impracticable.

The arrival of the relief party was well timed, the ammunition of the beleaguered men being almost expended.

The position they had chosen for defense was well adapted for the purpose, it being a little oasis, or basin, in a volcanic plain, the rim-rock nearly surrounding its circumference, which was, at several points, a little higher than the ground in the rear. Immediately on reaching this basin, the men took possession of these slight elevations and constructed rifle pits out of the loose rocks which were lying around in profusion. Thus they were able to hold the Indians at long range. In the little basin there were three clumps of willows, each of which contained a spring of good water. The men crowded their horses into the two larger bunches of willows, tying them as best they could, and in the smaller bunch they placed their provisions in charge of their German cook, who at once threw up a breast-work of sods on the exposed sides for a protection from the fire of the enemy.

Four rifle-pits, large enough to accommodate two men each, were constructed at such points as would cover the camp; a larger one that resembled a stone corral, and capable of holding all the men if necessary, was built the first night.

Over this miniature fortress the American flag was flown, its staff being the largest willow they could find in the basin. From this main fort, the men in the rifle pits were relieved at intervals. No regular meals were served; the position occupied by the cook and the provisions was about sixty yards from the main fortification, and since the intervening ground was swept by fire from the Indians' guns, refreshments were served usually at night.   These meals consisted of raw bacon, hard-tack and cold coffee. If the cook attempted to build a fire at night, it at once became a target.

One of the men composing the original party was named Thomas Caton.   He gave his residence as "Long Tom," Oregon.   He was a man of refined tastes and literary attainments.   Prior to the general attack at the Owyhee Crossing, the company had encountered several small predatory squads of Indians, and had annihilated them and taken their saddle animals.

Caton, who kept a diary in which he recorded events, had written up these encounters as they occurred from day to day.

During the second day of their besiegement, Caton and a comrade were assigned to a rifle-pit that protected the north side of the camp. Loose rock being scarce in that locality, the walls of the rifle-pit were low, and, consequently, the men kept their lonely and dangerous watch while in a recumbent position.   When Caton entered this post he began to write up his diary, and while in the middle of a sentence his attention had probably been attracted by the breaking of a twig, and, upon raising his head to look for the cause of the noise, he was shot in the forehead—his blood punctuating the last lines he had written.

His comrade remained in the rifle-pit with the dead man during the afternoon and evening, until it was sufficiently dark for him to make his escape without observation. He then came in and reported the tragedy, bringing the dead man's weapons and the diary that had ended so tragically. That rifle-pit was not regarrisoned, and although Caton's body was not removed until the second night after his death, his scalp was not taken nor was he mutilated in any manner by the Indians. He was buried in a shallow grave near the place where he was shot, and a mound of lava rocks was raised to mark the spot.

Since those strenuous days that little basin where the battle occurred, has become a watering place for thousands of sheep, and during each spring and early summer, the young lambs gambol above the ashes of him who met such a tragic end.

During the retreat, which covered about three miles and the more than three days' fight, Caton was the only man killed—one other being wounded, but he recovered.

The alarm that was sounded in Silver City and Ruby on the arrival of the scouts was communicated to the detached camps down Reynolds Creek, and reached the camp of the U. S. Infantry, who were located above Booneville. The captain in command ordered the pack-train driven in at once, and then mounting his men as best he could, without saddles, took the trail in pursuit of the volunteers, who had already started, and thus equipped, they arrived at the battle-ground within an hour after the citizen's rescue party reached that locality.

As before stated, court was being held in
Ruby City at the time Jennings' party was attacked, and when the news arrived that they
were surrounded with an overwhelming force,
and were liable to be wiped out, the presiding
judge announced that when court convened that
morning, he would adjourn for ten days to permit the members of the bar, and other attaches of
the court to go out and fight the Indians.   Thus,
the litigants were given an opportunity to reason
among themselves, and before the return of
the lawyers and fighting men, the famous "Poorman" case was settled by compromise, each of the
claimants receiving and retaining an interest in
the disputed property, the Poorman mine, which
was an exceedingly valuable property, and which
afterwards produced millions in wealth for its
fortunate owners.

The story of the discovery and development
of the Owyhee mines, and the subjection of the
Indians in that district would make a volume of
intensely interesting matter; but the writer de-
sires to avoid the criticism that his book is too
far apart between covers.   Hence, he cannot
devote too much space to one district.

A few days after the return of the volunteers, affairs in Owyhee county assumed their
normal condition, and the mining and reduction
of ore was given renewed impetus by the settlement of the Poorman controversy.

A few weeks later a general election was
held in the territory, at which one of the prom-

inent citizens of Owyhee county, a man named Fitzpatrick, was a candidate for congress on the Republican ticket, but, though he was a capable man and made a vigorous canvass, he was overwhelmingly defeated by E. D. Holbrook, the then incumbent.

Both conventions were held that year in Boise City, the Democratic in Riggs & Agnew's saloon, on the corner of Main and Sixth streets, and the Republican was held in a building which happened to be vacant on the corner of Main and Fifth streets.

Both conventions were lively affairs, but the Democrats outclassed the Republicans in the matter of sensational episodes, pistol shots having been exchanged between two of the delegates, W. W. Douthitt and H. C. Street, editor of the *Idaho World*. No one was injured by the shooting, and as soon as the smoke had escaped from the room, peace was restored and "all went merry as a marriage bell."

CHAPTER XIX.

SOLDIERS SUPPRESS LEGISLATIVE RIOT.

THE Fourth Session of the Idaho Territorial Legislature convened December 3rd, 1866, its membership being as follows:

COUNCIL.

E. A. Stevenson .... Ada County
H. C. Riggs .... Ada County
George Ainslie .... Boise County
S. P. Scaniker .... Boise County
H. C. Street .... Boise County
S. S. Fenn .... Idaho County
L. P. Brown .... Nez Perce County
M. A. Carter .... Oneida County
R. T. Miller .... Owyhee County
W. H. Hudson .... Shoshone County
George Ainslie, *President.*

HOUSE OF REPRESENTATIVES.

A. W. Flournoy .... Ada County
G. W. Paul .... Ada County
John Cozad .... Ada County
Nelson Davis .... Alturas County
B. J. Nordyke .... Alturas County
J. W. Knight .... Boise County
F. W. Bell .... Boise County
George Stafford .... Boise County

J. A. Abbott .... Boise County
A. P. Mitchell .... Boise County
W. L. Law .... Boise County
W. H. Parkinson .... Boise County
J. C. Harris .... Idaho County
A. McDonald .... Idaho County
W. W. Thayer .... Nez Perce County
J. S. Thayer .... Nez Perce County
A. Englis .... Owyhee County
Henry Ohle .... Owyhee County
D. G. Monroe .... Owyhee County
H. T. Caton .... Owyhee County
W. F. McMillen .... Shoshone County
A. W. Flournoy, *Speaker.*

Governor Ballard delivered his message to the legislature on the day it convened, both houses having promptly organized. The message contained a great deal of valuable information and was well received. Unfortunately during this session there were strained relations between the majority in both houses and the Territorial Secretary, S. R. Howlett, upon whom devolved the duties of disbursing officer, among them that of paying the salaries of the members, many of whom could not yet become reconciled to the outcome of the Civil War, which had ended the previous year.

This was shown by the roll-call in the Council, when the passage of the act repealing the official oath was effected, as provided for by act of the First Session.

The following is a copy of the proceedings

taken from the Session Laws of the Fourth Session, including the names of those councilmen
who voted to pass the measure, notwithstanding
the objections of the Governor:

AN ACT

*To Repeal an Act to Regulate Official Oaths, Ap-
proved December 28, 1863, and to Prescribe
an Oath to Be Administered to Public Officers in the Territory of Idaho:*

Preamble relating to Official Oaths;

Oath of members of legislative assembly,
Sec. 1;

Oath of officers, attorneys or counselors,
Sec. 1.

Oath, form and substance of, Sec. 1;

Oath, repeal of oath, approved Dec. 28, 1863,
Sec. 2;

Whereas,. At the Third Annual Session of
the Legislative Assembly of the Territory of
Idaho, "An Act to Repeal an Act to Regulate Official Oaths, approved December 28th, 1863, and
to Prescribe an Oath to be administered to public Officers in the Territory of Idaho," was
passed and transmitted to the Governor of the
Territory by the Committee on "Enrolled and
Engrossed Bills," and became a law by reason
of the Governor failing to return the same within
three days (Sundays excepted) as provided by
the Organic Act; and

Whereas, said Bill was published in the Idaho World, a newspaper published in the County

of Boise, and Territory of Idaho, by authority of the Legislative Assembly, but was not published and does not appear in the bound volume, among the Session laws of the Third Session of the Legislative Assembly; therefore,

Be It Enacted by the Legislative Assembly of the Territory of Idaho, as follows:

Section 1. That the only oath which shall be required of any member of the Legislative Assembly, or of any officer who may have been elected, appointed or chosen, or who may hereafter be elected, appointed or chosen, to' any office within the Territory of Idaho, under the laws thereof, before entering upon his duties, or of any Attorney or Counselor at Law or Solicitor in Chancery of any of the courts in this Territory, shall be required to take upon admission to practice, shall be as follows: I, (here name of the person and the office to which he has been elected, or appointed, or chosen) do solemnly swear (or affirm) that I will support the Constitution of the United States and the Organic Act of this Territory; and that I will faithfully and truly perform all the duties which may be required by law, to the best of my ability, so help me God.

Sec. 2. That "An Act to Repeal an Act to Regulate Official Oaths," approved December 28th, 1863, and to prescribe an oath to be administered to Public officers in the Territory of Idaho, enacted at the Third Session of the Legislative Assembly, and all and any acts contravening this Act, be and the same are hereby repealed.

Sec. 3. This act to take effect and be in force after ten days from the date of its becoming a law.

I hereby certify that the foregoing Council Bill No. 9 passed the Council December 27th, 1866, the question being: Shall the Bill pass; notwithstanding the objections of the Governor, Ayes—Messrs. Carter, Fenn, Miller, Riggs, Scaniker, Stevenson, Street, and Mr. President—8; Nays—Messrs. Brown and Hudson—2.

GEO. AINSLIE,
President of the Council.

Attest: CHAS. C. DUDLEY,
Secretary.

The folly of these men in thus perpetuating the bitterness of a civil war already ended, culminated in their refusal to take the oath of loyalty required by act of congress, which provided that "hereafter every person elected or appointed to any office of honor or profit, under the Government of the United States, in either civil, military or the naval department of the public service, excepting the President of the United States, shall, before entering upon the duties of such office, and before being entitled to any of the salary or other emoluments thereof, *take and subscribe* to the following oath or affirmation."

Then followed the obligation which a majority of the members of both houses of the Fourth

Session of the Idaho Legislature refused to take, and as a consequence, the Territorial Secretary, S. R. Howlett, would not pay them their per diem or mileage.

When informed of his decision, the members organized "rough houses," and proceeded to break the furniture and throw it out the windows. Governor Ballard requisitioned the commanding officer at Boise Barracks for troops to suppress the disturbance, and they were promptly furnished, appearing at rest in front of the legislative halls within an hour; and within the next half-hour the Idaho Solons had all subscribed to the oath and received their pay. Thus ended the most puerile happening that was ever enacted in the history of the Territory.

An effort was made to create a sentiment against Howlett, for refusing to pay the members unless they subscribed to the oath; but the law was explicit. The Department required that the oath, subscribed by each member, should accompany and be a part of his vouchers.

The foregoing unwarranted disgraceful occurrence was the closing event of the Fourth Session.

Fortunately for the interest of the taxpayers, congress amended the act providing for an annual session of the Idaho Legislature, and authorized the holding of biennial sessions; consequently the Fifth Session did not convene until December 7, 1868.

During the years 1867-1868, a noticeable

change had occurred in the types of new arrivals in the Territory, many of whom consisted of families who brought with them their household goods, and were prepared to make permanent homes. Especially was this apparent in the Payette and Boise valleys and their tributaries. The original locators having, in many instances returned to their former homes, their locations were occupied by the new arrivals, who, in most cases, intended to found lasting homes.

The Union Pacific and the Central Pacific railroads were nearing completion, and this fact, no doubt, had an influence in diverting immigration to South Idaho.

The vote cast for Delegate to Congress in 1868 revealed that the voting population had decreased during the previous two years. This was due to the fact that, while many permanent settlers had arrived during this time, a large number of placer miners had departed for their former homes, while others had abandoned the territory in search of new fields.

The fifth session of the Territorial Legislature which convened in Boise City on Dec. 7th, 1868 was composed with one exception of new members; they were a conservative body, and while they enacted but few laws, they adjourned at the end of the session without having done any harm.

The same tribute may be paid to the members of the sixth session which assembled on the 8th day of December, 1870.

The Seventh session began its labors on the second day of December, 1872, and adjourned on the 10th day of January, 1873. Its membership being composed of men who intended to remain permanently in Idaho, they were careful in the enactment of laws to avoid any unnecessary increase in taxes.

All new Territories suffer great inconvenience from the lack of surveys, which require both time and money to accomplish. Idaho suffered severely from neglect on the part of Congress to make the necessary appropriations to meet the contingency of making surveys of the agricultural lands to accommodate the requirements of actual settlers.

At the time Idaho Territory was organized the Nation was in the throes of civil war, and for many years thereafter its treasury was depleted by meeting the expenses incident to that contest; therefore it was not the fault of Congress, or neglect of our Delegates thereto, that appropriations for surveys, and other improvements incident to the development of a new country were deferred.

During the second session of the 38th Congress, Mr. Wallace, then Delegate from Idaho, succeeded in having the Sundry Civil Appropriation Bill amended so as to provide $10,000 "for surveys in Idaho," and the office of U. S. Surveyor General for Idaho was organized and opened for business in November, 1866.

The initial point from which all Townships

number to the north and south, and Ranges to the east and west, was established by Peter W. Bell, U. S. Deputy Surveyor, under contract No. 1, from the office of the U. S. Surveyor General, on April 19th, 1867, in Ada County, Territory of Idaho, and was composed of a "pine post in top of mound of stone, 6 ft. base and 6 ft. high, with a stone 14x12x4 inches marked with a x laid on north side of post." The foregoing described mound of stone was located on a high point of a rocky butte standing isolated upon the plain between Snake and Boise Rivers, in latitude 43 degrees, 26 minutes North and about 19 miles southwest from Boise.

Those assisting in establishing the monument, and the subsequent survey of the Boise Base Line were: D. F. Baker, A. B. Plume, J. C. Deaver and M. B. Hill, chainmen; assisted by Samuel Loft and B. C. Franklin, axmen.

The first public survey of any kind in Idaho was run on the Boise Base Line from the established initial point, west throungh T. 1. N., R. 1 W. on April 19th, 1867.

The first survey on the Boise Meridian, was run from the initial point in Ada county, through T. 1 S., R. 1 E. and R. 1 W. by Peter W. Bell, U. S. Deputy Surveyor, under his contract No. 1 on April 28th, 1867, with the same assistants he had in the survey of the Base Line.

The first Township subdivided in Ada county and in the Territory of Idaho, was T. 4 N. R 1 W. by Allen M. Thompson, U. S. Deputy Surveyor under contract No. 5, which survey was completed on September 8, 1867, and the plats were filed with the Register of the U. S. Land Office at Boise City on January 17th, 1868.

The first Township subdivided in Boise county was T. 5 N., R. 2 E., which was partly surveyed by Peter W. Bell; his survey was completed March 27, 1868. The plat of said township was filed with the Register of the U. S. Land Office at Boise City, on April 18, 1868.

The first Township subdivided in Idaho County was T. 30 N., R. 3 E., which was partly surveyed by Allen M. Thompson, U. S. Deputy Surveyor; his survey being completed on August 9, 1869. The plat of said township was filed with the Register of the U. S. Land Office at Lewiston, Idaho Territory on October 23, 1869.

The first subdivisional survey of a township in Nez Perce county was made in T. 34 N., R. 4 W. by David P. Thompson, U. S. Deputy Surveyor, who partly subdivided the same under his contract dated December 23, 1869, his survey being completed April 22, 1870. The plat of said survey was filed in the Lewiston Land Office on January 27, 1871.

The first mineral surveying in the Territory of Idaho, was let to James H. Slater as Contract No. 1 dated July 18, 1870, for surveying mineral claims in the mineral district of Alturas county.

During the subsequent decade, from 1870 to 1880 the appropriations made by Congress for surveying the public domain in Idaho were more

23 E. H. I.

liberal, but at all times prior to the admission of
the Territory as a State, and even since, the locations of settlers have been in advance of the
surveys.

CHAPTER XX.

INDIAN WARS IN IDAHO.

THE Eighth Session of the Idaho Legislature convened at the capital on the 7th day of December, 1874, and adjourned on the 15th day of January, 1875. The political divisions of the Territory represented in that session, together with the representation of each were as follows:

	Council	House of Representatives
Ada County	2	4
Alturas County	1	2
Boise County	3	8
Idaho County	1	2
Lemhi County	1	2
Nez Perce County	1	2
Oneida County	1	1
Owyhee County	1	4
Shoshone County	1	1
	12	26

One of the prominent incongruities of the early business management of Idaho Territory is found in the fact that the Legislature while providing for the collection of revenue to conduct the various departments of its government, left to the County Commissioners the duty of fixing the per cent. which the Tax Collector should retain out of all taxes collected as a recompense for his services in collecting the same.

The following is a sample of the fees allowed for collecting the Territorial portion of the revenue, in the counties named:

Alturas County charges ....38 per cent.
Ada County charges ....16 per cent.
Boise County charges ....23 per cent.
Lemhi County charges ....45 per cent.
Idaho County charges ....43 per cent.
Nez Perce County charges ....33 per cent.
Owyhee County charges ....21 per cent.
Oneida County charges ....28 per cent.
Shoshone County charges ....36 per cent.

The eighth session of the Territorial Legislature enacted a new revenue law which was approved January 15, 1875; section 104 of the act being as follows:

SEC. 104. The collectors of taxes in the counties of this Territory shall be allowed for collecting all taxes (except poll taxes) the following rates on all monies collected and paid over by them in each fiscal year, commencing on the first Monday of April, ten per centum on the first ten thousand dollars; four per centum on all over ten thousand and under twenty thousand dollars; three per centum on all over twenty thousand, and under fifty thousand dollars; two per centum on all over fifty thousand and under one hundred thousand dollars, and one per centum on all over one hundred thousand and under two hundred thousand dollars; *Provided*: that the assessor, as ex-officio tax collector shall be allowed on all collections on subsequent assessments assessed after the first Monday in August, twenty-five per cent on the first ten thousand dollars, and ten per cent on all over ten thousand dollars; but shall receive no per diem pay for making any subsequent assessment or for collecting poll or other per capita taxes.

It will be observed that under the preceding section it was greatly to the advantage of the assessor to delay the work of his office so as to obtain the fee of twenty-five per cent on all assessments made after the first Monday in August.

The decade including 1871 and 1880 was perhaps the most trying period in the history of Idaho Territory; up to 1870 the chief industry was placer mining, and the number of men employed in that enterprise, together with those in the towns and camps supported directly by the miners provided an excellent market for all kinds of farm produce raised in the valleys.

It seldom requires many years to exhaust the wealth of the average placer mining camp, and while the placer mines discovered in Idaho were no doubt more than average in extent and productiveness, yet hundreds of the best producing claims were exhausted within the first five years after their discovery; hence each succeeding year added to the melancholy of the situation, until eventually, and that too within ten years after the discovery of Boise Basin, hundreds of cabins on the hill-sides and in the gulches were left tenantless and alone among the whispering pines.

While it is true that many valuable properties continued to produce sufficient gold dust to justify the employment of a large number of men for many years later, yes even up to present writing, yet the great rush had come and gone between the years 1863 and 1870, and those who remained were required to adjust themselves to the changed condition.

During the decade to which reference is made many rich mineral lodes were discovered, carrying lead, silver, gold and copper; especially were the counties of Alturas and Shoshone found to be rich in the precious metals, but owing to lack of transportation, many of the properties which afterwards became famous, had not been sufficiently developed to give employment to many men, hence the attention of new arrivals in the country was directed to its possibilities in agriculture and stock raising.

Those farmers who from the first settlement of Boise and Payette valleys, as well as those who had settled in Idaho and Nez Perce counties, had proved the character and fertility of the soil and left nothing to conjecture as to the future possibilities of Idaho as an agricultural state.

Experiments in farming had been successfully made not only in the localities mentioned, but also in Malad Valley, Cache Valley, Bear Lake Valley and in other then isolated localities.

The experience of those who first attempted farming in Idaho county, revealed that while the valleys of Snake river, and its tributaries in South Idaho, required irrigation to admit of successful cultivation, the bench lands or plateaux adjacent to Craig's Mountain and the Coeur d'Alenes are not surpassed in fertility by any other agricultural lands of equal area in the United States, the rainfall there being sufficient to insure bountiful harvests. As soon as this became known to the public, a rush of homeseekers followed, and Idaho, Nez Perce and what is called the Palouse country today, were quickly settled and transformed into fertile, productive farms.

The foregoing advance of what is called "civilization" was accomplished by appropriating the hunting and Camas grounds of the Indians who, for generations, yes perhaps since time began, had owned and occupied them. We simply moved in, and without asking for permission, took possession.

When we admit, as we must, that the occupation by the whites of the most fertile valleys and the best grazing lands brought the pinch of hunger to many an Indian tepee, is it to be wondered that the brigandage we practiced was resented in the only manner they recognized—an appeal to arms? I am aware that in those days many men declared that the only "good Indian is a dead one,' but that does not alleviate the sadness of it all.

In their efforts to conquer the wilderness, which included the Indian, many lives were lost, many homes made desolate, but upon the ashes of these and similar tragedies had arisen not only the commonwealth of Idaho, but the Union of States of which she is an important factor. Our only justification lies in the claim, that "the march of progress means the survival of the fittest."

Resentment of the advent of the first settlers in Bear Lake Valley was so pronounced, and the danger of hostilities so imminent, that the families were grouped in what is now Paris, the county seat of Bear Lake county, each family being apportioned a small tract of ground for a house and garden, while the male members of the family located land up and down the valley, as near as practicable to their families; a company of minute men was organized, with horses ever saddled and ready to fall into line to proceed to the rescue, or defense of the women and children if occasion required; a lookout being posted to give the agreed signal if hostilities were observed. The fears of those fathers, or the tears of those mothers whose little ones were exposed to such terrible danger can hardly be imagined by those who visit that peaceful valley today.

The hostilities of those Indians, allied with others, finally culminated in a battle with a body of U. S. troops led by General Connor. The battle occurred on Bear River at the confluence of a little creek, since known as "Battle Creek," the engagement being fought a few miles from the present location of the prosperous town of Preston in Oneida county. The battle was fiercely contested by both Indians and soldiers and raged for several hours, but the troops were finally victorious, although great bravery was displayed by the Indians, most of them fighting to their death, and the few who escaped brokenhearted and dispirited, never ralied to offer other resistance to their invaders.

Although the early history of Idaho is replete with Indian outbreaks entailing heavy loss and much suffering upon the settlers, such outbreaks were usually local in character and consequently being met and quelled by volunteers did not attain to the magnitude of a "war," but eventually an Indian war was precipitated upon the settlers in Idaho county which swept portions of that county with the besom of destruction, leaving in its wake the horrors and atrocities of Indian warfare.

Chief Joseph, the leader and head of a powerful branch or tribe of the Nez Perce nation of Indians, being resentful of wrongs, real, or imaginary, without warning, swooped down upon the unsuspecting and unprepared settlers on Salmon River and Camas Prairie, leaving in the wake of himself and warriors, a trail of desolation and woe, never to be forgotten so long as any of the witnesses of the tragedy or their descendents live to relate the details of the horrors enacted.

U. S. troops under General Howard were despatched to the scene of the massacre as quickly as possible, and they, supported by local volunteers took the field against the Indians. Several engagements occurred but no decisive victory was gained over the Indians, who finally crossed the Clearwater River and took the Lo-Lo Trail into Montana, where they were afterward surrounded and captured, Joseph and his remaining warriors being exiled to Oklahoma and after being held there for a time they were returned to the Colville Reservation in the State of Washington, where he died a few years later.

Those who fell victims of the Joseph outbreak were in no manner responsible for the violation of treaty obligations which he claimed as the cause for his resort to arms, yet under the methods of Indian warfare all who were white suffer alike. Innocence is no defense.

It is an injustice to charge the Indian war of 1877 to the Nez Perce Indians as a Tribe. The contest was precipitated by Chief Joseph and his band; and while it is true they were Nez Perce Indians, yet their tribal organization was separate and distinct; Joseph being their chief. The Nez Perces proper were always friendly to the whites, and so remained during the Chief Joseph imbroglio.

The Indian outbreak of 1877, was succeeded the following year, 1878, by an uprising of the Bannock Indians, who being eventually joined by renegade remnants of other tribes, after leaving Camas Prairie the scene of their first murderous attack, spread over the country westward and to the south glutting their savage instincts with murder and rapine; crossing Snake River they swept through Owyhee county into Oregon, extending their depredations as far west as John Day Valley. Although pursued almost from their start by both volunteer and regular soldiers, the movements of the Indians were so rapid and erratic, that it was difficult to force them into a general engagement, although several desperate skirmishes were fought, in which many of the Indians, as well as several soldiers were killed, finally to avoid capture or annihilation they scattered into small bands and taking to the hills and mountains made their way back as best they could to the protection of their reservation.

The Bannock war with all its attendant horrors, cost of suppression, destruction of property, and loss of life, was precipitated by an error made by a clerk or stenographer in transcribing the treaty, which was written and ratified by the U. S. Senate Feb. 16, 1869, and provided that, "It is agreed that whenever the Bannocks desire a reservation to be set apart for their use, or whenever the President of the United States shall deem it advisable for them to be put upon a reservation, he shall cause one to be selected for them in their present country, which shall embrace reasonable portions of the Port-Neuf and Kansas Prairie countries." There being no such prairie as "Kansas Prairie" and Camas Prairie being one of the most valuable possessions of the Bannock Indians, it is reasonable to suppose that it was agreed in the treaty that the Indians should be allowed to retain a part of their Camas ground, but the clerk who transcribed the Treaty had probably never heard of the blue flowered lily of the north-western states called "Camas," and being familiar with the name "Kansas" wrote in "Kansas Prairie," when it was the intent of the treaty makers that the Bannocks should be allowed to retain a reasonable portion of Camas prairie.

Those whose duty it was to see that the treaty was carried out, should have performed that duty, and prevented the settlers from encroaching upon the ground where the Indians were acustomed to harvest their annual crop of camas, but no protection was given to the treaty rights of the Bannocks, and when they discovered their harvest being destroyed by the white man's hogs, forbearance ceased to be a virtue, and they appealed to the only arbiter they knew, the God of Battle. The writer being one of the first trespassers on Camas prairie, must admit that the Indians under their code of morals and government, had ample justification for the methods they pursued.

Many valuable lives were lost, much suffering endured, and property destroyed during the Bannock war; besides which the development of the country was retarded, and the government as well as the Territory compelled to meet an enormous expense in its suppression, all originating, as is shown to be probable, by an error in the use of a word.

During the year 1879, central Idaho, including the Salmon river country, was afflicted with what proved to be but a miniature Indian war, but insignificant as were its proportions it cost the lives of many persons, and required the employment of several companies of regular soldiers accompanied and aided by volunteer scouts, to suppress and capture the "hostiles," which was finally accomplished.

The Indians who were engaged in this outbreak were what were known as "Sheep Eaters," a small aggregation composed of Shoshones, Bannocks and renegades from other tribes. It is doubtful whether they numbered more than one hundred and fifty, all told, but they were mountain Indians, and like all of that type, were strong, active men and women, capable of enduring great hardship, and if need be, could subsist for days on very meager rations; born and reared as most of them had been among the canyons and crags of the Salmon river mountains, they were familiar with every gorge, defile and trail, from the Rocky Mountains on the east to the Blue Mountains on the west; consequently the task of overtaking and capturing them was an arduous one. The regular troops detailed to make the capture were reinforced by a body of Umatilla Indian scouts, and a company of citizen scouts under the command of Colonel Orlando Robbins, than whom no better trailer or fighter could have been chosen; and the men directly under his command were of the best the country could afford, all trained in the use of arms, and experienced in Indian warfare, good trailers, good shots, and brave to the verge of recklessness. It is not possible in this narrative to mention the name of each individual scout who distinguished himself while serving under Colonel Robbins in this or the two preceding campaigns; as a troop, as a unit, no body of men could have performed better or braver service; always at the front, theirs were the posts of greatest danger. This tribute to their gallantry and worth is not designed to detract from the merit of the brave officers and men of the U. S. army who served through the same campaigns; there were no drones, no cowards, in the field during those strenuous years.

I would be doing less than my duty to the memory of an old comrade and one-time fellow officer if I closed this synopsis of Idaho's Indian wars without making more particular mention of the brave chief of scouts who fought through them all, Col. Orlando Robbins, who was widely and familiarly known as "Rube" Robbins. He first appeared prominently before the people of

Idaho Territory during the summer of 1862. He
was chosen to act as one of the floor managers
at a ball to be given in Florence July 4th that
year, his associate manager being a man named
Jakey Williams.

Florence at the time named for the ball was
in the heydey of its mining prosperity, and the
giving of a ball was designed to provide amusement and entertainment for the respectable element in the town; those wives who had accompanied their husbands to the new Eldorado in
search of wealth were to supply the respecta-
bility.

To manage such a ball as the one proposed,
and preserve a proper semblance of decorum was
a difficult problem, owing to the cosmopolitan
character of the population of Florence at that
time. It was the recognition of that fact which
led to the selection of Rube and Jakey to act
as managers.

It was after the festivities had fairly commenced and many eyes spoke love to other
men's wives, that a noted gambler made his
appearance in the ball room, bringing with him
the well known mistress of another gambler.
The indignation of the ladies present was made
known to the floor managers with the request
that the two objectionable characters be requested to leave the room. The floor-managers
complied with the request, and the gambler and
his partner, when told that their presence was
not agreeable, quietly left the hall. The forego-

ing episode resulted in an attack being made by
the paramour of the woman who was requested
to leave the ball, and the man who took her
there, on the managers. The difficulty was precipitated the following day, and resulted in a
double funeral, both gamblers being killed in the
pistol duel which ensued. Cherokee Bob chose
Rube as the object of his wrath and in doing
so made a fatal mistake. The ball given on the
evening of July 4th, 1862, and its attendant
tragedy, was a prominent event in the history
of that erstwhile city, and has been recorded in
a former chapter.

Rube Robbins' name was a synonym for
honesty and bravery, and during his eventful
and useful life he filled many positions of honor
and trust. He was feared, yet respected by
every bad man and "gun-fighter" who ever so-
journed in Idaho, and it is doubtful if any officer made more arrests of that class than he. He
was brave to the limit, yet tended-hearted as a
child; vigorous of mind and body, he endured
the hardships of the frontiers, survived the dangers of many battles, and finally followed the
majority of his pioneer friends and comrades
who had preceded him. He now lies peacefully
in the beautiful Boise Valley, awaiting the final
call. He was in life a sturdy and brave comrade, a true and loyal friend.

CHAPTER XXI.

CONSTITUTIONAL CONVENTION.

THE years following 1880, and including 1889, witnessed the most extensive and permanent improvements yet made within the Territory, railroad building being extensively prosecuted during those years.

During that era the Oregon Short Line, the Utah Northern, and the Wood River and the Boise branches were completed; also the Northern Pacific, and the Moscow branch of the O. R. & N. A line of railroad had also been built into Wardner and Wallace, giving impetus to the development of the Cœur d'Alene mines, the permanency and value of which had already been determined. New and prosperous towns sprung into existence like magic, while the old and fossilized marts of trade took on new life. Each succeeding month brought new arrivals of men and women who brought their household goods and were prepared to make Idaho their future home. School houses were built, churches erected, and a spirit of peace and prosperity prevailed.

The Indians which had caused so much trouble were assigned to their respective reservations, and confidence in the future of Idaho had arrived to remain. The mines were yielding their annual output of the precious metals, without stint or diminution, the hills and valleys were dotted with flocks and herds, the farmers rejoiced in bountiful harvests, and the enjoyment of peaceful homes. The rollicking cowboy, the modest and retiring shepherd, the lusty miner and the boisterous lumber-jack, all, all, were happy and content.

But little historical interest is attached to any of the proceedings of the succeeding sessions of the Idaho Territorial Legislature, except it may be of interest to future residents of this country to know that it was the practice for a number of years for the Territorial Legislature to dissolve the bonds of matrimony; the members not only enacted laws, but sat as a divorce court.

The following is a sample of the manner in which divorces were formally granted in Idaho Territory:

DIVORCING—FALLON & FALLON.

AN ACT

To Dissolve the Bonds of Matrimony now Existing Between Martin Fallon and Mary Fallon, his Wife.

Be it enacted by the Legislative Assembly of the Territory of Idaho, as follows:

Section 1. That the bonds of matrimony heretofore and now existing, between Martin Fallon and Mary Fallon, his wife, be, and the same are hereby dissolved, and declared void.

Sec. 2.   This act shall take effect and be in force from and after its passage.

Approved February 9, 1881.

The foregoing is but one of several similar acts recorded in the General Laws of Idaho Territory.   (See Enactments of Ninth, Tenth and Eleventh Sessions, 1876-1881.)

While the resources of Idaho were undergoing such rapid development during the decade between and including the years 1880 and 1889, the adjacent territories of Montana, Wyoming, and Washington were enjoying a similar degree of prosperity, the territories of Montana and Washington having outstripped the Territory of Idaho in population.

All the territories were now anxious to be admitted to statehood, but especially persistent were the two Dakotas, Montana, Washington and Idaho.   The four first mentioned were believed to have sufficient population and taxable wealth to entitle them to admission, consequently enabling acts were passed looking to that object, but the population of Idaho, as well as that of Wyoming, was deemed insufficient to entitle them to equal rank with the older and larger commonwealths. Both the territories of Wyoming and Idaho, being especially favored with the possession of that particular type of genus homo in whom tenacity of purpose is largely developed, resolved to continue their efforts for admission.

On April 2, 1889, the Territorial Governor, Hon. E. A. Stevenson, issued a proclamation re-

questing the people to elect delegates to a constitutional convention to meet in Boise City at noon,
the fourth day of July of that year. This meeting was to be held for the purpose of framing a
constitution for the proposed state of Idaho and
the proclamation prescribed the qualifications
and apportionment of members, who were to
total seventy-two. The proclamation thus issued
was not authorized by law, and consequently the
county commissioners could not appoint election
officers, or use public funds to pay them for their
services; nor was there any provision to pay the
per diem and mileage of the delegates.

The foregoing call failed in its purpose of
convening a constitutional convention, and Hon.
George L. Shoup, who was appointed April 1,
1889, to succeed Governor Stevenson to the office
of Governor of Idaho Territory, issued another
call on May 11, 1889. Governor Shoup's call
was slightly different from the one issued by
Governor Stevenson and resulted in the choosing of delegates to a convention to be assembled
at Boise City July 4, 1889—at the same time and
place named in the former call.

There were, and perhaps are, even today,
persons who cannot conceive how it might be
possible for an assemblage of citizens, such as
composed the convention which framed the constitution of Idaho, to be called without an effort
being made to secure some advantage for one
of the political parties. But, if such an effort
was made, it failed in its accomplishment, for in

no manner could there have been chosen an equal number of delegates who would have been more earnest in their endeavor to promote in an unselfish and non-partisan manner the welfare of the proposed state of Idaho. They labored faithfully and arduously, and the result of their efforts was a constitution than which no better was ever presented to any constituency for ratification.

All questions likely to interest the people were covered, and it provided for an economical administration of state government.

Its various articles were discussed, section after section, by the able lawyers who were members of the convention—not as the attorneys of certain interests, but as patriotic and loyal citizens, which they were.

The members concluded their labors and affixed their signatures to the instrument which they had drafted, on the sixth day of August, 1889.

The following persons were duly accredited delegates to the convention which framed the constitution of the State of Idaho, all of whom affixed their signatures thereto except P. J. Pefley, of Ada County:

Wm. H. Claggett, *Pres.*	Wm. H. Hammell.
Geo. Ainslie.	H. S. Hampton.
W. C. B. Allen.	H. O. Harkness.
Robt. Anderson	Frank Harris.
H. Armstrong.	Sol. Hasbrouck.
Orlando B. Batten.	C. M. Hays.

Frank W. Beane.

Jas. H. Beatty.

J. W. Ballentine.

A. D. Bevan

Henry B. Blake

Frederick Campbell.

Frank P. Cavanah.

A. S. Chaney.

Chas. A. Clark.

I. N. Coston.

Jas. I. Crutcher.

Stephen S. Glidden.

John S. Gray.

John T. Morgan.

Aaron F. Parker.

A. J. Pinkham.

P. J. Pefley.

W. D. Robbins.

Aug. M. Sinnott.

Drew W. Standrod.

Frank Steunenberg.

Sam F. Taylor.

J. L. Underwood.

John Lemp.

N. I. Andrews.

J. W. Brigham.

W. B. Heyburn.

John Hogan.

J. M. Howe.

E. S. Jewell.

Geo. W. King.

H. B. Kinport.

Jas. W. Lamoreaux.

John Lewis.

Wm. C. Maxey.

A. E. Mayhew.

W. J. McConnell.

Henry Melder.

John H. Meyer.

A. B. Moss.

A. J. Pierce.

J. W. Poe.

Jas. W. Reid.

Wm. H. Savidge.

James M. Shoup.

Homer Stull.

Willis Sweet.

Lycurgus Vineyard.

J. S. Whitton.

Edgar Wilson.

W. W. Woods.

Samuel J. Pritchard.

Mr. Pefley explained his reason for refusing to sign the instrument he had ·helped to create as follows:

"I always think consistency is a jewel highly prized, and inasmuch as there are sections in there that I could not endorse when they passed as sections or articles, I cannot now conscientiously sign the constitution and therefore ask to be excused."

Mr. Pefley objected to the preamble, which is as follows: "We, the people of the state of Idaho, grateful to Almighty· God for our freedom, to secure its blessings and promote our common welfare, do establish this constitution."

John S. Gray, who was also a member from Ada county, explained Pefley's action by stating that Pefley had had a "falling out with God," and was not willing to tender him an expression of gratitude.

A committee of ten members was appointed to draft an address to the people, the following being a copy of the address they reported:

ADDRESS TO THE PEOPLE OF IDAHO.

BOISE CITY, *August 6, 1889.*

To the People of Idaho:

The convention convened at Boise City on July 4, 1889, to frame a constitution for the state of Idaho, has completed its labors.

The constitution so framed will be submitted to you for approval or rejection on November 5, 1889.

Before adjournment, the convention by resolution appointed the undersigned as a committee to lay before you the reasons why the constitution should be adopted, and this duty we now fulfil.

DISADVANTAGES OF A TERRITORIAL GOVERNMENT.

The territorial system of government under which we have lived for the past twenty-six years is in direct conflict with the spirit of republican and democratic institutions.

We have no voice in the selection of the most important officers who administer our local affairs, no voice in the enactment of laws by congress to which we must yield obedience; and no voice in the election of the chief magistrate of the Republic, who appoints the principal officers, by whom the executive and judicial affairs of our territory are administered.

We are held in a state of political vassalage, similar in many respects to that in which the American colonies were held by Great Britain.

Governments are instituted for the purpose of securing to all men their natural and inalienable right to life, libery and the pursuit of happiness, and all rightful governments derive their just powers from the consent of the governed.

Taxation without the right of representation, among all people who love freedom, has ever been held a valid complaint against the governing power.

While a territory, congress, in which we have no voice or other adequate representation, can at any time annul any act passed by our legislature, and under a present law of congress placing limitations and restrictions upon the power of the Territorial legislature, no great public work or improvement in the interest of the people, no matter how necessary it may be to the development of our mineral or agricultural resources, can be inaugurated or carried out.

Under the congressional alien land act, no alien can own or hold lands in the territory, and this prohibition shuts the door to the influx and the investment of foreign capital in our mines containing precious and useful metals, thus retarding and almost paralyzing the development of our unlimited resources, and depriving labor of its most encouraging and inviting fields of employment.

Our school lands lie unoccupied, returning no revenue for the education of our children, and are not open to purchase by those seeking homes among us, thus retarding immigration, and that great increase in population to which our natural resources and unexampled healthfulness of climate entitle us.

A territory cannot have a settled public policy. The fact that congress may at any time annul its legislation on any matter of pure local concern, prevents active co-operation by the people on those higher planes of public life which result in the establishment of a permanent state policy.

The abuse of the veto power of alien governors who in the past have been, and who in the future may again be sent among us, is one of which we have had more than one example of sad experience by which the people have been discouraged.

The most intolerable evil, however, under which we have lived for the past twenty-five years, has been the changing and shifting character of our judicial decisions, by which we have been deprived of the inestimable benefit of judicial precedents as a safeguard to our rights of person and property.

Scarcely has one judge, sent to us from abroad, obtained even a slight insight into the laws and customs of the territory, before another coming into his room has undone the work of his predecessor, and this chronic condition of change has left all of our business and property interests in a constant state of doubt and uncertainty.

To make confusion worse confounded, we have been denied an appeal from these raw and inexperienced decisions to an independent supreme court, under the territorial system of having the judge below review his own judgments on appeal, while the small judicial force of the territory (unable or incompetent to perform the duties devolving upon it) causes our calendars to be overburdened with causes, and such justice as we at last obtain to be delayed until litigants are ruined.

To meet this great want of the people, the constitution has provided a Judicial Department, ample, but not too great to promptly decide all questions of controversy and secure a revision of all decisions by an independent supreme court.

Although the expense of this department is

large, it is no greater than our necessities compel, and in the prompt determination of all causes, the people will find that their burdens, direct and indirect, will be greatly lessened.

Statehood will Save Annually $55,290 to the Taxpayers of Idaho.

Some objection has been urged against statehood on the ground that the cost of government will be greatly increased.

In framing the constitution the convention has kept this objection constantly in mind, and it affords us great satisfaction to announce to the taxpayers of Idaho that the aggregate cost of the state and county governments under the proposed constitution will be $55,290 less annually than under the present territorial government.

This result is reached by the following statement of the cost of the new state government, to-wit:

Annual expense of Executive Department ....$ 20,220
Annual expense of Judiciary Department 38,220
Annual expense of Legislative Department 15,110
Annual expense of Insane Asylum 20,000
Annual expense of Penitentiary 23,075
Annual interest on all outstanding bonds 10,200
Annual expense of State University 11,000
All other expenses 300

Total cost of State Government under the proposed constitution $138,125
Total annual cost of present territorial government to the taxpayers of Idaho ....$ 84,365

Increase of cost of state government ....$ 53,760

By changing the system of county government now in vogue to that proposed by the constitution, by which officers are to be paid fees instead of salaries, there will be saved annually to the counties of the state the following amounts, to-wit:

Salaries of Sheriffs	$ 36,000
Salaries of Auditors and Recorders	15,000
Salaries of Probate Judges	10,260
Salaries of County District Attorneys	34,200
Salaries of County Superintendents of Public Instruction	7,020
Salaries of Clerks of District Courts	6,570
Total annual saving in county government under the constitution	$109,050
Increase in cost of state over territorial government	53,760
Annual net saving to taxpayers	$ 55,290

In addition to the above in many instances the fees of officers will amount annually to a sum greater than the maximum compensation allowed them.

This excess will go into the county treasury for the benefit of the taxpayers. It is believed that in few instances will any minimum compensation have to be made up. Thus it will be seen that the state and county governments under the proposed constitution will cost the taxpayers $55,290 per annum less than the present territorial and county governments.

Diminution of School Taxes to Be Obtained by Statehood.

The school land which will belong to the new state of Idaho will consist of Sections 16 and 36 of every Township, and 500,000 acres granted under Section 2378 of the Revised Statutes of the United States, all of which in round numbers will amount to over 3,340,000 acres, and at $10 per acre are valued at $33,400,000.

Of these the constitution provides that no more than 25 sections, 16,000 acres, shall be sold annually. In ten years there would be sold 160,-000 acres. Estimated at the minimum price of $10 per acre, the total sum realized by the sale of this land in ten years will be $1,600,000. This sum should certainly yield six (6) per cent net, which would give an annual income of $96,000. Besides this revenue, the lands thus sold are immediately subject to taxation, and the revenue obtained from these lands in the way of taxes will decrease the general annual levies.

As the school tax constitutes a large part of the expense of government, and as the revenue derived from school lands will enable the legislature in a short time to reduce the school levies to almost nothing, it is easy to see that your taxes will be greatly reduced, in this respect, by a state government.

With statehood there will be available other public lands, as follows:

University grant .... 46,000 acres
Penitentiary lands .... 160 acres
Agricultural College lands .... 90,000 acres
Scientific School lands .... 100,000 acres
Normal School lands .... 100,000 acres
Charitable institutions .... 300,000 acres
Public Buildings .... 32,000 acres

The proceeds from the sale of these lands will provide all necessary buildings for the respective purposes mentioned, and eventually furnish a sufficient income for their maintenance. Until statehood is secured all these public lands are unavailable for the purpose of relieving taxation and furnishing homes for settlers.

Character of the Constitution.

The convention that framed the constitution was in no sense a partisan one. In its organization both political parties were represented by delegates from every county. Strong Republican counties sent minorities of Democratic, and democratic counties minorities of Republican delegates. This happy combination of political forces was reflected in the spirit which at every stage of its deliberations animated the convention.

Every material, industrial and professional interest was represented in its membership, and it was wholly free from outside influences.

The business and taxpaying portion of our people was especially prominent and watchful of every interest of vital concern.

We believe that the constitution finally adopted is in an eminent degree a conservatively progressive one. The powers conferred upon the legislature are commensurate with the needs of the state, while the restrictions placed upon legislative action are such as experience in other states has shown to be wholesome or necessary.

A careful perusal of its provisions will, we think, satisfy any candid mind that a state government administered in harmony with its spirit and intent, will cause an immediate and wonderful increase in population, and in the wealth and the happiness of the people.

For a quarter of a century the pioneers of Idaho have been patiently laying the foundation of the future state. They have at all times upheld the power and dignity of the nation. Those who emigrated hither in the first flush of early manhood, are now gray with age, and surrounded by their children and grandchildren.

They have partly redeemed the wilderness which they found, and by their heroic sacrifices paved the way for the higher civilization upon which they are entering. They remember with inexpressible tenderness their old homes in the East, and long to be again restored to the full rights of citizenship under the constitution of the United States.

To accomplish this end we respectfully invite you to give the constitution submitted herewith a candid consideration, and ratify the same by your suffrages.

WM. H. CLAGGETT, *Shoshone County.*

A. J. PINKHAM, *Alturas County.*

CHAS. M. HAYS, *Owyhee County.*

WM. J. McCONNELL, *Latah County.*

HENRY ARMSTRONG, *Logan County.*

GEO. AINSLIE, *Boise County.*

JAS. W. REID, *Nez Perce County.*

S. F. TAYLOR, *Bingham County.*

CHAS. A. CLARK, *Ada County.*

FRANK P. CAVANAH, *Elmore County.*

The foregoing address to the people of Idaho was given wide circulation throughout the Territory, and the electors were given ample opportunity to consider whether it was desirable for the territory to become a state, approximately three months being allowed to intervene before the constitution was submitted to the voters for adoption or rejection.

A constitutional election was held November 5, 1889, at which election the constitution was ratified by an almost unanimous vote.

The citizens of Idaho were then in a position to ask the congress of the United States to admit Idaho as one of the Unions of States; a bill was accordingly prepared and introduced entitled "An Act to Provide for the Admission of the State of Idaho into the Union." Hon. George L. Shoup who was then governor of the territory, ex-Governor Stevenson, James McNab, and the writer, W. J. McConnell, went to Washington as a volunteer delegation to aid our then delegate, Hon. Fred T. Dubois, in securing the passage of the admission act.

It was apparent soon after the introduction of the bill that the admission of Idaho was regarded with favor by the prominent members of both houses regardless of political affiliations, and accordingly the bill was passed and received the approval of the president July 3, 1890. With that stroke of the president's pen closed the career of the infant Idaho, and ended her eventful history as a territory, thus closing the last chapter of this narrative.

APPENDIX

TO

THE EARLY HISTORY OF IDAHO

*Including a Roster of the Ter-
ritorial Delegates and the
Record Made by Each.*

APPENDIX.

DELEGATES FROM IDAHO TERRITORY.

DELEGATE	CONGRESS	YEARS
William H. Wallace, *Lewiston*	38th	1863-1865
E. D. Holbrook, *Idaho City*	39th	1865-1867
E. D. Holbrook, *Idaho City*	40th	1867-1869
Jacob K. Shafer, *Idaho City*	41st	1869-1871
Samuel A. Merritt, *Idaho City*	42nd	1871-1873
John Hailey, *Boise City*	43rd	1873-1875
Thomas W. Bennett, *Boise City*	44th	1875-1877
Stephen S. Fenn, *Mount Idaho*	44th	1875-1877
Stephen S. Fenn, *Mount Idaho*	45th	1877-1879
George Ainslie, *Idaho City*	46th	1879-1881
George Ainslie, *Idaho City*	47th	1881-1883
Theodore F. Singiser, *Boise City*	48th	1883-1885
John Hailey, *Boise City*	49th	1885-1887
Fred T. Dubois, *Blackfoot*	50th	1887-1889

THIRTY-EIGHTH CONGRESS, FIRST SESSION.
December 7th, 1863, to July 4th, 1864.

Wallace, William H., Remarks by, on

MR. WALLACE, of Idaho. I move that the House
proceed to the business upon the Speaker's table, to
take up House Bill No. 15, to provide a temporary government for the Territory of Montana, and that the
House further insist upon its disagreement to the amendments of the Senate, and ask for a further free conference on the disagreeing votes between the two houses.

MR. PENDLETON. I ask to have entered a motion to
adhere.

MR. WALLACE. That would kill the bill.

The previous question was seconded and the main
question ordered.

MR. PENDLETON demanded the yeas and nays on the
motion to insist.

The yeas and nays were ordered. The question was
taken and it was decided in the affirmative—yeas 69,
nays 55. So the motion was agreed to.

MR. WALLACE moved to reconsider the vote just tak-
en; and also moved that the motion to reconsider be
laid on the table. The latter motion was agreed to.

HOUSE BILL NO. 405.

To Provide Internal Revenue to Support the Government,
to Pay Interest on the Public Debt, and
for Other Purposes.

MR. WALLACE. I move to amend this section by striking out the proviso, which is in these words: *Provided:* That all such duties accruing upon gold and silver produced as aforesaid shall be due and payable in coin or bullion. Mr. Chairman, I think this is the only instance in this bill where a distinction is made in the character of the payments required to be made by the people. The miners are required to pay in coin or in gold or silver bullion. I ask the committee whether there is any fair and good reason for making such a distinction. The government of the United States has flooded the Pacific coast with paper money. Every person engaged in business there, whether he is running a rum-mill, a billiard-saloon, or a bowling-alley, can pay the tax required of him in the paper currency of the country issued by the government itself. But when you come to the miner, the most meritorious class of people in that section of the country, you require him to pay his taxes in gold or silver. When the tax-gatherer comes around, and the miner presents to him the paper currency issued by the government, it is repudiated. Why should congress place the government in that position, repudiating its paper, and requiring the miner to pay in coin or gold or silver bullion, while every other person can pay his taxes in the currency of the country? For that reason, and believing that this is an inequality which is odious and offensive, I have offered the amendment.

Tellers were ordered on the amendment. So the amendment was agreed to.

INDIAN APPROPRIATION BILL.

MR. WALLACE. I apprehend if the gentlemen from Iowa were familiar with the cost of transportation there he would not have moved this amendment. This appropriation is based on an estimate made by the Indian department, who are aware of the cost of transportation from year to year. If the Missouri river is navigable at the time, the cost of transporting these goods may be less than $17,000; but if, on the other hand, the river is not navigable, it is questionable whether that sum will cover the transportation. I will say to my friend from Iowa that the Missouri river at that point is navigable in the most favorable seasons only two months out of the twelve, and frequently goods which have been sent up to that point have had to be landed at points three, four, and five hundred miles below, and then transported by land.

For these reasons I hope that the motion made by the gentleman from Iowa will not prevail. (The motion of Mr. Hubbard of Iowa was to strike out $17,000 and insert $10,000.) So the Hubbard amendment was agreed to.

MR. WALLACE. I move to amend by striking out "$20,000" and inserting "$25,000." I will state that the appropriation made for similar objects in all the other territories is $25,000, while in the Territory of Idaho now there is a larger area of country and more Indians to take care of, and consequently more danger of collision between them and the whites than in any other Territory. I think the appropriation should be at least as large as for the other territories.

The amendment was agreed to.

THIRTY-EIGHTH CONGRESS, SECOND SESSION.
December 5, 1864, to March 3, 1865.

Wallace, William H., Remarks by, on Sundry Civil Appropriation Bill.

MR. WALLACE. The amount of $10,000 is not enough to meet the wants of Idaho. There is, and has been, a great demand for lands upon which to settle, and the settlers want these lands surveyed, so that they may pay the price to the government and secure their titles. Unless this appropriation is made that cannot be done. I know the immigration that is flowing into the territory of Idaho; I know the wants of these people, and I know, sir, that this appropriation is needed. * * * * * * * The squatters are not interfered with, yet so long as the lands are unsurveyed, and they cannot procure patents from the government, the settlers are unwilling to go on and make the improvement that they otherwise would do. In order that the lands may be surveyed and these improvements may go on, I ask this appropriation may be made.

The question was taken on Mr. Wallace's amendment and it was agreed to.

THIRTY-NINTH CONGRESS, FIRST SESSION.
December 4, 1865 to July 28, 1866.

Holbrook, E. D. No remarks in this Session. Branch Mint in Idaho.

MR. HOLBROOK, by unanimous consent, submitted the following preamble and resolution, which was read, considered and agreed to:

Whereas, The recent discoveries of the vast and extensive mineral fields of the interior, which the patient

and laborious toil of miners has developed, demonstrates
that the deposits of precious metals in the Territory of
Idaho are unsurpassed in richness and extent by those
of any other country, and which it will take the continued labor of ages to exhaust; and whereas the unnecessary delay, expense, and danger attending the transportation of said precious metals a great distance for the
purpose of coinage would be entirely removed by the
construction of a United States branch mint in the
immediate vicinity of this great mineral center, would
tend to a rapid and full development of the mineral resources, and be of incalculable advantage and benefit to
the inhabitants of that section of our country as well as
a source of revenue to the Government, therefore, be it

Resolved, That the Committee on Mines and Mining
be instructed to inquire into the expediency of changing
the location of the United States branch mint from The
Dalles, in the State of Oregon, to Boise City, in the
Territory of Idaho, and that they report by bill or
otherwise.

THIRTY-NINTH CONGRESS, SECOND SESSION.
December 3, 1866 to March 3, 1867.

Holbrook, E. D.   No remarks in this Session.

FORTIETH CONGRESS, FIRST SESSION.
March 4, 1867, to December 2, 1867.

*Holbrook, E. D., Remarks by, on.   Presented one Petition
and Introduced one Bill.   No remarks this session.*

FORTIETH CONGRESS, SECOND SESSION.
December 2, 1867 to November 10, 1868.

Holbrook, E. D., Bills Introduced By.

No. 261.   To establish post routes in the Territory of
Idaho.

No. 262.   Authorizing a survey of the southern
boundary line of the Territory of Idaho.

No. 263.   Amendatory of the Organic Act of Idaho
Territory by extending the jurisdiction of justices of the
peace.

No. 264.   To locate and establish an assay office in
the Territory.

No. 265.   To reimburse the people of the Territory
of Idaho for losses sustained by Indian depredations and
for moneys expended in protecting their property against
hostile Indians.

No. 266.   To reimburse the citizens of Wasco, Umatilla, Union, Grant and Baker counties for losses sustained by Indian depredations.

No. 299. Extending the preemption and homestead laws of the United States in the Territory of Idaho.

No. 408. Granting aid in the construction of a railroad and telegraph line from the Union Pacific railroad to Idaho; Portland (Oregon), Montana and Puget Sound.

No. 652. To increase the compensation of registers and receivers in the Territory of Idaho.

Holbrook, E. D., Resolutions Submitted by.

In relation to the payment of salaries to territorial officers absent from their duties.

Holbrook, E. D., Remarks by, on Sundry Civil Appropriation Bill.

The Clerk read the following: For surveying the public lands in Idaho, at rates not exceeding fifteen dollars per mile for standard line, twelve dollars for township, and ten dollars for section lines, $15,000.

MR. HOLBROOK. I move to amend the paragraph just read by striking out "fifteen" and inserting "twenty-five." I desire to state in connection with this amendment that the land officers of Idaho Territory recommended the appropriation of $35,000 as being absolutely necessary for carrying on the surveys of public lands in that Territory. The Commissioner of Public Lands recommended to the Secretary of the Interior an appropriation of $25,000, which is small enough. This is the amount proposed in my amendment, which I hope will be adopted.

(The committee divided and the tellers reported—ayes 43, nays 55. So the amendment was not agreed to).

I desire to ask the gentleman from Illinois (MR. WASHBURNE) a question in this connection. I desire to know why it is that he appeals to members of this House and asks them to vote an appropriation of $15,000 for the survey of lands in Washington Territory, and why he asks an appropriation of $25,000 for Colorado, and refuses a like appropriation for Montana, when there is the same amount of population today settled in the Territory of Montana, where there never has been a survey made, where there is absolutely more need of it than in either of the places I have mentioned, where mineral lodes are being taken up, and where surveys have to be made before a person can acquire title to any mineral lands that he may locate. As has been mentioned by the gentleman from Montana (MR. CAVANAUGH) there are hundreds of valleys in that Territory where there are settlers who desire to make improvements. They do not know whether those improvements are going to become theirs permanently, or whether, when the surveys are completed, a portion of the lands they have taken up, and upon which they have constructed their houses and planted their orchards, will not be divided by township lines, and that their improvements are not going into the hands of some one who has done nothing to improve the valleys of that vast section of country. I trust that the amendment offered by the gentleman from Montana will be adopted, and I appeal to the members of the House not to make this discrimination against that Territory.

The gentleman from Illinois (MR. WASHBURNE) has not yet answered my question, and I again ask him to do so. I want him to tell this House why this discrimination is made against Montana Territory. They have reported in favor of $15,000 for Washington Territory; $25,000 for Oregon; $15,000 for Idaho Territory; $25,000 for Colorado Territory, etc., while only $5,000 is appropriated for Montana Territory.

MR. WASHBURNE. We found there was no land to be surveyed there, and therefore there was no necessity for any appropriation for that purpose.

On the Resolution to Print the Report of J. Ross Browne.

MR. HOLBROOK. I would ask the gentleman (MR. ASHLEY of Nevada) if he does not know that four-fifths of the report is taken up with the description of mines in his own state, and more particularly of one mine—the Comstock ledge.

Mr. Speaker, I have only a word to say in regard to this proposition. The gentleman from Nevada (MR. ASHLEY) in his remarks on this subject, seems to suppose that I am opposed to the printing of this report. Such is not the case. I believe the country will derive a vast amount of information from the report. It will call the attention of the eastern section of the country to our mines in the distant west. It will doubtless be the means to some extent of inducing capitalists to make investments in that country, which we at the present time very much need. But, sir, I cannot allow that report to go unchallenged and uncontradicted, so far as its statements concern the territory of Idaho. I do not mean to censure Mr. Browne for the report which he has made. Considering the comparatively small amount of the appropriation made by congress for the purpose of carrying out this examination, it was impossible for Mr. Browne to go there and devote to the work the time necessary to enable him to make an accurate and truthful report. No man starting from New York and crossing this continent, passing over hundreds of thousands of square miles of mineral territory, and spending there a period of only about sixty days, could undertake to make a full and accurate report in regard to the mineral resources of that country.

A great portion of that report, however, I can heartily endorse, believing it to contain information valuable to the country; and I rose only for the purpose of correcting the impression which might have been created by the remarks of the gentleman from Nevada, that I oppose the printing of the report. My object was not to advertise the mines of Idaho.

April 15, 1868, indefinite leave of absence was granted to Mr. Stewart, Mr. Holbrook and Mr. Laflin.

FORTIETH CONGRESS, THIRD SESSION.
December 7, 1868, to March 4, 1869.

Holbrook, E. D., Remarks by, on Indian Appropriation Bill.

MR. HOLBROOK. I would like to make an inquiry of the gentleman from Massachusetts (MR. BUTLER). In proposing to strike out "eleven" and to insert "twelve," as the number of superintendents he states it is for the purpose of providing a superintendent for the Crow Indians. I wish to call his attention to the fact that in the Indian appropriation bill of last year the superintendencies of the Territories of Montana and Idaho were united. I think the gentleman is now convinced that a superintendency embracing those two Territories is too large; that it is impossible for one superintendent to attend to all the business for those two Territories. I therefore ask the gentleman to amend his amendment so as to increase the number of superintendents to thirteen. I have a letter here in my possession from the first person who was appointed to the superintendency of these territories after they were united. He has had much experience with various tribes of Indians in the west, and he states that it is an utter impossibility for one superintendent to attend to all the business pertaining to those two Territories. *   *   *   I believe that I have consulted with every member but one of the Committee on Appropriations, and they have agreed that the Territories of Montana and Idaho should be separated, and each have a superintendent.

MR. BUTLER. When we reach the proper place in this bill it is my intention to move an amendment which will give a superintendent to each of those Territories.

MR. HOLBROOK. Now, Mr. Chairman, there are some facts connected with the Indian affairs in the Territory of Idaho, with which I presume the gentlemen of this House are familiar. There are more Indians in the Territory of Idaho than in any other separate territory in the United States. I presume gentlemen are not unaware of the fact that citizens of the Territory of Idaho within the last two years have lost more property because of the Indian war and Indian disturbances than the people of all the rest of the territories combined. Why, sir, we have lost more than two millions of property in a single county of that territory through the hostile acts of the Indians. The Committee on Appropriations have reduced the appropriations for Idaho to the same amount which is allowed to the Territory of Utah, where they have not had an Indian war for many years past. I therefore move that the appropriation for Idaho Territory be increased to $30,000 and I trust that there will be no objection to the amendment.

The amendment was disagreed to.

MR. HOLBROOK. I am not replying to the Committee on Appropriations, because they stated the other day that they had made a pro rata reduction in the appro-

priation for the Territory of Idaho without taking into
consideration the outside surrounding circumstances connected with the case.   And after the gentleman having
charge of this bill saw fit to silence delegates here by
raising points of order, and making assertions which he
knew at the time he made them to be unqualifiedly
false——

The SPEAKER. The Chair must arrest the remarks
of the gentleman from Idaho. He certainly is not now
in order.

MR. HOLBROOK. I am aware that what I have said
is not parliamentary.

MR. BENJAMIN. I ask that the words used by the
Delegate from Idaho (MR. HOLBROOK) be taken down in
writing, read from the Clerk's desk, and ruled upon by
the speaker.

The words having been reduced to writing, were
read by the Clerk as follows:

And after the gentleman having charge of this bill
saw fit to silence delegates here by raising points of
order, and making assertions which he knew at the time
he made them to be unqualifiedly false——

The SPEAKER. The Chair rules that these words
are out of order, both as being unparliamentary and as
being indecorous.   Where a member states that what
another member has said is not true that is not unparliamentary, because it is possible that the member may
have been mistaken.   But when a gentleman states that
a member on this floor has declared that which he knew
to be unqualifiedly false, that is the most insulting language that can be uttered in a parliamentary body.

MR. HOLBROOK. I would like to ask a question of
the Chair.

MR. BENJAMIN. I object, until the words which the
Chair has declared to be unparliamentary have been re-
tracted.

MR. HOLBROOK. I do not propose to retract any
words I have used.

The SPEAKER. The gentleman from Idaho (MR.
HOLBROOK) is not in order. The gentleman from Massachusetts (MR. BUTLER) is entitled to fourteen minutes
remaining of his hour.

MR. SCHENCK. I offer the following resolution, and
on it demand the previous question: *Resolved,* That
E. D. Holbrook, Delegate from the Territory of Idaho,
having distinctly uttered in the presence of the House
the following words in debate: "and after the *   *   *
(see statement of Mr. Holbrook, 10 and 11). The resolution was adopted.

The SPEAKER. The sergeant-at-arms will execute
the order of the House.

Mr. Holbrook appeared at the bar of the House, accompanied by the sergeant-at-arms.

The SPEAKER. Mr. Holbrook, oftentimes in a deliberative body, in the discussion of exciting questions,
language is used which, when attention is called to it,
is promptly withdrawn. We are all fallible, and hence

are liable to yield sometimes to the temptation to indulge in language not seemly or proper; but when the remark employed is offensive in its character, and apparently, from the construction of the sentence, intended to be insulting, and when, an opportunity being given for its withdrawal, that opportunity is not taken advantage of, thus reiterating the insult, to a fellow-member uttered upon the floor of the House, it has always been deemed by deliberative assemblies censurable by the body with which both members are connected. This instance is, in the opinion of the House, of that character, and the House has instructed its speaker to censure you at the bar. I therefore by the order of the House, pronounce upon you its censure for the language which you have uttered in its hearing. You will resume your seat.

Following this censure Mr. Holbrook submitted a few remarks on the Army appropriation bill, not important; likewise on the Deficiency and Sundry Civil appropriation bills.

FORTY-FIRST CONGRESS, FIRST SESSION.
March 4, 1869, to April 10, 1869.

Shafer, J. K. No Remarks during this Session.

FORTY-FIRST CONGRESS, SECOND SESSION.
December 6, 1869 to July 15, 1870.

Shafer, J. K.

Mr. Shafer introduced fifteen bills and resolutions, none of importance.

Remarks by, on Deficiency Appropriation Bill.

MR. SHAFER. Mr. Chairman, I have no objection to the clause as it stands except that it appropriates these amounts to certain individuals, specifically naming them. Now, the fact is that many of those claims since they have become due have been assigned to one party or another. And all I desire is that where the claims have been assigned to other parties the parties to whom they have been assigned shall have the benefit of this act. If the paragraph passes in its present form it will be ineffectual and nugatory, as far as one-half, or one-third of these claims are concerned. And therefore I desire the insertion at each of the places I have indicated of the words "or their assigns." (The amendment was not agreed to).

FORTY-FIRST CONGRESS, THIRD SESSION.
December 5, 1870 to March 4, 1871.

Shafer, Jacob K., Remarks by, on the Bill Relating to a Government for Wyoming and Utah Territories.

MR. SHAFER. I wish to be understood that this law has been applicable for several years to the Territory of

Idaho, and that the people of that Territory regard it as bad in principle and worse in practice. In some of the more remote counties from the capital of the Territory but a single term of the court has been held in each year. Every lawyer knows that there ought to be two terms of the court in every county in each year. If this thing is allowed to go on in the other Territories as it is now in Idaho the courts will not be held as they ought to be. They have not been held regularly in that Territory, and I have no reason to believe they will be held more regularly in the other Territories.

Sundry Civil Appropriation Bill.

MR. SHAFER. I move in line four hundred and thirteen, to strike out "$20,000" and insert "$30,000." The appropriations for surveys heretofore made for this Territory of Idaho have been extremely limited, and the inconveniences which have resulted have been such that I have to ask the House to make this appropriation larger. In southern Idaho there is one settlement of about fifteen hundred persons who have been living there for four, five, or six years, and not one single acre of land has ever been surveyed. I have abundant assurance that next spring there will be a large immigration to the Bear river and Bear lake country. In northern Idaho also our surveys have been extremely limited, and it is very desirable, as that portion of the country has been settled up for five or six years, that those surveys should be made, so that the men who have settled there may acquire title to their lands.

There is another reason also for my amendment. There is a large body of mining lands in the Territory of Idaho, none of which have ever been surveyed, and it is desirable that they also be surveyed. I have therefore to ask the House to increase this appropriation from $20,000 to $30,000. I believe that in offering this amendment I have the concurrence of the chairman of the committee on Appropriations, and I trust there will be no objection to it. (The amendment was agreed to).

FORTY-SECOND CONGRESS, FIRST SESSION.
March 4, 1871, to April 20, 1871.

Merritt, Samuel A., Remarks by, on Deficiency Appropriation Bill.

MR. MERRITT. I move to amend by adding to the thirty-seventh amendment of the Senate the following:

That the appropriation for the survey of the boundary line between Idaho and Utah Territories, contained in the act making appropriations for sundry civil expenses of the Government for the year ending June 30, 1872, and for other purposes, approved March 3, 1871, is hereby made subject to present use.

The object of this amendment is to allow the Secretary of the Interior to expend immediately the amount appropriated by the Forty-first Congress for the establishment of the boundary line between Idaho and Utah. A portion of the boundary line is yet undefined, and consequently there are one thousand or fifteen hundred people who claim to belong to either Territory, according to circumstances. When the tax collector of Utah comes around they claim to be citizens of Idaho; when the tax collector of Idaho comes around they claim to be citizens of Utah. The best season to make the survey is during the months of May, June and July. After the water of the rivers has risen it will be impossible perhaps to make the survey, because a great portion of the line will be overflowed. The amount to be expended is only $6,400, and I imagine it cannot make much difference whether it is expended in the months of May, June and July, or in the months of July, August and September. I have consulted in regard to this amendment with the Delegate from Utah (MR. HOOPER) who has no objection to it. (So the amendment was agreed to.

FORTY-SECOND CONGRESS, SECOND SESSION.
December 4, 1871 to June 10, 1872.

Merritt, Samuel A., Remarks by, on Territorial Penitentiaries.

MR. MERRITT. I ask unanimous consent to offer for immediate consideration the following resolution:

Resolved: That the Attorney-General is directed to furnish to this House, at the earliest practicable time, a statement showing the cost of equipping and maintaining the penitentiaries in the Territories of Colorado, Montana and Idaho, from the time the marshals of said Territories took charge of said penitentiaries up to this date; also the number of persons confined therein convicted of offenses against the laws of the United States and of said Territories; also what contracts have been made with said Territories for keeping territorial convicts, and the sum of money paid by said several Territories for keeping territorial prisoners. (There being no objection, the resolution was adopted).

FORTY-SECOND CONGRESS, THIRD SESSION.
December 2, 1872, to March 3, 1873.

Merritt, Samuel A., Remarks by, on the Bill Relating to Territorial Penitentiaries.

MR. MERRITT. The territorial prisons are now in charge of the United States government, which pays for maintaining them, and the Territories pay so much for the maintenance of territorial prisoners, not less than one dollar, and sometimes as high as two dollars per day. I have here a statement furnished by the Department of Justice, as follows: * * * * * From that statement it will appear that the Colorado penitentiary cost for sixteen months the sum of $24,796.99. The amount received from the territory was $13,631.57. There was one Federal prisoner there for four months at a cost of $2,771.35 per month, or rather more than it would cost to maintain several members of Congress during that time. In Montana the cost of maintaining the penitentiary for sixteen months was $23,143.73; the amount received from the territory was $8,271. There was one federal prisoner maintained there for sixteen months at a cost of $929.54 per month. The cost of maintaining the Idaho State Penitentiary for 16 months was $8,398.32; the amount received from the territory was $1,729. The cost of maintaining three federal prisoners for thirteen months was $513.02 each per month.

MR. HOLMAN. From the statement of the gentleman this would appear to be a favorable arrangement.

MR. MERRITT. It will be advantageous to the Government, and advantageous to the Territories. There are very few Federal prisoners in the Territories, very few infractions of the Federal law. By the arrangement proposed in this bill the government will have to pay but a small sum in comparison with the present cost. I think this is a good arrangement for both the government and the Territories.

On the Bill regulating the Compensation of Members of Territorial Legislatures.

MR. MERRITT. I wish to correct the gentleman from Indiana (MR. HOLMAN). These bills were prepared to be reported by the committee on the Territories during the last session. This bill was ready to be reported at the last session. There was no disposition on the part of the committee—certainly none on the part of the gentleman who introduced the bill—to keep it back.

I will say further though in some of the Territories members of the legislature get six dollars per day, in others they get but four dollars, and in others three dollars—an amount totally inadequate to pay the ordinary expenses of such officers. We do not want, I hope, to starve members of Territorial Legislatures. They have no political influence, and there is just where the rub is. These salaries were fixed on the basis of thirty years ago, when we first organized the Territories. Everyone knows that the price of living is much higher now. The cost of living is greater, all the necessaries of life are much higher; and I say the governor of any one of the Territories cannot live as a gentleman at any such salaries in the Territories of Utah, Montana, Idaho, and some of the other Territories, as that which they now receive. A governor cannot live on a salary of $2,500 even if he is so fortunate as to have only one wife. How much less can it be done if he should happen to have **more than one wife?**

Now, while I may be in favor of just economy, we ought not to be so niggardly as to starve these men who are serving the government in these positions. (The pending amendment was agreed to).

FORTY-THIRD CONGRESS, FIRST SESSION.
December 1, 1873 to June 23, 1874.

Hailey, John.

No remarks during this session. Introduced ten bills.

FORTY-THIRD CONGRESS, SECOND SESSION.
December 7, 1874, to March 3, 1875.

Hailey, John.

No remarks in this session. No bills introduced. Presented one petition.

FORTY-FOURTH CONGRESS, FIRST SESSION.
December 6, 1875, to August 15, 1876.

Bennett, Thomas W., Resolution offered by

That the committee on Judiciary inquire into the expediency of granting to citizens of the Territories the privilege of voting for President and Vice-President. Referred.

Remarks by, on Legislative, Executive and Judicial Appropriation Bill.

MR. BENNETT. Mr. Chairman, I have with some care examined the bill reported to the House by the committee on Appropriations and now under consideration. And I am well convinced that many of its provisions, in relation to the governments in the Territories, should they become law, will work great hardship to the people of the Territories, seriously embarrass the administration of their governments, and greatly retard the growth of their people and the development of their resources.

I have several amendments prepared, which I propose to offer to the bill, as the proper sections are read by the Clerk, and at this time I desire only to submit some general remarks upon the bill as it applies to the Territories, in the hope that the House may reverse what I deem the hasty and unwise conclusions of the committee. Sweeping reductions have been reported in the appropriations for the Territories. These reductions were doubtless honestly made by the committee in the supposed interest of economy and retrenchment, and in so far as they subserve those purposes, I cheerfully acquiesce.

Mr. Chairman, neither myself nor the people whom I have the honor to represent are unaware of the universal demand of the American people for retrenchment, in the public expenditures of the Government, nor of the pressing necessity therefor. Everywhere, all over the country, in public and private life, in official and social circles, in politics and religion, are to be seen the ugly evidences and baneful influences of extravagances and its consequent demoralizations and corruptions. And he who attempts to fasten this stain upon the garments of any one class, or of any one party, simply insults the common intelligence, controverts the common history, and does violence to the common experience of the country. The evil has pervaded all elements of society and infected all political parties. We need not be at a loss to discover the prime cause of all this disorder and loss of public and private virtue, for it is but the natural result of a great civil war, and the demoralization which it created. Neither is it profitable to discuss the responsibilities of that war, for its causes, its operations, and its results have passed into history, and the brave men who met each other in the deadly strife where

> Once was felt the storm of war
> When it had an earthquake's roar,
> And flashed upon the mountain height
> And smoked along the shore——

now sit happily together under the "banner of beauty and glory," with each other vieing in the prayer:

> Peace, thy olive wand extend,
> And bid wild war his ravage end.

*   *   *   *   *

But the bill now under discussion aspires to apply the corrective in the direction of retrenchment. And to this the whole country gives its profound and grateful sanction. Too long have the people waited, watched, and prayed for this reform, while they have been answered with "a maximum of words and a minimum of deeds."

But, Mr. Chairman, I submit that the cheapest is not always the best, and every reduction of expense is not always economy. It is neither economy nor good husbandry to indiscriminately cut and prune the barren and the fruitful alike. Neither is it a good system of pruning which adopts an inflexible rule to cut all vines alike by a fixed percentage of measurement.

Mr. Chairman, I think I can show that the committee in their zeal for retrenchment have not used a proper discrimination, and that the per cent rule which they adopted worked great injustice and utterly fails to accomplish reform, but inflicts only evil where good was intended.

I will take the Territory of Idaho as an average example. This Territory was organized by an act of Congress, and is in every sense the creature of the Gov-

ernment. In area, the Territory is three times as large
as the State of Indiana. In beautiful scenery of snow-
capped mountains and lovely valleys, of grand cascades
and calm lakes, it far surpasses the famed land of the
Swiss, for I have seen them both. In beauty and salu-
brity of climate it is the peer of Italy, for I have enjoyed them both. Its great mountains are permeated
everywhere with quartz ledges and lodes of gold and
silver, while amid the sands of its streams and its bars
the freed golden dust glitters in the sun, forming a fabu-
lous array of marvelous deposits which will require the
industry of ages to develop and exhaust, while pasturage,
timber, fish and game are in inexhaustible supply. Talk
of your Hawaiian Island, and your treaties of reciprocity with them, here in Idaho we offer a reciprocity
backed by resources contrasting with those of the Ha-
wiian Islands as this great Republic of ours contrasts
with the land and hereditaments of his majesty King
Kalakua. The people who live out there are your sons
and your brothers   *   *   *   *   .   *   *   *

But you ask how can these things be avoided? I
answer that the Constitution should be so amended as to
do away entirely with the cumbrous and unfair machinery of an electoral college, and each qualified voter
of the Republic should be allowed to vote directly for
president, whether he is a citizen of the United States
residing in a state, or a citizen of the United States
residing in a territory.

Again, the people of the territories should be allowed
to elect their own officers, as do the people of the states.
In this way the people there would get their choice of
rulers and a great source of political patronage removed.
A bill is now pending before the committee on Territories for this purpose, and I understand will be reported
adversely to the House, for what reason I am unable to
perceive, unless it comes from that inordinate desire of
all sons of Adam to have somebody to rule over. Since
the war has enfranchised the negro and given him the
right of choosing his own rulers and of representation
in Congress, there is nobody left disfranchised but your
brothers in the territories.

Then, again, the people of the territories have no
representation in either house of congress. It is true
they are allowed the privilege of sending a delegate to
this House, who, if he conducts himself modestly and
does not meddle too much in public business is allowed
a chair to sit down in when he is tired, and listen to the
wit and the wisdom of the men who represent his old
home in the states who has never obeyed the injunc-
tion "Go west and grow up with the country," and be
disfranchised. It is true he is allowed to debate, but
after he has had his say, after he has exercised his
great constitutional right of "jaw-bone" and sits down
feeling that he has made the subject luminous with his
eloquence and his logic, the roll is called, and the representatives of the people in the states, including the colored brethren, vote, it may be, unanimously against his

26 E. H. I.

proposition, and he is not even allowed to vote for it, that he may go back to his constituents and parade his record in self-defense. And worse than that, the delegates are excluded from the committees of the House; even those committees whose business directly concerns the people of the territories, as for instance those of Mines and Mining, Indian Affairs, Military Affairs, Public Lands, Private Land Claims, Pacific Railroads, Commerce, and Post-offices and Post-roads. On all of these committees a delegate from his experience could be of invaluable service to the committee, to his constituents, and to the country, and having no vote, could not possibly do harm if he desired. * * * * *

Mr. Chairman, I shall not urge appropriations at this session outside our regular sums for the territorial government. I shall yield to the great demands of the people for retrenchment. We in Idaho are poor and needy. We have no capitol buildings, no United States court-house, our navigable rivers are obstructed, and we have no railroad or telegraph built by government subsidy, yet all I shall ask is to be let alone, and not robbed of our necessary and just appropriations because others have been extravagant. And to this end I beg, in the name of common justice, common honesty, common sense, common decency, and common brotherhood, that you let us keep what little we have, and, if you want to retrench, do it where it can be safely done, but be sure you do not mistake injustice for economy and cripple where you ought to sustain. The best economy is that which fosters industry, develops the resources of a country, and does justice to all.

If you will not let us vote for our rulers, if you will not give representation along with our taxation; if you will not let us be on your committees; if you will not allow us to pay our own officers increased compensation; if you will squander money on worthless Indians; if you will refuse us public lands within our own borders to build us a railroad; and if you will disfranchise us, in the name of American honor I insist that you shall not kill us in the name of economy.

On Bill to transfer the Office of Indian Affairs from the Interior Department to the War Department.

MR. BENNETT. There is another thing which ought to be stated, and that is the Indians do not always get the beef which is charged to them. I had occasion, upon a visit to the Indians in Idaho, to take the testimony in writing of an Indian chief. Although I saw from the accounts of the Indian agent that he had been furnished with beef to the amount stated out of the annual appropriation of $20,000 to that tribe for five or six years, yet the chief told me that he had never seen any of the beef of all that has been charged to these Indians. He positively testified that he had never seen any beef, notwithstanding the large account which had been charged to him by the agent. The truth is, in many cases the

Indians are fed on shadowy beef, while the soldier sees he gets tangible beef, and beef of the best quality, and from the block.

FORTY-FOURTH CONGRESS, FIRST SESSION.
Report No. 624.

HOUSE OF REPRESENTATIVES.
Contested Election Case of Fenn vs. Bennett.
June 5, 1876.— Ordered to be Printed.

MR. HOUSE, from the Committee on Elections, submitted the following report:

The Committee on Elections, to whom was referred the case of S. S. Fenn, claimant to a seat in the House of Representatives of the Forty-fourth Congress as a Delegate from the Territory of Idaho, make the following report:

The returns from the various voting precincts, as made to the clerks of the boards of county commissioners, the parties to whom the precinct returns were to be made, show that S. S. Fenn, the claimant, received a plurality of one hundred and five votes over T. W. Bennett, the sitting member. The returns made to the state board of canvassers show the same plurality for the claimant. The territorial canvassers were the Secretary of the Territory and the United States Marshal of the Territory, who were required to canvass the returns in the presence of the Governor of the Territory. The territorial canvassers refused to canvass the following votes returned, viz., two hundred and forty-six votes given for Hon. S. S. Fenn in Oneida county; four hundred and twenty-three for S. S. Fenn, and eighty-seven for T. W. Bennett, in Nez Perce county; also one hundred and thirty-four votes given for T. W. Bennett, and one hundred and two votes for S. S. Fenn, in Lemhi county; also one hundred and sixty-three for S. S. Fenn, and twenty-three for T. W. Bennett, in Idaho county. The reason alleged by the territorial board of canvassers for rejecting two hundred and forty-six votes for S. S. Fenn in the county of Oneida is that there was the prefix "Hon." to said votes. The sitting member, at the hearing, waived the objection to the counting of those votes from Oneida county, and they are accordingly counted for the claimant. The returns from the county of Nez Perce were rejected by the territorial canvassers for the reason that the votes of the county were canvassed under the law of 1864, which gave the canvassing of the votes to the clerk of the county commissioners, and two county officers to be selected by the clerk, and not under the act of 1869, which gives the county commissioners jurisdiction to canvass the votes of the several precincts of the county. Although the question as to the proper board to canvass the precinct returns is a very important one for the territorial canvassers to consider, your committee do not regard it of much importance in coming to a decision in this case, as the

question for the House to consider is, who, in fact, received the highest number of votes, and the precinct returns are proved, which very clearly show that the actual vote cast in this county was four hundred and
twenty-three for S. S. Fenn and thirty-seven for T. W.
Bennett; and although the territorial canvassers acted
rightly in rejecting the returns from this county, as they
were not canvassed by the county commissioners, your
committee, from the precinct returns, find that four
hundred and twenty-three were, in fact, given for S. S.
Fenn, and should now be counted for him; and eighty-
seven votes were, in fact, given for T. W. Bennett, and
should be counted for him.   The vote of Idaho county
was rejected on the ground that the returns for the
Delegate to Congress were not on a separate sheet of
paper.   The law of the Territory, act of December 22,
1864, provided that the clerk of the county commissioners shall make an abstract of the votes for Delegate to
Congress on the sheet, the abstract of votes for members of the legislative assembly on one sheet, and the
abstract of votes for district officers on the sheet, and
the abstract of votes for county and precinct officers on
another sheet.   The returns from this county had all of
the votes for the several officers voted for on the same
sheet; but your committee regard the law in this matter
as merely directory, and do not find that the vote is
thereby vitiated, but count the votes from this county
for the parties for whom they were cast.   In Lemhi
County both the contestant and contestee agree that the
votes from this county should be counted, viz: one hundred and thirty-four for T. W. Bennett, and one hundred and two for S. S. Fenn, as it is clear the votes were
intended and actually cast for them.   The votes thus
counted give the claimant a plurality of one hundred
and five votes, and your committee, therefore, recom-
mend the passage of the following resolutions:

1. *Resolved*, That T. W. Bennett was not elected,
and is not entitled to a seat in the House of Representatives for the Forty-fourth Congress as a Delegate
from the Territory of Idaho.

2. *Resolved*, That S. S. Fenn, was elected, and is
entitled to a seat in the House of Representatives of the
Fourth-fourth Congress as a Delegate from the Territory of Idaho.

MONDAY, *June 5, 1876.*

MR. HOUSE.   I rise for the purpose of submitting a
report from the Committee of Elections in the case of
Fenn *vs.* Bennett.

I move that the report be laid upon the table, and
ordered to be printed, merely asking now that the resolutions accompanying the report be read.

The Clerk read as follows:

Resolved, That T. W. Bennett was not elected, and
is not entitled, to a seat in the House of Representatives

of the Fourty-fourth Congress as a Delegate from the
Territory of Idaho.

Resolved, That S. S. Fenn was elected, and is entitled, to a seat in the House of Representatives of the
Fourty-fourth Congress as a Delegate from the Territory of Idaho.

The motion was agreed to; and the report was laid
on the table, and ordered to be printed.

FRIDAY, *June 23, 1876.*

The above resolutions were agreed to.

Mr. S. S. Fenn appeared at the bar of the House,
and was duly qualified by taking the oath prescribed by
law.

FORTY-FOURTH CONGRESS, FIRST · SESSION.

July 26, 1876.

Fenn, S. S., Remarks by

Mr. FENN. Mr. Speaker, I observe in the Record
what has been referred to by the gentleman from New
York, (Mr. TOWNSEND.) on yesterday I was absent at
the time the argument took place on this floor in the
Virginia contested-election case. I will state now that I
received the unanimous democratic nomination by the
democratic convention of the Territory for Delegate, and
afterward I canvassed a large portion of the Territory
—as much as I could in the intervening time before the
election. Mr. T. W. Bennett, who has been appointed
governor of the Territory by President Grant, and who
had served in that office between two and three years,
who is looked upon as an able and rather unscrupulous
republican politician, after the meeting of the republican
territorial convention announced himself as an independent candidate for Delegate to Congress, and within
forty-eight hours thereafter the republican convention
indorsed him and placed him before the people as their
candidate.

The county of Oneida in our Territory has quite a
large Mormon population, but I was never in that county
until several months after the election. I will state further, that I sent no man to that county, to work in my
interest; that Governor Bennett did send men to work
in his interest, and tried to secure the Mormon vote in
that county. I am proud to say that I received four-
fifths of the legal vote case in that county at that
election, and I will say that Mr. Hailey, my democratic
predecessor as Delegate upon this floor from Idaho, received five-sixths of the entire vote in Oneida county at
the preceding election.

During the remainder of this session Mr. Fenn introduced five bills.

FORTY-FOURTH CONGRESS, SECOND SESSION.
December 4, 1876 to March 3, 1877.

Fenn, Stephen S. Remarks by, on Indian Appropriation Bill.

Mr. FENN. Now, Mr. Chairman, in regard to the amendment I wish to say I do not know that I have any special objection to make to it. I reside in the Territory of Idaho, and from information which comes to me it appears these Indians are advancing in the arts of civilization; that they are quiet and peaceful, and that the white people are perfectly satisfied with them.

But I wish to add, so far as the appropriation for the Fort Hall reservation is concerned, $20,000 would not be a sufficient sum if the law were faithfully carried out. There is no advance in civilization on the part of the Snake, Bannock and Sheepeater bands of Indians, who ought to go upon the reservation, are wandering vagabonds, while the bands of the same tribes at Fort Lemhi reservations are peaceful and quiet, advancing in civilization and, as I have said, the white people are perfectly satisfied with them. The Indians who ought to be removed and kept upon the Fort Hall reservation are wandering all over the country, notwithstanding from year to year this appropriation is made for the purpose of removing them to that reservation. If this appropriation of $20,000 is made for this purpose it will only be squandered as heretofore, and not all expended for the removal of these Indians. Therefore, I am willing that $5,000 in accordance with the suggestion of the gentleman from Montana, shall be transferred where it will do some good, and be a benefit to the Bannocks, Snakes, Sheepeaters.

FORTY-FIFTH CONGRESS, FIRST SESSION.
October 15, 1877 to December 3, 1877.

Fenn, Stephen S. No remarks in this session.

FORTY-FIFTH CONGRESS, SECOND SESSION.
December 3, 1877 to June 20, 1878.

Fenn, Stephen S., Remarks by, on the Bill to Transfer the Indian Bureau from the Interior to the War Department.

MR. FENN. Mr. Speaker, the committee on Indian Affairs have reported a bill (H. R. 3541) to transfer the office of Indian Affairs to the War Department. Representing as I do a constituency vitally interested in a proper settlement of that question I should be derelict in duty if I failed to give my reasons for advocating the bill, and I take this opportunity to do so; and what I have to say will not be the expression of sentiments drawn from Cooper's works of fiction, read in my boyhood, nor from Longfellow's metrical imaginings, but from the lessons taught by thirty-seven years' experience in the frontier settlements of our country and among the Indian tribes.   *   *   *   *   *

No sickly sentimentality will solve this question. The cry that it is better to feed than fight the Indians has produced its legitimate fruits of murder and devastation.

Your system of farming out the Indian agencies to different religious denominations as a means of civilization has only resulted in depopulating reservations and producing Indian hostilities, while your religious agents and religious teachers have plundered the Indians, plundered the government, and produced naught but discord and disorganization by attempting to force their peculiar religious faith upon savages and barbarous or partly civilized people. The fact should not be forgotten that the whole Indian race, by all their traditions, taught them from their childhood are impressed with the belief that the height of human virtue is to deprive their enemies of their property and take their lives, whether these enemies be the white race or the surrounding Indian tribes; that they all look upon and feel the white race to be their natural enemy; that before you can have the respect of an Indian he must feel that in some respect you are his superior. These facts are felt and known by every man who has had personal experience with the Indian race.

The Indians on our western frontiers who have endeavored to improve themselves, who are striving to be self-sustaining, who have profited by the examples of the early missionaries, who practiced what they preached, and the early pioneers who with those missionaries taught them by example the blessings of industry have been totally neglected under the policy of the last few years, until it has become proverbial among the Indians that those who endeavor to assist themselves receive no assistance from the Government, while the turbulent, threatening reptiles are pampered in their idleness. How can that state of affairs be remedied? The answer is plain and simple: By turning the Indian Bureau over to the War Department. The power will then be at hand to enforce obedience. The mass of machinery will be in the hands of men who have had experience with Indian character in frontier service, who will make pledges to be fulfilled, and threats, if you please, or rules and regulations to be enforced.

The Christianizing influences will not be ignored. Schools, industrial habits and honest Christian missionary labor will be fostered. The vital subject of improving the Indian race and making them self-sustaining will be enforced by the Government, and the appropriation for that purpose will insure an honest administration of affairs.

Mr. Speaker, our Indian policy has been radically wrong from its inception. It has been an anomaly, a monstrous incongruity, a burlesque upon us as a nation.

The policy of treating savage tribes within the limits of our Government as independent nations, making solemn treaties with them as civilized nations, allowing them all the attributes of sovereignty, and while doing so considering them as the nation's wards, to be supported in idleness, will always interpose a barrier to the advancement of the Indians in civilization. Let the reservation system and tribal authority be abrogated as soon as possible. Give every Indian, whether within or without a reservation. the same right to the enjoyment of the privileges of the homestead laws as white citizens. Let their land be inalienable and non-taxable for a term of years, say fifteen or twenty; break up your reservation as soon as possible, and with them all tribal relations. Give the Indian the first chance for selecting homesteads on the reservation so broken up. The suicidal policy that has been adopted and enforced by the Interior Department under your peace policy of making the Indian agencies, the United States forces in the field, and the military posts, "cities of refuge" for the protection of red-handed, indiscriminate murderers of men, women and children, the brutal outragers of mothers and daughters—committing their crimes, not in a state of war, but by stealth, in peaceful communities—to which the fiends can flee and have protection against trial and punishment for their crimes, has only been a premium offered to outrage, crime and bloodshed.

> "The fear o' hell's a hangman's whip,
> To hau'd the wretch in order."

And the fear of certain and exemplary punishment for crime alone will restrain the brutal, be they of the white or Indian race.

Last summer when the Nez Perce war broke out and there was imminent danger of the emissaries of the Nez Perces involving the Spokanes and other tribes in the conflict, and a white man had been killed by renegade Indians but a few miles from the main settlement of the Cœur d'Alenes, and the white settlers in their unprotected state abandoned their homes, leaving household goods and all their effects unprotected and their growing crops subject to destruction, the Cœur d'Alenes became the protectors of the abandoned property of the settlers and guarded it fully and completely until the return of the owners.

I now desire to bring to the support of my argument the facts as to the working of the present system in the Territory of Idaho, which I have the honor to represent on this floor, and in the eastern portion of Washington Territory, which has fallen specially under my observation for some years. In southern Idaho we have the Fort Hall reservation, provided for the Shoshones and Bannocks, which for several years has had liberal appropriations from the Government. It was assigned to the Methodist church, although there were no Methodists among the Indians within its limits or among those expected to be removed or settled there. Faithful Roman Catholic fathers had long prior thereto established a mission among them. Large numbers had embraced that faith and were rapidly advancing in civilization without one dollar expense for them or aid from the Government. Now for the sequel: Instead of the Christianizing and civilizing efforts of your religious peace-policy having produced any beneficial results, notwithstanding large appropriations for that purpose, there are not one-half as many Indians on the reservation as were located within its limits when the same was established.

None of the thousands who were expected to be located or removed there are to be found upon the reservation. Those driven off are scattered abroad, creating discord, robbing, stealing, and begging, a source of alarm to the settlers over one-third of Idaho; not only threatening hostilities at the reservation, and throughout the country, but they have actually commenced their murders. Troops have been hurredly assembled there to protect life and property, and a general outbreak is imminent and will only be averted by the presence of a large military force, or by the removal of the cause, namely, the present agent, held there by his church, and a change of policy, as in this bill provided, that will remove the root of the present deplorable state of affairs. At the Lemhi agency, in eastern Idaho, we are blessed with Rev. Mr. Sowers, who by his want of knowledge of Indian character, his stealings, plundering, and general unfaithfulness and inefficiency, has driven off one-half the Indians from the reservation in the last ten months, who are treatening to return with torch and rifle.

The white settlers in the country, alarmed, are stockading, and steps are being taken to station troops for their protection, and nothing but a speedy change will arrest a bloody denouement.

I now come to a commentary upon the present policy that would to God I had been spared the duty of making. I refer to the late Nez Perce war and its causes and the present state of that afflicted country, and the imminent dangers of another war in northern Idaho and eastern Washington that will dwarf the late Nez Perce war into comparative insignificance. This agency was assigned to the Presbyterians when the unholy system of farming out reservations to churches was inaugurated. A Presbyterian mission had been established within what is now the Nez Perce reservation some forty years ago, by Rev. Mr. Spaulding, a worthy missionary, who labored long and ardently for the advancement of the Nez Perces. At the time of farming out the agencies to church organizations was inaugurated, there were as many Methodists as Presbyterians among the Nez Perces, and more Catholics than either.

Under the blighting church influence, J. B. Monteith was appointed agent in February, 1871. From the day of his entering upon his duties as agent he commenced sowing the seeds that during the summer of 1877 produced their harvest of Indian war and desolation. On the 13th, 14th and 15th of June last twenty of my neighbors, men, women and children were horribly murdered by the Nez Perce Indians. Wives and mothers were outraged by the brutal fiends. Large numbers escaped, wounded and disabled, to carry with them through life an evidence of Indian mercy when scourged to madness by outrages perpetrated by their Indian agent. The country was laid waste. The loss of life among our citizens in northern Idaho in defending their homes and families; the murders and devastation in the Territory of Montana and in the county of Lemhi, Idaho Territory, while on their march; the heavy losses of life by the United States army in the field and among the citizen soldiery of Idaho and Montana; the enormous expense incurred in the conflicts, are familiar to this House and the country.

And I here proclaim upon this floor, and I speak from personal knowledge, that in my opinion and in the opinion of nearly every man who lives anywhere in the vicinity of the scenes of hostilities in northern Idaho, I may say every man except a few who have been the tools and parasites of the agent, said J. B. Montieth, the United States Indian agent for the Nez Perces, was the primary cause of every drop of blood and of every dollar's destruction of property and every dollar's expense either by the Government or by individuals in the course of the Nez Perce war; unless it should be considered he was but a tool in the hands of the Presbyterian Missionary Society, and if so, he may divide with them the responsibility. This may appear strange to persons who are not cognizant of the facts, but such will be the record made by the impartial historian.

I will as briefly as possible give the facts as they existed, as they will prove a stronger argument in behalf of the pending measure than volumes of theory. Until the advent of J. B. Monteith among them as agent the Nez Perces had been proverbially peaceful and the friends of the white settlers. Very few difficulties had ever occurred between the whites and the Indians. They were considerably advanced in civilization. Large numbers of them were farmers, nearly all stock raisers, and many laboring faithfully for the white settlers at remunerative wages. I have not time to detail all of his iniquities fully, but I will say he first commenced a bitter warfare upon the old missionary, Rev. Mr. Spaulding, who was beloved by the mass of the tribe of every faith, and followed the onslaught upon him by an equally bitter warfare upon Rev. Mr. Cowle, Presbyterian missionary, beloved by the Indians under his charge, until he was driven from his field of labor, and is now proving his usefulness among the Spokanes without government aid. He (Monteith) bitterly opposed allowing Catholic services on the reservation, although they were the most numerous denomination of Christians located on the reservation and of those who lived without its limits. Money was raised for building a Catholic church upon the reservation—much of it furnished by persons not of the Catholic faith, the donors knowing full well that the Catholic missionaries ever labored in behalf of peace, quietude and good will. Agent Monteith refused to allow the church to be built. Then followed a long correspondence with the Interior Department, the agent denying the right of the Catholics to erect the church, and protesting against it, resulting in an order from the Indian department directing Father Cataldo, the priest in charge, should be allowed to erect a "church and necessary missionary buildings on the Nez Perce reservation."

The church was erected some seven miles from the agency. Soon thereafter steps were taken to erect a school house near the church. This was met by an order from Agent Monteith not to erect the school house, claiming it was not "a necessary missionary building."

He has persecuted the Methodists, and allowed his father, a Presbyterian minister and employe of his at the agency, without reproof or reparation, to threaten with uplifted cane and drive from a church at the agency, built by government funds for the use of the Indians for their purposes of worship, a native Methodist Indian preacher, named Timothy, a talented and worthy son of an important chief, who was an early convert to Christianity under the missionary labors of Rev. Mr. Spaulding, simply because in the course of his sermon, he (Timothy) saw fit to claim tolerance for his faith in common with others. But the crowning infamy of Monteith was his base and slanderous charges made to the Interior Department, in the early part of the year 1877, against the Rev. Father Cataldo, the priest at the Nez Perce Catholic mission, for the purpose of excluding him from the reservation, that he was using his influence to keep Joseph and the non-treaty Indians who were without the reservation from coming thereon, and that he was stirring up dissentions; all of which, he, Monteith, was compelled to admit to a council held with the Nez Perces in May last, in the presence of General Howard, was false in every particular. He has continually evidenced favoritism in the distribution of annuities, pampering a few parasites at the expense of the tribe; interfered with the election of chiefs, and used his power to elect his tools; been false to every pledge made by which, in the early part of his administration, he induced Indians residing without the reservation to leave or dispose of farms and come upon the reservation; *   *   *   *   *

Information was sent time and time again by the settlers to both the military authorities at Fort Lapwai and to the agent that an outbreak was imminent and hourly expected; but so little regard had the agent for the lives and property of the white citizens, or so limited was his knowledge of the character of the Indians under his charge, and so slight his appreciation of the legitimate results of his own vicious administration, that while it was notorious to the country that the disaffected Indians were holding councils and performing their military exercises daily within a short distance of the reservation, and making every arrangement for the conflict, and within twenty days of the outbreak, he, J. B. Monteith, by letter, authorized the selling of ammunition to the Indians to enable them more effectually to carry out their hellish designs.   *   *   *   *   *

The interests of humanity, economy, efficient public service, permanent advancement of the Indians in civilization, and an early disposition of the whole vexed Indian question by rendering them self-supporting, demands the passage of the bill under consideration.

FORTY-FIFTH CONGRESS, THIRD SESSION.
December 2, 1878 to March 3, 1879.

Fenn, Stephen S.

No remarks during this session.

FORTY-SIXTH CONGRESS, FIRST SESSION.
March 18, 1879 to July 1, 1879.

Ainslie, George.

Introduced eleven bills. No remarks this session.

FORTY-SIXTH CONGRESS, SECOND SESSION.
December 1, 1879 to June 16, 1880.

Ainslie, George.

Introduced thirteen bills. Petitions and papers presented by, from fourteen persons and associations. No remarks this session.

FORTY-SIXTH CONGRESS, THIRD SESSION.
December 6, 1880 to March 3, 1881.

Ainslie, George.

Introduced three bills. Presented eight petitions. No remarks in this session.

FORTY-SEVENTH CONGRESS.
(*Special Session of the Senate*).
March 4 to May 20 and October 10 to October 29, 1881.

FORTY-SEVENTH CONGRESS, FIRST SESSION.
December 5, 1881 to August 8, 1882.

Ainslie, George.

Introduced twenty bills.

Remarks by, on Alaska, Admission of Delegate from.

MR. AINSLIE. I desire to say a word in regard to this matter. I am glad to hear the claim made by the chairman of the committee on Elections that this is a question of privilege—the question whether the people of Alaska are entitled to representation on this floor.

I am not acquainted with the gentleman who is claiming the seat; I never saw him in my life. But I am glad to find the committee on Elections, represented by its honored chairman, claiming that this is a question of privilege, and declaring that the people of an unrepresented portion of the United States are entitled to some little consideration in this House.

I have been here for nearly three years; I have been on the roll of the House, and I have drawn my salary very regularly, but I have never known my people to be represented at least by a vote. We have just the same rights that the colonists had a hundred years ago when they rebelled against Great Britain; we are under taxation without representation.

I am glad the committee on Elections is claiming the right now of a portion of the population of the United States, even though they be among the icebergs of Alaska, to be represented on this floor. Whether it is a question of privilege or not I do not know. But I hope it will be considered a question of privilege that the people of all portions of the United States shall be represented, and I hope the committee will frame a bill that will give the people of the territories a right to be represented by a vote on this floor.

FORTY-SEVENTH CONGRESS, SECOND SESSION.
December 4, 1882 to March 3, 1883.

Ainslie, George.

No remarks during this session.

FORTY-EIGHTH CONGRESS, FIRST SESSION.
December 3, 1883 to July 7, 1884.

Singiser, Theodore F.

Introduced fourteen bills. No remarks in this session.

FORTY-EIGHTH CONGRESS, SECOND SESSION.
December 1, 1884 to March 3, 1885.

Singiser, Theodore F.

Appointed on committee to attend opening of New Orleans Exposition. No remarks during this session.

FORTY-NINTH CONGRESS, FIRST SESSION.
December 7, 1885 to August 5, 1886.

Hailey, John, Remarks by, on Idaho and Washington Territories.

MR. HAILEY. Mr. Speaker, I desire to say but little on this question. This pan-handle of Idaho, about which there has been so much talk, has been a bone of contention for the last twenty years. A large majority of the people living in that portion of the territory have wanted annexation to Washington Territory. There is no doubt about that fact in my mind. The people of the southern portion of Idaho, however, have objected to it until the last two years. Up to that time their objection was a serious one. Three years ago last fall the people of the north were so embittered against the people of the south because they could not be annexed that both political parties in these northern counties refused to participate in the territorial conventions. They called an independent convention for the purpose of nominating a man to run on the annexation question with a view of sending him to Washington city to work for the annexation of those counties to Washington Territory whether he was elected or not. But the Republican candidate was a little sharper than the Democratic candidate, and he rushed up north and pledged himself to go for annexation, and they took him as their candidate with the understanding down south, I am told by good authority, that he did not intend to work very hard for it.

However, he secured almost the unanimous vote of these northern counties, and was elected. But although he was elected, he did not secure their annexation. At the recent election, or rather at the conventions which preceded the election, the Republicans placed a section in their platform pledging their party to do all in their power to secure the annexation, and their delegate also was pledged to do whatever was in his power, if elected, to annex these northern counties to Washington Territory. The Democratic party took the matter under advisement, talked it over, and after some consideration of the subject, concluded that they would also put the same plank in their platform, or substantially the same thing, favoring this annexation. I gave them due notice that if the plank was inserted in the platform and they nominated me, that if elected I would try to give this portion of the territory away to Washington Territory.

I now propose to keep good the pledges made by my party and myself by trying to have them annexed to Washington Territory. They have expressed a desire to go to Washington, and I do not propose to keep them from going; they have been very troublesome. I hope the bill will pass to annex them to Washington Territory, because we can get along very well without them. It has been clearly understood for years that the people of those counties themselves wanted to be annexed to Washington Territory. The legislature in 1885 passed a memorial requesting that these counties be annexed to Washington Territory, but with the proviso that they should pay their portion of the debt of the territory just as this bill provides.

Now at this late date some of these northern counties, I understand, are kicking about it when they find that they can really be annexed to Washington Territory, and they do not want it near so bad as they thought they did. Some of them say they prefer to go to Montana Territory, and for that reason they send in here and oppose the passage of the bill which proposed to give them they very thing they have been asking for so many years, and I therefore insist upon the passage of the bill.

FORTY-NINTH CONGRESS, SECOND SESSION.
December 6, 1886 to March 3, 1887.

Hailey, John.

No remarks during this session.

FIFTIETH CONGRESS, FIRST SESSION.
December 5, 1887 to October 20, 1888.

Dubois, Fred T., Remarks by, on Polygamy.

Resolved, That the Attorney-General be requested to furnish to the House of Representatives the number of convictions for polygamy, adultery, and unlawful co-habitation had in the Territories of Utah and Idaho under the provisions of the anti-polygamy law of 1882, and the act of 1882 amendatory thereof, and the act of March 3, 1887, and the dates thereof as shown by the records of the Department of Justice, together with the amount of fines, forfeitures and costs collected from said prosecutions, with the date of judgments under which said several sums were collected; a list of pardons granted by the President of the United States to persons convicted of such crimes of polygamy, adultery and unlawful co-habitation, respectively, in the said territories of Utah and Idaho, giving the name, date of sentence, time of imprisonment, amount of fine, date of pardon, and the reason for granting the same in each case.

Mr. Dubois. Mr. Speaker, I am very glad that the committee on Judiciary saw fit to enlarge the scope of the resolution which I had the honor to introduce. I am satisfied that a great deal of valuable information will be furnished as a consequence of the adoption of the resolution. In addition to the request which was embodied in my original resolution, that a list should be furnished of the pardons which have been granted to those convicted of unlawful co-habitation, adultery and polygamy, the committee have added a request that the number of convictions had for these various crimes shall also be furnished. This information will absolutely and utterly refute a statement which has been brazenly made and reiterated by the agents of the Mormon church here that only one and one-half per cent, or less, of their people are in polygamy.   *   *   *   *   *   *

I stand by the statement which I had the honor to make before the Senate committee, that about one-half of the adult Mormons in Utah are in polygamy. As regards Idaho, I had the evidence before me as United States marshal of the territory to demonstrate that at least one-third of the adult Mormons in that territory are in polygamy.   *   *   *   *   *   *

Remarks on Tariff.

Amended by striking out "lead ore and lead dross, three-fourths of 1 cent per pound."

MR. DUBOIS. Mr. Chairman, in behalf of the territory I represent, I desire to enter my protest against the section of this bill. The fact that one hundred thousand people living in Idaho have no vote upon this measure, the fact that millions of dollars, in labor as well as in cash, would be affected by its provisions if it should become a law, ought to add weight to the protest that I now make.

The development of Idaho has been carried to just that extent that great lead and silver mines have been opened, and enormous sums invested in the machinery necessary to develop them. The territory has just started upon a career of unexampled prosperity. But, the mines of Idaho, those that are attracting the most attention and contributing most to the growing wealth of the country are low-grade silver-lead mines, that need the fostering care of the government.   *   *   *   *   *   *

FIFTIETH CONGRESS, SECOND SESSION.
December 3, 1888, to March 3, 1889.

Dubois, Fred T., Remarks by, on Admission of Idaho.

MR. DUBOIS. Mr. Speaker, I take it for granted that there will be no objection, founded on sound public policy or justice, to the admission of North and South Dakota, Montana, and Washington.

There seems to be a doubt in the minds of some members as to the expediency of admitting New Mexico. No argument has been advanced to prove that the citizens of New Mexico are not law-abiding and attached to the principles of our government.   *   *   *   *

The remarks which have been made by the various delegates whose territories are included in the bill under discussion apply with full force, clearness and fairness to Idaho. They could be iterated and reiterated in a hundred different ways, yet the truth would not be half told. .

I will not at this particular time in this discussion insist on a recognition of the just claims of the Terri-

tory of Idaho, because it might retard the justice which
I believe and hope you are prepared to mete out to our
sister territories. I will please my fancy in the hope
that the journey on this road of fairness to those brave
and loyal people, who have been harassed and handi-
capped so long beyond the usual probationary period of
territorial government will bring such unqualified peace
and contentment to your minds that you will quickly
recognize and pass upon the appeal of Idaho.

I do not ask immediate statehood. My people do not
claim admission at once. We ask an enabling act which
will definitely fix a time when we can assume the responsibilities and blessings of a state. We care not what
conditions you impose as to population or resources. It
makes no difference to us whether we come in under the
ordinance of 1787, which requires 60,000 free inhabitants, or whether we are to have the number equal to
the ratio of representation for a member of Congress.

STATEMENT OF MILEAGE PAID TO DELEGATES FROM IDAHO, TERRITORY OF.

*Thirty-Eighth Congress to Fiftieth Congress, Totals Paid
to Each.*

NOTE—These figures were taken from the personal
ledger accounts of the delegates, the ledgers being found
in the Treasury Department. The figures are authentic
and correct, having been compared.

William H. Wallace (Sworn in Feb. 3, 1864).   Cr.
38th Congress, 1863-65.   1863
                        Dec. 7, by mileage $6,192.00
                                   1864
                        Dec. 5, by mileage   6,192.00

                        (@ 40c per mile) $12,384.00

E. D. Holbrook   Cr.
39th Congress, 1865-67.   1865
                        Dec. 4, by mileage
                          (7,500 @ 40c) $6,000.00
                                   1866
                        Dec. 4, by mileage,
                          (7,500 @ 20c) 3,000.00

                                          $9,000.00

E. D. Holbrook   Cr.
40th Congress, 1867-69.   1867
                        Dec. 2, by mileage ..$3,000.00
                                   1868
                        Dec. 7, by mileage,
                          (@ 20c per mile)   3,000.00

                                          $6,000.00

27 E. H. I.

Jacob K. Shafer   Cr.
41st Congress, 1869-71.   1869
                                     Mar. 4, by mileage
                                       (1st Ses., 7,500
                                       @ 20c) $3,000.00
                                     Dec. 4, by mileage
                                       (2nd Ses., 3,066
                                       @ 20c) 1,226.40
                                       1870
                                     Dec. 6, by mileage
                                       (3rd Session) 1,226.40
                                                          _____
                                                           $5,452.80

Samuel A. Merritt   Cr.
42nd Congress, 1871-73.   1871
                                     Mar. 4, by mileage
                                       (3,065 @ 20c) $1,226.00
                                     Dec. 4, by mileage .. 1,226.00
                                       1872
                                     Dec. 2, by mileage .. 1,226.00
                                                          _____
                                                           $3,678.00

NOTE—Each member of this Congress was paid mileage; this ledger account (Merritt's) shows that he was
credited with the mileage as set forth opposite and that
he was paid such mileage as appears from the debit side
of his ledger account. The account was closed at the
expiration of the 42nd congress, and balanced. This
supplemental account appears following the accounts of
each member of that congress:

Samuel A. Merritt
42nd Congress.
  1873   Dr. | 1873   Cr.
Mar. 4, to mileage* 3,678.00|| Mar. 4, by in-
Mar. 4, to Speaker's || creased compen-
  certificate (cash) 1,322.00|| sation $5,000.00
                   _____|| _____
                   $5,000.00 || $5,000.00

This credit of $5,000 was under the provisions of the
so-called "Salary Grab Act" approved March 3, 1873,
which increased the compensation of each member and
delegate of the 42nd congress in the sum of $5,000 or at
the rate of $2,500 per annum, *with the proviso* that from
that sum of increase should be deducted such sum or
sums as were paid to each *for mileage* during the 42nd
congress. Thus while mileage was paid for the 42nd
congress, the amount of the mileage was deducted from
the extra compensation paid to such members under the
Act of March 3, 1873.
  * Deducted from extra compensation.
  (This account to illustrate that mileage *was paid*
during 42nd Congress).

John Hailey   Cr.
43rd Congress, 1873-75.   1874
                        Feb. 4, by *expenses* $ 430.00
                               1875
                        Jan. 4, by mileage   1,065.60
                                            _____
                                            $1,495.60

NOTE—For the first session of the 43rd congress, actual traveling expenses were paid in lieu of mileage.

T. W. Bennett   Cr.
44th Congress, 1875-77.   1875
                        Jan. 12, by mileage $1,141.20

Note on the ledger: "Succeeded by S. S. Fenn."

S. S. Fenn   Cr.
44th Congress, 1875-77.   1876
                        June 24, by mile'ge $1,323.20
                        Dec. 15, by mileage 1,323.20
                                            _____
                                            $2,646.40
(First *debit* on this account is June 24, 1876).

S. S. Fenn   Cr.
45th Congress, 1877-79.   1877
                        Dec. 11, by mileage $1,323.20
                               1878
                        Dec. 6, by mileage   1,323.20
                                            _____
                                            $2,646.40

George Ainslie   Cr.
46th Congress, 1879-81.   1879
                        Dec. 17, by mileage, $1,111.20
                               1880
                        Dec. 11, by mileage, 1,111.20
                                            _____
                                            $2,222.40

George Ainslie   Cr.
47th Congress, 1881-83.   1881
                        Dec. 19, by mileage $1,111.20
                               1882
                        Dec. 9, by mileage,   1,111.20
                                            _____
                                            $2,222.40

T. F. Singiser   **Cr.**
48th Congress, 1888-85.   1883
                                Dec. 10, by mileage $1,120.00
                                      1884
                                Dec. 11, by mileage   1,120.00
                                                     _____
                                                     $2,240.00

John Hailey   **Cr.**
49th Congress, 1885-87.   1885
                                Dec. 21,by mileage, $1,070.40
                                      1886
                                Dec.   9, by mileage   1,070.40
                                                     _____
                                                     $2,140.80

Fred T. Dubois   **Cr.**
50th Congress, 1887-89.   1887
                                Dec. 16, by mileage $ 990.40
                                      1888
                                Dec.   4, by mileage   990.40
                                                     _____
                                                     $1,980.80

Printed in the USA
CPSIA information can be obtained
at www.ICGtesting.com
LVHW021920050923
757178LV00040B/832